MONETARY POLICY IN AN
UNCERTAIN WORLD

Monetary Policy in an Uncertain World

Ten Years After the Crisis

Edited by
James A. Dorn

CATO
INSTITUTE
Washington, D.C.

ISBN: 978-1-948647-14-4
eBook ISBN: 978-1-948647-15-1

Library of Congress Cataloging-in-Publication Data available.

Printed in the United States of America
Cover design: Jon Meyers and Mai Makled

Cato Institute
1000 Massachusetts Avenue, N.W.
Washington, D.C. 20001

www.cato.org

CONTENTS

Editor's Preface

Ten years after the 2008 financial crisis we are again facing the possibility of economic turmoil as the Fed and other central banks exit their unconventional monetary policies by raising interest rates and shrinking their balance sheets. Although central banks will move gradually, unforeseen circumstances could trigger a flight to safety and a collapse of asset prices that had previously been stimulated by near-zero interest rates and large-scale asset purchases, popularly known as "quantitative easing."

This book brings together leading scholars and former policymakers to draw lessons from the decade of unconventional monetary policies relied upon to stimulate the global economy in the aftermath of the financial crisis. The articles included in this book combine historical perspectives and forward-looking views of the Fed's exit strategy and monetary normalization, along with the arguments for a rules-based monetary policy both at the domestic and international levels.

Kevin Warsh, a former member of the Board of Governors of the Federal Reserve System, reminds us in his article that, although the economy has improved since the crisis, the tasks facing the Fed are still large. "So we should resist allowing the policy debate to be small or push aside ideas that depart from the prevailing consensus. The Fed's job is not easier today, and its conclusions are not obvious." The contributors to this volume meet Warsh's challenge by questioning the status quo and offering fresh ideas for improving monetary policy.

The financial crisis highlighted the uncertainty that confronts policymakers. Having failed to prevent the 2008 financial crisis and the Great Recession, the Federal Reserve and other major central banks all subsequently adopted similar policies characterized by near-zero interest rates, quantitative easing and forward guidance. Those unconventional monetary policies were designed to increase risk taking, prop up asset prices, increase spending and restore full employment.

While asset prices have risen and unemployment is at historic lows, the Fed's balance sheet ballooned from about $800 billion before the crisis to more than $4 trillion today, and the long period of near-zero interest rates has created a series of asset bubbles, which risk being burst as interest rates rise again.

Moreover, the Fed has engaged in preferential credit allocation through its large-scale asset purchase program, in which it has acquired billions of dollars' worth of mortgage-backed securities and shifted out of short-term Treasuries to longer-term government debt.

In order to expand its balance sheet, the Fed has radically changed its operating procedure. Instead of engaging in open market operations nudging the policy rate toward a single target rate by buying and selling short-term Treasuries, the Fed now establishes a target range for the funds rate—with the rate of interest on excess reserves (IOER), introduced in October 2008, as its upper limit and the Fed's overnight reverse repurchase (ON RRP) agreement rate as its lower limit.

Because the IOER exceeds comparable market rates, some banks now find it worthwhile to accumulate excess reserves instead of trading them for other assets. The economy is, in other words, kept in a purpose-made "liquidity trap," so that the traditional monetary "transmission mechanism" linking increases in the monetary base to changes in bank lending, overall spending, and inflation, no longer functions as it once did. Under the new operating arrangements, the Fed changes its policy stance by changing its IOER and ON RRP rates, thereby influencing not the supply of but the demand for the Fed's deposit balances.

Meanwhile, the Fed's regulatory powers have increased dramatically as well. The Federal Reserve System, which was intended to be decentralized so that policymakers would take account of divergent ideas, has become even more centralized with each new crisis. As a result, monetary policy has also become more politicized.

Finally, the lack of any systematic policy rule to guide long-run decisions has increased regime uncertainty. The so-called knowledge

problem—and the limits of monetary policy—need to be widely recognized. Policymakers err by paying too much attention to short-run
remedies and too little attention to the long-run consequences of current decisions. If human judgments were perfect, then purely discretionary monetary policy would be ideal. However, as Karl Brunner
(1980: 61) wisely noted, the reality is that:

> We suffer neither under total ignorance nor do we enjoy full
> knowledge. Our life moves in a grey zone of partial knowl-
> edge and partial ignorance. [Consequently], a nonactivist
> [rules-based] regime emerges . . . as the safest strategy. It
> does not assure us that economic fluctuations will be avoided.
> But it will assure us that monetary policymaking does not
> impose additional uncertainties . . . on the market place.

Before serious consideration can be given to implementing any
rules-based monetary regime, the Fed needs to normalize monetary
policy by ending interest on excess reserves and shrinking its balance
sheet to restore a precrisis federal funds market. Once changes in
base money can be effectively transmitted to changes in the money
supply and nominal income, the Fed can then implement a rules-
based regime to reduce uncertainty and spur investment and growth.

The ideas put forth in this volume for monetary reform are meant
to inform policymakers and the public about the importance of maintaining a credible monetary policy regime both for financial stability
and economic prosperity. Ensuring long-run price stability, letting
market forces set interest rates and allocate credit, and keeping nominal income on a steady growth path will create new opportunities
and widen the scope of markets to promote economic performance.

I thank the contributors to this volume for their work which will
help us better understand the complexities of monetary policy and
the remedies that can help us prevent future crises. Special thanks go
to The George Edward Durell Foundation which has long supported
the Cato Institute's work on monetary policy. All the articles in this
volume were first presented at the annual monetary conferences and
appeared in various issues of the *Cato Journal*, with the exception of
George Selgin's article, which first appeared in *Alt-M*.

Finally, I would like to thank my colleagues at the Center for
Monetary and Financial Alternatives for ongoing conversations that

have deepened my knowledge of monetary history and policy, and to our donors who have generously supported our efforts to give monetary and financial institutions the attention they deserve.

—J. A. Dorn

Reference

Brunner, K. (1980) "The Control of Monetary Aggregates." In *Controlling Monetary Aggregates III*, 1–65. Boston: Federal Reserve Bank of Boston.

PART 1

LESSONS FROM THE CRISIS

1
RETHINKING CENTRAL BANKING
Gerald P. O'Driscoll Jr.

Central banks are a relatively recent development in monetary history (Smith [1936] 1990). Money can and has been created privately and competitively.[1] In many cases, princes coined money but their coins had to compete for acceptance with other coinage both princely and privately produced. The Maria Theresa Thaler was first struck in Vienna in 1741, and it was adopted globally for international trade. The dollar is a government monopoly in the United States, but globally the greenback must compete for usage.

The creation of the Federal Reserve System was an innovation. It was not created to conduct discretionary monetary policy but to manage the gold standard. "There was no provision in the Federal Reserve Act for discretionary monetary policy" (Jordan 2016a: 373). So, both theoretically and historically, there are alternatives to central banking.

The Federal Reserve's foray into credit allocation has moved it into a form of central planning. In this article, I initially focus on the problems inherent in conducting discretionary monetary policy in a central bank. I then offer a public choice analysis of why we are nonetheless stuck with discretion. Finally, I present policy reforms that need to be implemented if we are to move from discretion to a

---

Gerald P. O'Driscoll Jr. is a Senior Fellow at the Cato Institute. This article is reprinted from the *Cato Journal*, Vol. 37, No. 2 (Spring/Summer 2017). He thanks Jim Dorn, Jerry Jordan, Edward J. Kane, Patrick J. Lawler, Maralene Martin, and John B. Taylor for their comments.

[1]On the theory and experience of free or competitive banking, see Dowd ([1988] 1996), Dowd and Timberlake (1998), Selgin (1988), and White (1984, 1989).

policy rule. Congress, or at least the House of Representatives, has indicated a willingness to mandate rule-based monetary policy. It is important that these reforms be implemented in order that a rule-based policy can be successfully executed.

The Knowledge Problem

The knowledge problem is most closely associated with F. A. Hayek, who emphasized that the knowledge needed for decision-making is localized and dispersed across the population.[2] In markets, prices economize on information and communicate what is needed for economic actors to make allocational decisions. That part of Hayek's argument is generally understood.[3]

There is more to Hayek's argument, however. Much relevant economic knowledge is tacit. Individuals have unarticulated knowledge vital to decisionmaking but no understanding or theory of why what they do works. As Caldwell (2004: 337) observed, "The dispersion of such knowledge is a permanent condition of life." It is permanent because tacit knowledge by its nature cannot be articulated and, hence, cannot be transmitted.

The knowledge problem is an obstacle to achieving intertemporal equilibrium even if money were neutral. The existence of monetary shocks greatly complicates the formation of intertemporal expectations. It also complicates the conduct of monetary policy. A central bank confronts the problem of assembling dispersed knowledge, some of which cannot even be conveyed. The problem of implementing an optimal monetary policy is conceptually the same problem confronting a central planning authority. Implementing optimal monetary policy requires surmounting the knowledge problem, which is impossible.

Milton Friedman presented his own take on the knowledge problem in Friedman (1968). He offered two propositions, the first being that monetary policy should do no harm. Too often, central banks violate that norm. Second, he argued that monetary policy should provide "a stable background for the economy" (Friedman 1968: 12–13). "We simply do not know enough" to engage in discretionary

---

[2]This section borrows from O'Driscoll (2016).

[3]Hayek developed his argument in a number of papers collected in Hayek (1948). O'Driscoll (2016) provides specific citations to these papers.

monetary policy (Friedman 1968: 14). His analysis of the knowledge problem is what led to his advocacy of a simple monetary rule. The rule would minimize harm and provide a stable background. He did not believe that monetary policy was capable of increasing the economic growth rate. That depended on "those basic forces of enterprise, ingenuity, invention, hard work, and thrift that are the true springs of economic growth" (Friedman 1968: 17).

Friedman's awareness of the knowledge problem and his adoption of policy rules as a solution to it predate his AEA presidential address or even his work on money. "Friedman was already advocating rules . . . before his monetarist theoretical position came to fruition. But Friedman's case for rules did rely on a strong theoretical motivation: in particular, the possibility that stabilization policies might give rise to destabilization of the economy" (Nelson 2015: 204). The conviction that, in a world of uncertainty, stabilization policies might actually destabilize the economy is what most united Hayek and Friedman. Both the Great Depression and the Great Recession exemplify that dynamic—stabilization policies destabilizing the economy.

Other monetary economists followed in the Hayek-Friedman mold of emphasizing uncertainty in policymaking. Karl Brunner and Allan Meltzer are notable examples, and Meltzer (2015) reprises their contribution. Axel Leijonhufvud (1981) emphasized the role of information in economic coordination. These monetary economists all had a UCLA connection, which is where Chicago and Vienna intersected. Other, nonmonetary UCLA economists who contributed to the economics of uncertainty were Armen Alchian (1969) and Thomas Sowell ([1980] 1996). Today, John Taylor's work follows closely in that tradition. The Monetary Policy Rule website provides a useful compendium of recent articles (Taylor 2016a).

Fed Governance: Bureaucracy and Incentives

Conti-Brown (2016) is highly critical of the Fed's structure, which he views as causing governance problems and a lack of democratic accountability. He recommends changing it by eliminating the private-component resident in the reserve banks from monetary policymaking. Reserve banks are private institutions and their presidents are not political appointees. According to Conti-Brown, the Fed's structure is a mistake and it needs to be fixed.

Decades earlier, Kane (1980) looked at the same reality and found the "murky lines of internal authority" serve identifiable political goals. "Once the Fed is viewed as a policy scapegoat for elected officials, these developments emerge as intelligible adaptations to recurring political pressures" (Kane 1980: 210).[4] In Kane's analysis, if macroeconomic outcomes are good, politicians can claim credit for them. If outcomes are bad, politicians can blame the Fed. Central bank discretion and "independence" benefit both sides. Fed officials are not bound by rules and thus enjoy the sense of power that comes with discretion. Politicians are happy to grant that discretion because it allows them to scapegoat the central bank. If the Fed were effectively rule-bound, then politicians could only blame themselves for choosing the rule.

The last thing politicians want is to have the buck stop at their desk. So they tolerate ambiguity in Fed governance, nontransparency in policymaking, and long tenure for Fed officials. These features provide plausible deniability for both the administration and Congress. Fed officials, in turn, get power and prestige, which are valuable nonpecuniary returns. There is symbiotic rent seeking by Fed officials and politicians. The two sides feed off each other to their mutual benefit.

Conti-Brown (2016: 109) is particularly critical of the Reserve Bank structure because it impedes democratic accountability. In a public-choice analysis, however, the last thing politicians crave is accountability. With respect to fiscal policy, politicians love to spend without levying taxes to pay for the spending. So future, unspecified taxes (debt finance) are preferred to present taxes. If taxes are levied, nontransparent taxes are preferred. The corporate income tax is an example.

The preference for dispensing benefits without providing for the financing of those benefits exhibits blame avoidance, which Weaver (1986) identified as the main goal of politicians generally. Voters exhibit "negativity bias." Perceived losses are punished more than perceived benefits are rewarded. So politicians engage in strategies to avoid blame. Two of those are passing the buck and finding a scapegoat (Weaver 1986: 386–88). Creating independent agencies

---

[4]Kane (2016: 210) described "the Fed's special bureaucratic features" as "its independence, its acceptance of impossible policy assignments and its murky lines of internal authority."

is one way to pass the buck, and scapegoating is a fall back. So Weaver (1986), drawing from the political science literature, confirmed the intuition of Kane (1986), which focused just on monetary policy.

When it comes to monetary policy, it is in the interest of Congress and the president not to compel the Fed to specify a complete monetary strategy. "The advantage that I see is that by leaving the Fed high command a substantial amount of ex ante discretion, elected officials leave themselves scope for blaming the Fed ex post when things go wrong" (Kane 1980: 206). What for Conti-Brown is a defect in Fed governance is for a public-choice theorist like Kane a desirable feature for rent-seeking politicians and Fed officials.

A public-choice analyst would agree with Conti-Brown that nothing like optimal policy would be the outcome of the current system. But the analyst would also agree with Kane (2016: 200) that it is a "utopian conception of Fed intentions" to characterize monetary policy as pursuing optimality.

Monetary policy is not neutral. For instance, some identifiable private interests are inordinately sensitive to changes in interest rates. What Kane (1980: 207) describes as "the low-interest lobby" resists increases in interest rates. The lobby puts political pressure on their representatives to avoid rate hikes. Politicians need a central bank that is responsive to these pressures. Incompleteness in monetary strategy is the answer.

The Federal Reserve has been signaling for approximately two years its intentions to implement a program of rate increases. It succeeded in implementing only a one-quarter point increase in short-term interest rates in December 2015. It did not raise rates again until December 2016, again a one-quarter point increase.

A letter to the Editor of the *Wall Street Journal* by Congressman Scott Garrett (2016) specifies one channel by which political pressures are applied to the Fed.

> As I pointed out to Chairwoman Janet Yellen during a congressional hearing last year, her own calendar reflects weekly meeting with political figures and partisan special-interest groups. Even more troubling, there is a long history of Fed chairs or governors serving as partisan figures in the Treasury or the White House before their appointment. So while the Fed is quick to decry any attempts at congressional oversight, it cannot credibly claim to be politically independent.

Garrett's letter reveals that, while all elected politicians share a common interest to stay elected and retain power, their interests divide along partisan lines. There are also conflicts between the branches of government.

In sum, a public-choice approach to analyzing monetary policy is useful in rendering intelligible otherwise murky aspects of monetary policy and Fed governance. The analysis reveals there is political symbiosis between the central bank and government. And, finally, it clarifies that the Fed is not politically independent (Cargill and O'Driscoll 2013).

Central Banking and Central Planning

The dollar is an evolved currency that was in use in the American colonies long before it was adopted and defined by the Currency Act of 1792. Dollar notes were issued by private banks against specie. The Union issued Greenbacks to finance the Civil War. The National Banking Act established a new system of private currency issue denominated in dollars. After the Civil War until 1879 (the resumption of gold payments), the Greenbacks circulated side by side with gold. The National Bank System was in place until the creation of the Federal Reserve System in 1913 (Friedman and Schwartz 1963).

As already noted, the Federal Reserve System was not created to engage in discretionary monetary policy. (It would be anachronistic to impute such an idea to the System's creators.) Only in 1933 was the link to gold severed domestically; only with the closing of the gold window in 1971 was the linkage broken internationally. The dollar was only then a purely managed currency (Eichengreen 2011).

There is no playbook for a managed fiat currency that also serves as the global currency. It has been a work in progress. Domestically, the Great Inflation was followed by the Volcker Era and then the Great Moderation. Many observers thought the Fed and other central banks had finally got it right (Friedman 2006). A housing bubble was already pumped up, however, and soon we had a housing bust and a global financial crisis (Taylor 2009).

Under Chairman Ben Bernanke, the Federal Reserve responded with unprecedented and unconventional monetary policy. There were many aspects to the policy; I will focus on just one: credit allocation. The credit allocation took many forms: special loans to particular financial firms (both banks and nonbanks), and even to commercial firms, was one channel. So, too, were the aggressive purchases of mortgage securities and long-dated Treasuries. Those purchases benefited the financial firms selling them to the Fed, who might otherwise have been forced to sell the securities at market prices. Additionally, the housing industry benefited by what amounted to a bond-support program for housing securities. These aggressive asset purchases called into question any claim of Fed independence.

The Fed celebrates the 1951 Accord with the Treasury as its Independence Day (Hetzel and Leach 2001: 33). By committing to maintaining short-term interest rates near zero and long rates at low levels, however, the Fed effectively surrendered that independence (Meltzer 2016).

The Fed for now has suspended quantitative easing. Janet Yellen's speech at the 2016 Jackson Hole Conference, however, put future bond purchases squarely in the Fed's toolkit (Yellen 2016). In any case, the Fed continues to maintain the size of its balance sheet by replacing maturing securities. It remains a significant holder of mortgage securities and thus continues to influence the allocation of credit. That was the intent of the bond-buying program when Bernanke announced it at the 2010 Jackson Hole Conference (Hummel 2011: 510).

Hummel (2011) strongly criticized Bernanke's credit allocation policies, now also followed by Yellen. Hummel (2011: 512) charged that "central banking has become the new central planning." The new policy is dangerous for the economy and for the central bank itself.

As an institution, the Fed was formally held in high esteem. Not so anymore. On the political right and left, there is great hostility to the institution. Fed Chairwoman Janet Yellen commands respect from only 38 percent of Americans while Alan Greenspan, in the early 2000s, gained the confidence of more than 70 percent (Hilsenrath 2016: A6).

The Fed jealously guards its political independence and acts aggressively to maintain it. Fed officials have vigorously opposed efforts by Congress to institute a policy audit—even though the Fed's expanded balance sheet and forays into credit allocation are the greatest threats to its putative independence. As former Fed Governor Kevin Warsh (2016: A11) recently put it, "Central bank power is permissible in a democracy only when its scope is limited, its track record strong, and its accountability assured." Today's Fed fails on all three counts.

Reforming the Fed

Downsizing the Fed's balance sheet is a necessary condition for implementing a sound monetary reform. Any central bank with a balance sheet of $4.5 trillion is going to find itself in the business of allocating credit. In the Fed's case, its balance sheet grew because of its foray into supporting housing finance. Even if it had ballooned its balance sheet by traditional purchases of Treasury securities, there would be calls for the Fed to support this or that sector. There have already been calls for the Fed to purchase student loans. There will surely be calls to bail out public pension funds (*Wall Street Journal* 2016). Come the next major municipal bond crisis, surely some will suggest a central bank bailout. Who will save the finances of the state of Illinois if not the Fed?

If the Federal Reserve were the politically independent institution that it claims to be, its overseers would long since have begun to shrink its balance sheet to avoid being called upon to implement financial rescues of politically connected groups. In its downsizing, the Fed should have rid itself of mortgage-backed securities. Yet Fed officials luxuriate in their role of dispensers of public capital. As the editors of the *Wall Street Journal* (2016) have observed, "the Fed is now a joint venture partner with the biggest banks."

There are also technical problems created by the Fed's expanded balance sheet and its move out of short-term, highly liquid Treasury securities into long-dated bonds.[5] Commercial banks are no longer reserve-constrained. Nearly all of the reserves on the Fed's balance sheet are in excess of what is required for banks to hold. For that reason, few federal funds are traded. Influencing the availability and cost of federal funds has been the traditional way the Fed has conducted monetary policy. There is scant demand for federal funds in a world in which reserves are abundant.

Traditionally, when the Fed wanted to tighten money and credit, it would sell Treasury bills to absorb reserves and put upward pressure on the fed funds rate. But the Fed has not had bills on its balance sheet for some time, so it cannot affect the fed funds rate directly by acting on the asset side of its balance sheet. Instead, the Fed has taken actions on the liability side of the balance sheet by

---

[5]Jordan (2016b) deals with these issues in more detail.

paying interest on reserves (IOR) and on reverse repurchase agreements.[6] It is counting on arbitrage to move the fed funds rate in tandem. Even if somewhat successful so far, the policy actions are a rather meaningless exercise. The fed funds market no longer plays the role it once did in allocating credit among banks. And the administered rates the Fed is paying are not succeeding in keeping other, market-set short-term interest rates moving in tandem. For instance, when IOR is 50bp and interest on reverse repurchase agreements is 25bp, the four-week Treasury bill was 10bp on September 26, 2016, and 16bp on September 27th. These are not cherry-picked rates. As Jordan (2016b: 26) details, after the Fed's December 2015 hikes in administered rates, "yields of market-determined interest rates subsequently *fell* and remain below the levels that prevailed before the increase in administered rates."

At a minimum, the Fed should commence letting maturing obligations roll off its balance sheet. It should also sell some longer-term securities to move the process of downsizing the balance sheet along. The goal is get banks reserve-constrained so that the Fed can conduct conventional monetary policy. The Fed has thus far refused to do either. In its statement on "Policy Normalization Principles and Plans," the FOMC promised to "normalize the stance of monetary policy." It will do so "when it becomes appropriate." The statement is vague not only as to timing but also as to what its balance sheet will look like after normalization (Taylor 2016b: 716–17).

Reigning in emergency lending (Section 13 (3) of the Federal Reserve Act) is essential to keeping the Fed out of credit allocation and lending to politically favored entities (banks and nonbanks). As long as the central bank retains emergency lending powers, it will be in the credit allocation business. Any lending to markets for liquidity reasons can be accomplished via open market operations.

With these changes in place, advocates of monetary rules have a way forward. There would be no more technical impediments to implementing the Taylor rule or NGDP targeting, or still another monetary rule. Serious discussion of which rule to choose could begin. With the bloated Fed balance sheet, however, such discussions are premature.

[6]Jerry Jordan was among the first to observe that the Fed is now operating entirely on the liability side of the balance sheet.

Reserve Banks

I want to deal briefly with the recurring question of the status of the reserve banks and their presidents. Conti-Brown (2016) has most recently resurrected the issue. He treats their existence as solely the result of a political compromise by President Woodrow Wilson between two competing plans (the 1910 Aldrich Plan and the 1912 Glass Plan). He thus views the reserve banks solely in political terms (Conti-Brown 2016: 20–23). He all but ignores the economic function of the presidents. The closest he comes to acknowledging that is when he quotes Wilson: "We have purposely scattered the regional reserve banks and shall be intensely disappointed if they do not exercise a very large measure of independence" (Conti-Brown 2016: 22).

The economic justification today for the regional reserve banks is to provide economic policy perspectives from around the country. Without that input, only the policy elites of Washington and New York would be heard. To say they are insular and out of touch with people in most of the rest of the country would be an understatement. The energy industry is concentrated in the Kansas City and Dallas Federal Reserve districts; agriculture is concentrated there and in other districts; and so on. Simply put, the reserve bank presidents are there to prevent group think and be able to back up their views by voting on monetary policy. That, I submit, is the gravamen of Woodrow Wilson's argument.

If I were to criticize the presidents, it would be for not dissenting more often. Too many have gone along to get along. If the presidents don't exhibit their independence more often, they will undermine the best argument for their existence. Happily, at the September 2016 FOMC meeting, three presidents dissented from the policy: Esther George (Kansas City), Loretta Mester (Cleveland), and Eric Rosengren (Boston).[7] Perhaps the presidents have got back their policy mojo, and the FOMC will function as intended.[8] The unanimous vote for a rate increase at the December meeting involved the

---

[7]Three dissents at a meeting is a large number, but not unprecedented. Thornton and Wheelock (2014) analyze the history of FMOC dissents.

[8]Fed governors, once active dissenters, have almost ceased to dissent. There have been only two dissents by governors since 1995 (Thornton and Wheelock 2014: 225).

committee's adopting the policy advocated by the dissenters at the earlier meeting. Dissenting worked as it should.

I will not respond to Conti-Brown's arguments in detail. He thinks the reserve banks are unconstitutional, but other legal scholars disagree.[9] He is mightily offended because the banks are private entities performing a public function. When they were created, however, providing a national currency was not considered an inherently governmental function. Moreover, operating a clearinghouse, which the reserve banks took over from clearinghouse associations owned by commercial banks, was not considered an inherently governmental function. So banker involvement in the reserve banks made sense. Conti-Brown (2016: 105) grudgingly acknowledges that the involvement of commercial bankers in Federal Reserve banks has been reduced. I, for one, would have no objection if it were reduced further. But getting rid of the decentralization in the Federal Reserve System would be a policy blunder. Meltzer (2016) argues the role of reserve banks should be strengthened and suggests allowing all 12 presidents to vote at every FOMC meeting.

My principal objection to Conti-Brown's jihad against reserve banks is that it is beside the point and a distraction in the current circumstance. Abolishing the reserve banks would not address any pressing monetary policy issue of the day. It would not address the Fed's bloated balance sheet, credit allocation, emergency lending, or lack of monetary rules. Conti-Brown wants the Fed to be more democratic. From a public-choice perspective, that goal translates into the Fed being even more political. It has already become too political; no more of that influence is needed.

Conclusion

In 1913, Congress took a wrong turn when it enacted the Federal Reserve Act. Other, better reforms were available. An asset-based currency would have provided an elastic currency (Selgin 2016). In both the Great Depression and the Great Recession, the Federal

---

[9]Walker Todd (2016) is one who disagrees. According to him, the reigning precedent is McCulloch v. Maryland decided in 1819. The structure of the Federal Reserve System has survived all constitutional challenges.

Reserve failed to provide elastic credit in a timely fashion.[10] Before the Fed, the existing clearinghouses provided emergency cash in times of liquidity crises. That provision was found to be extra-legal. The practice could have been legalized without creating a central bank.[11]

We are where we are. That statement is not to take a position on alternatives to central banking. The most likely alternative would involve the development of digital currencies with wide usage. There are many obstacles to the emergence of alternative currencies, however, of which anti-money laundering laws are just one. We are certainly talking a decade or more before a private currency alternative to central banking could emerge.[12]

What to do in the interim? We cannot simply wait and see how quickly the world of digital money develops. There will be lot of monetary misconduct in the interim. The goal should be to restrain and contain the Fed in the future and to roll back central bank overreach. That includes downsizing the Fed's balance sheet and ending emergency lending.[13] Credit allocation should cease, and the Fed's regulatory powers under the Dodd-Frank Act need to be curtailed.

[10]In the summer of 2008, the Fed was sterilizing credit provided to individual institutions. In effect, Chairman Bernanke failed in his famous promise to Milton Friedman never to repeat the mistakes of the 1930s.

[11]For more on the alternatives and the Fed's historical performance, see Selgin, Lastrapes, and White (2012).

[12]And there are contrary forces working against digital currencies. See Lemieux (2016).

[13]The Dodd-Frank Act includes a limited reform of emergency lending. The Fed can no longer employ emergency lending to bail out a single institution, but only to "any participant in any program or facility with broad-based eligibility" (quoted in Conti-Brown 2016: 156). I agree with Conti-Brown's skeptical assessment, however, that "the Fed's lawyers have shown themselves to be very able at defining structures and entities in a way that is consistent with the law's letter but still aimed at unfettered deployment of emergency funds" (Conti-Brown 2016: 300, n14). It would take more than this limited provision to curtail emergency lending by the Fed. Walker Todd, a former Fed lawyer himself, points out that the really effective emergency lending in the 1930s was accomplished by the Reconstruction Finance Corporation, an agency created by an act of Congress. It moved from lending to equity investments in companies. Whatever one's view of the desirability of bailouts, it is fiscal policy. Fiscal policy is properly the prerogative of Congress rather than a central bank. See also Taylor (2016b: 717).

There was a time when ordinary people did not know who or what a Fed chair was. High Federal Reserve officials were not the most important economic policymakers for the country. Genuine reform of the Federal Reserve would restore anonymity to the Fed and put economic policymaking back where it belongs—with Congress and the president. This position is in the spirit of Friedman's admonition that monetary policy should provide a framework within which private planning and decisionmaking take place.

Congress has unquestioned authority on monetary policy. Getting it to assert that authority means overcoming its inclination to delegate excessively its authority (passing the buck). At least the House of Representatives has shown a willingness to do so, as evidenced by the passage of H.R. 3189, the Fed Oversight Reform and Modernization (FORM) Act, which would require the Fed to choose a monetary rule.[14]

Reforming the Fed and implementing better monetary policy will not by themselves cure the economic malaise in the United States. Reform of the economy is needed to unleash Friedman's "forces of enterprise, ingenuity, invention, hard work, and thrift that are the true springs of economic growth." That effort must include tax reform and deregulation. Our tax system is complex and costly. Regulation at all levels stifles the formation of new businesses and job creation.[15] Monetary policy is only one arrow in the policy quiver, but an important one.

The Fed's intrusion into credit allocation has allowed government planning to be substituted for private initiative. Additionally, the very low interest rate policies have enabled government deficit spending, promoting the state over the market. Finally, the sheer size of the Fed's balance sheet threatens the market economy. Reforms outlined in this article urgently need enactment and implementation.

---

[14]Consideration of the FORM Act drew a remarkable letter from Fed Chair Janet Yellen (2015). That letter, in turn, drew a spirited response from John Taylor (2015).

[15]Wallison (2016) connects slow global economic growth to regulations and offers a glimmer of hope.

References

Alchian, A. A. (1969) "Information Costs, Pricing and Resource Unemployment." *Economic Inquiry* 7: 109–28.

Caldwell, B. (2004) *Hayek's Challenge: An Intellectual Biography of F. A. Hayek*. Chicago: University of Chicago Press.

Cargill, T. F., and O'Driscoll, G. P. Jr. (2013) "Federal Reserve Independence: Reality or Myth?" *Cato Journal* 33 (3): 417–35.

Conti-Brown, P. (2016) *The Power and Independence of the Federal Reserve*. Princeton: Princeton University Press.

Dowd, K. ([1988] 1996) *Private Money: The Path to Monetary Stability*. Hobart Paper 112. London: Institute of Economic Affairs.

Dowd, K., and Timberlake, R. H. Jr. (1998) *Money and the Nation State*. Oakland, Calif.: Independent Institute.

Eichengreen, B. (2011) *Exorbitant Privilege: The Rise and Fall of the Dollar and the Future of the International Monetary System*. Oxford: Oxford University Press.

Federal Open Market Committee (FOMC) (2014) "Policy Normalization Principles and Plans," as adopted effective September 16, 2014. Available at www.federalreserve.gov /monetarypolicy/files/FOMC_PolicyNormalization.pdf.

Friedman, M. (1968) "The Role of Monetary Policy." *American Economic Review* 58 (1): 1–17.

_____ (2006) "He Has Set a Standard." *Wall Street Journal* (January 31).

Friedman, M., and Schwartz, A. J. (1963) *A Monetary History of the United States, 1867–1960*. Princeton: Princeton University Press.

Garrett, S. (2016) Letter to the Editor. *Wall Street Journal* (September 6): A14.

Hayek, F. A. (1948) *Individualism and Economic Order*. Chicago: University of Chicago Press.

Hetzel, R. L., and Leach, R. F. (2001) "The Treasury-Fed Accord: A New Narrative Account." *Federal Reserve Bank Richmond Economic Quarterly* 87 (Winter): 33–55.

Hilsenrath, J. (2016) "Fed Stumbles Fueled Populism." *Wall Street Journal* (August 26): A1, A6.

Hummel, J. R. (2011) "Ben Bernanke versus Milton Friedman: The Federal Reserve's Emergence as the U.S. Economy's Central Planner." *The Independent Review* 15 (Spring): 485–518.

Jordan, J. (2016a) "The New Monetary Framework." *Cato Journal* 36 (2): 367–83.

_____ (2016b) "Rethinking the Monetary Transmission Mechanism." Paper prepared for the 2016 Cato Institute Monetary Conference (November 17).

Kane, E. J. (1980) "Politics and Fed Policymaking: The More Things Change the More They Remain the Same." *Journal of Monetary Economics* 6: 199–211.

Leijonhufvud, A. (1981) *Information and Coordination.* New York: Oxford University Press.

Lemieux, P. (2016) "In Defense of Cash." *Library of Economics and Liberty* (October 3): www.econlib.org/library/Columns/y2016 /Lemieuxcash.html.

Meltzer, A. H. (2015) "Karl Brunner, Scholar: An Appreciation." Paper prepared for the Swiss National Bank Conference in Honor of Karl Brunner's 100th Anniversary, September 2016.

_____ (2016) "Reform the Federal Reserve." *Defining Ideas* (October 12).

Nelson, E. (2015) *Milton Friedman and Economic Debate in the United States: Book 1,* 1932–1972. Unpublished manuscript.

O'Driscoll, G. P. Jr. (2016) "Monetary Policy and the Knowledge Policy." *Cato Journal* 36 (2): 337–52.

Selgin, G. (2016) "New York's Bank: The National Monetary Commission and the Founding of the Fed." Cato Institute Policy Analysis No. 793 (June 21).

Selgin, G.; Lastrapes, W.; and White, L. H. (2012) "Has the Fed Been a Failure?" *Journal of Macroeconomics* 34: 569–96.

Smith, V. C. ([1936] 1990) *The Rationale of Central Banking.* Indianapolis: Liberty Press.

Sowell, T. ([1980] 1996) *Knowledge and Decisions.* New York: Basic Books.

Taylor, J. (2009) *Getting Off Track.* Stanford: Hoover Institution Press.

_____ (2015) "The Fed's Letter to Congress and the FORM Debate." *Economics One* (November 18): https://economicsone .com/2015/11/18/the-feds-letter-to-congress-and-the-form -debate.

_____ (2016a) Monetary Policy Homepage: http://web.stanford .edu/~johntayl/PolRulLink.htm.

_____ (2016b) "Interest on Reserves and the Fed's Balance Sheet." *Cato Journal* 36 (3): 711–20.

Thornton, D. L., and Wheelock, D. C. (2014) "Making Sense of Dissents: A History of FOMC Dissents." Federal Reserve Bank of St. Louis *Review* (Third Quarter): 213–28.

Todd, W. (2016) Private Email Communication (October 13).

Wall Street Journal (2016) Review & Outlook: "The Federal Reserve's Politicians" (August 29): A10.

Wallison, P. J. (2016) "The Regulatory Tide Recedes." *Wall Street Journal* (October 10): A15.

Warsh, K. (2016) "The Federal Reserve Needs New Thinking." *Wall Street Journal* (August 25): A11.

Weaver, R. K. (1986) "The Politics of Blame Avoidance." *Journal of Public Policy* 6 (Oct.– Dec.): 371–98.

White, L. H. (1984) *Free Banking in Britain: Theory, Experience, and Debate, 1800–1845*. Cambridge: Cambridge University Press.

_____ (1989) *Competition and Currency: Essays on Free Banking and Money*. New York: New York University Press.

Yellen, J. L. (2015) Letter to The Honorable Paul Ryan and The Honorable Nancy Pelosi (November 16).

_____ (2016) "The Federal Reserve's Monetary Toolkit: Past, Present, and Future." Speech at the Federal Reserve Bank of Kansas City Symposium, Jackson Hole, Wyoming (August 26).

2
SORTING OUT MONETARY AND FISCAL POLICIES
Mickey D. Levy

Monetary and fiscal policies have both have gone off track. Excessively easy monetary policy, marked by a massive increase in the Federal Reserve's balance sheet and sustained negative real interest rates, has failed to stimulate faster economic growths but has distorted financial behavior and involves sizable risks. Fiscal policies have resulted in an unhealthy rise in government debt, and projections of dramatic further increases heap burdens on future generations and involve incalculable risks. Monetary and fiscal policies interact in undesirable ways. The Fed's expanded scope of monetary policy has blurred the boundaries with fiscal and credit policies, and the ever-growing government debt may eventually impinge on the Fed and its independence.

A reset of monetary and fiscal policies is required. The Fed has begun to normalize monetary policy so, at this point, a shift in fiscal policy is much more pressing.

The Fed must continue to raise interest rates and unwind its balance sheet but be more aggressive than indicated in its current strategy. The Fed should aim to reduce its balance sheet to the point in which excess reserves are kept relatively low, and it should

Mickey D. Levy is Chief Economist for the Americas and Asia at Berenberg Capital Markets, LLC, and a member of the Shadow Open Market Committee. This article is reprinted from the *Cato Journal*, Vol. 38, No. 1 (Winter 2018). It is based on testimony presented to the U.S. Congress, House Financial Services Committee, July 20, 2017. The views expressed are the author's and do not reflect those of Berenberg Capital Markets.

fully unwind its holdings of mortgage-backed securities (MBS). A full normalization of monetary policy would benefit economic performance and improve financial health. Equally important, the Fed must acknowledge the limitations of monetary policy and step back from policy overreach, including removing itself from credit allocation policies and toning down its excessive focus on short-term fine-tuning.

The longer-run projections of government debt are alarming and must be taken seriously. General government debt has risen to 100 percent of GDP, up from 61 percent before the 2008–09 financial crisis, while publicly held debt, which excludes debt held for accounting purposes by the Social Security Trust Fund and other trust funds, has risen to 78 percent from 40 percent. The Congressional Budget Office (CBO) estimates that under current law, the publicly held debt-to-GDP ratio is projected to rise to nearly 150 percent by 2047. Congress must develop and implement a strategy that guarantees sound longer-run finances. This requires tough choices, particularly as it addresses the ever-growing entitlement programs, but the costs of inaction are rising. Many acknowledge the risks of rising debt for future economic performance, but in reality the burdens of the government's finances are already affecting current economic performance and the government's allocation of national resources. Witness how the persistent increases in entitlement programs and concerns about high government debt squeeze current spending on infrastructure, research and development, and other activities that would enhance economic performance. Under current laws, these budget constraints—those at the federal level as well as those facing state and municipal governments—will only increase in severity.

Congress's fiscal agenda must be two-pronged. First, Congress must develop and enhance programs and initiatives that directly address the sources of undesired economic and labor market underperformance while restructuring and trimming spending programs that are ineffective and wasteful. This requires transforming the government's annual procedure of budgeting of appropriations for the array of the so-called discretionary programs and dealing with the entitlement programs from a "deficit bean-counting" exercise into a strategic process that carefully assesses the structure of key programs and their objectives—whether they are meeting their policy and social objectives; whether they are doing so effectively; their unintended side effects; and how they may be enhanced, modified, and cut.

Second, Congress must enact laws that gradually phase in reforms of the entitlement programs that constrain the projected growth of *future* spending in a fair and honest way, improving the benefit structures of the programs with the objectives of protecting lower income retirees and providing sufficient time for older workers to plan for retirement.

The Proper Roles of Monetary and Fiscal Policies

I fully understand the frustrations stemming from the underperformance of the economy in recent years—the sizeable pockets of persistently high unemployment and low wages facing many working-age people, and weak trends in business investment and productivity that underlie disappointingly slow growth. We all want better performance. But the issue is how to achieve it.

Neither the Fed's sustained monetary ease nor high deficit spending addresses structural challenges facing labor markets, business caution in expansion and investing, weak productivity, and other critical issues. This is particularly apparent with the unemployment rate at 4.3 percent, below standard estimates of its "natural rate" (so-called full employment).

The reality is monetary policy cannot create permanent jobs, improve educational attainment or skills, permanently reduce unemployment of the semi-skilled, or raise productivity and real wages. Rather, monetary policy is an aggregate demand tool. The major sources of underperformance involve structural challenges that are beyond the scope of monetary policy to address. Yet in recent years, there has been excessive reliance on the Fed. All too frequently, analysts and observers opine "fiscal policy is dysfunctional so the Fed has to ease policy." This assumes that monetary policy and fiscal policy are two interchangeable levers. They are not. Monetary policy is not a substitute for fiscal policy. Monetary policy involves the Fed's control of interest rates and the amount of money in the economy, which influences aggregate demand and longer-run inflation.

Fiscal policy operates differently. Government spending programs and tax structures allocate national resources—for income support, national defense, health care, public goods like infrastructure, and an array of other activities—and create incentives favoring certain activities while discouraging others. In a critical sense, the magnitude and mix of spending programs and the structure and details of tax policies—along with the magnitudes of deficit spending—reveal the nation's priorities set by past and current fiscal policymakers. These allocations of national resources and how specific spending and tax provisions influence households and businesses are key inputs to economic performance, productivity, and potential growth.

In recent decades, the most pronounced change in the federal government's budget is the rapid expansions of Social Security, Medicare, and Medicaid. According to the CBO (2017), outlays for Social Security, Medicare and Medicaid, and health-care related entitlements have risen from 47 percent of total federal outlays (10.1 percent of GDP) in 1992 to 62.9 percent of federal outlays (13.2 percent of GDP) in 2017. These programs are projected to rise dramatically further to 65.3 percent of federal outlays (15.4 percent of GDP) by 2027.

The objectives of these entitlements are laudable, and they are critical for government and society. However, the growth in these programs has been the primary source of the rising government debt (and projections of further increases), and has significantly increased the share of government spending allocated to income support and health. Consequently, spending on other programs has been squeezed, including those that would enhance longer-run productive capacity. For virtually every state, Medicaid spending is one of the largest and fastest growing spending programs. Faced with rigid balanced-budget constraints on their operating budgets, states have cut back on the provision of some basic government goods and services.

Can these government programs be improved, made more efficient, or modified in ways that maintain their objectives? Yes. Congress must cut through budget categorizations like "mandatory spending" and "discretionary spending programs" and identify ways to improve the efficiency of these programs while maintaining their intent.

Aside from monetary and fiscal policies, labor market performance and business decisions are affected by a growing web of economic and labor regulations imposed by federal, state, and local governments. Private industries add to the list of regulatory requirements, including the expanding imposition of occupational certification requirements and other practices like "noncompete" job contracts. Certainly, while some of these government regulations and industry rules serve important roles, many constrain the mobility of a sizeable portion of the labor force, limit job opportunities, and are very costly to the economy. Obviously, these are beyond the scope of monetary and fiscal policy.

Regulatory policies deserve attention, in the discussion about the efficacy of monetary and fiscal policies, because they have unique economic effects that may work at cross-purposes to monetary and fiscal policies. In order to establish public policies that improve standards of living, we need to address the sources of economic and labor underperformance with the proper policy tools, rather than rely on standard monetary and fiscal stimulus that are unlikely to have desired outcomes but are costly and generate unintended side effects.

The Fed's Expanded Scope

The Fed deserves credit for its quantitative easing (QE) in 2008–09 that helped to restore financial stability and end the deep recession. The paralysis in the mortgage and short-term funding markets was scary and truly a crisis. The Fed's aggressive interventions and asset purchases, including its large-scale purchases of MBS and its "bailout" of AIG, directly involved the Fed in credit allocation and fiscal policy. At the time, Fed Chairman Ben Bernanke (2008) explicitly identified these Fed interventions as temporary emergency measures, and stated that the Fed would exit them on a timely basis.

But the efficacy of the Fed's unprecedented monetary ease well after the economy had achieved sustainable growth and financial markets had stabilized—the dramatic expansion of its large-scale asset purchase programs (LSAPs) and targeting the Fed funds rate below inflation—is questionable, and the expanded scope of monetary policy involves substantial risks. These policies and the Fed's forward guidance have stimulated financial markets and asset prices, but the economy has been largely unresponsive. Nominal GDP has not accelerated—it has averaged 3.6 percent annualized growth since the Fed implemented QE3 in Fall 2012—and real growth has been subnormal. Business investment has been disappointing despite the Fed's successful efforts to lower the real costs of capital. Productivity gains have been weak, and estimates of potential growth have been reduced significantly. Labor markets have clearly improved, but large pockets of underemployment persist.

Nonmonetary factors including government tax and regulatory policies have hampered credit growth and economic performance (Levy 2017). In banking, the burdensome regulations imposed by Dodd-Frank and the Fed's stress tests have deterred bank lending (Calomiris 2017). The Fed's low rates and forward guidance aimed at keeping bond yields low have dampened expectations. Meanwhile, the Fed's policy of paying interest on excess reserves (IOER), which began in October 2008, at a rate above the effective fed funds rate, has increased the demand to park reserves at the Fed rather than lend them out (Selgin 2016). Despite the dramatic surge in the Fed's monetary base, M2 has grown at a modest 6 percent rate in recent years. The response of aggregate demand has been tepid, and velocity has declined. This reflects several factors. Lower interest rates have increased the demand for money. The Fed's forward guidance has reinforced a sense of caution in the economy. In addition, burdensome regulations have inhibited the supply of bank credit and the monetary policy channels have been clogged. As a result, the high-powered money created by the Fed's LSAPs remain as excess reserves on big bank balance sheets and have not been put to work in the economy (Ireland and Levy 2017).

In the nonfinancial sector, the array of taxes and regulatory burdens and mandated expenses imposed by federal, state, and local governments have constrained business and household spending. Of note, these government-imposed burdens have led businesses to raise their required hurdle rates for investment projects and many job-creating expansion plans have been scuttled. Capital spending has been disappointing in light of the low real costs of capital and strong corporate profits and cash flows.

The Fed takes far too much credit for the sustained economic expansion and labor market improvement of recent years. Without the sustained aggressive monetary ease, the economy would have continued to expand and jobs would have increased. History shows clearly that economic performance has not been harmed when the Fed has normalized interest rates following a period of monetary ease. Not surprisingly, the three Fed rate hikes since December 2015 have had no material impact on economic performance.

Through most of the expansion, the Fed viewed the low wage gains and inflation as a rationale to enhance and maintain its efforts to use monetary policy to stimulate economic growth. Effectively, the Fed's mindset has evolved into the belief that its role is to manage the real economy. The Fed has rejected the notion that its persistently easy policies have been ineffective—much less the possibility that its policies may have had negative effects. Recently, the Fed has changed its tune. In a speech in March 2017, entitled "From Adding Accommodation to Scaling it Back," Fed Chair Janet Yellen identified "unwelcome developments" affecting economic performance that "reflect structural challenges that lie substantially beyond the reach of monetary policy." She continued to state that "Fiscal and regulatory policies—which are of course the responsibility of the Administration and Congress—are best suited to address such adverse structural trends" (Yellen 2017).

Along with weak productivity gains, the failure of nominal GDP to accelerate in response to the Fed's unprecedented monetary ease has been a key reason why wage increases have remained modest and inflation has remained below the Fed's 2 percent target. The slow (and nonaccelerating) growth of aggregate product demand has influenced wage and price setting behavior, reducing the flexibility of businesses to raise product prices and reducing their willingness to grant higher wages. Slow growth in nominal GDP—it has averaged 3.4 percent so far this expansion compared to 5.3 percent in the 2001–07 expansion and 5.6 percent during the 1990s—is statistically significant in explaining the slow wage gains despite the low unemployment rate (Levy and Reid 2016). Additionally, inflation has been constrained by declining quality-adjusted prices of select goods and services stemming from technological innovations and product improvements. Most notably, the PCE deflator for durable goods has fallen persistently since the mid-1990s. These innovations have increased consumer purchasing power and benefitted the economy.

The Fed's historic tendency to fine-tune the economy and financial markets has been accentuated during this expansion. This was apparent when the Fed implemented QE2, Operation Twist, and QE3 in an explicit effort to lower unemployment, and since 2014 when the Fed delayed tapering its asset purchases and then stuck to its reinvestment program to maintain its oversized portfolio. The Fed has been heavily influenced by short-term fluctuations in the economy, and by global and domestic asset markets. It has modified its employment mandate to include focus on the labor force participation rate and wages. These are beyond the Fed's mandate and well beyond the scope of monetary policy. Such short-term focus and expanded role historically have led to policy mistakes.

The Fed's Balance Sheet

As a result of these short-run concerns, the Fed maintains a balance sheet of $4.5 trillion, including $2.5 trillion of U.S. Treasury securities of various maturities and $1.8 trillion of MBS, primarily with long maturities. The Fed is now the largest holder of each, with 17 percent of outstanding federal publicly held debt and 12 percent of MBS outstanding. (The Fed's holdings of Treasuries are counted as publicly held debt because the Federal Reserve Banks are legally capitalized by the private sector banks in their districts). Prior to the financial crisis, the Fed's balance sheet was roughly $850 billion, composed nearly entirely of short-term Treasuries and other liquid securities.

The Fed has begun a strategy of gradually and passively unwinding a fairly even portion of its Treasury and MBS holdings by reinvesting all but a small portion of principle of maturing assets. Although the Fed has not been clear about the ultimate size of balance sheet it wishes to maintain, several Fed members have indicated that its ultimate aim is to maintain a large buffer of excess reserves. This strategy should be modified. The Fed's holdings of MBS are inappropriate, directly involving monetary policy in credit allocation, and should be totally unwound. The Fed's MBS holdings effectively favor mortgage credit over other types of credit. While the initial MBS purchases during the height of the financial crisis had a distinct purpose—to stabilize a completely dysfunctional and illiquid market that posed a threat to global markets—continuing to hold MBS makes little sense. Mortgage markets are functioning normally with sufficient liquidity. The Fed's ongoing explicit subsidies of the housing sector are irrational, and the Fed should go back to an all-Treasuries portfolio.

The Fed's intention to maintain a large buffer of excess reserves implies a shift from pre-financial crisis operating procedures, in which the Fed's much smaller asset portfolio resulted in a minimal amount of excess reserves. The Fed has built an argument that maintaining a large amount of excess reserves going forward would benefit the Fed's conduct of monetary policy and enhance its ability to stabilize financial markets. The maintenance of a large buffer of excess reserves would require the Fed to continue to pay IOER and manage the effective Fed funds rate through a "floor system." I prefer a strategy of maintaining a smaller balance sheet that would involve less excess reserves in the banking system, like the Fed used through most of its history prior to the financial crisis in 2008–09. With minimal excess reserves, the Fed used a market-based "corridor system" in which it managed the effective funds rate close to its target rate through open-market purchases and sales of assets. Going back to its traditional operating procedure would allow the Fed to lessen its exposure in the overnight reverse repo market and in general constrain its overall footprint in financial markets. However, this operational preference is of less importance than the higher priorities of fully winding down the Fed's MBS holdings and reining in the scope of monetary policy.

Monetary Influences on Fiscal Policy

The Fed's balance sheet, low policy rate, and forward guidance aimed at keeping bond yields low temporarily have combined to reduce budget deficits and the government's debt service costs. The Fed effectively is operating a massive positive carry strategy by borrowing short and lending long. This will generate profits and reduce budget deficits as long as interest rates stay low. The Fed's remittances to the U.S. Treasury reached a peak of $117 billion in Fiscal Year 2015. They have receded in 2016 and 2017 as the average yield on the Fed's portfolio has receded and the Fed's rate hikes have increased the interest it pays to commercial banks under IOER. These large remittances to the Treasury have materially reduced recent budget deficits.

While this deficit reduction may sound good superficially, it involves sizeable risks—to current and future taxpayers—and entangles the Fed's monetary policy in the government's budget and fiscal policies in unhealthy ways. Congress seems to perceive that the Fed's outsized profits remitted to the Treasury are risk-free and permanent, when in fact they involve sizeable interest rate risks. Moreover, the Fed's balance sheet exposes monetary policy to undesirable budget practices and may undercut the Fed's independence and credibility.

At a recent congressional hearing held by the House Financial Services Committee on the interaction between monetary and fiscal policies, Congressman Brad Sherman (D–CA) heaped praise on the outsized net profits the Fed remits to the Treasury and asked, "What would the Fed need to do to double (to $200 billion) the amount of profits it remits to the Treasury?" This question may seem amusing to monetary economists, but it illustrates a lack of understanding about the proper role of monetary policy and highlights the Fed's potential vulnerabilities. The Fed should not understate the political-economy risks of maintaining such a large balance sheet. By suppressing deficits and debt service costs, the Fed's outsized remittances have eased pressure on Congress to address the growing budget imbalance. Also, as illustration of how Congress may misuse the Fed's large remittances, in December 2015, Congress's enactment of the FAST Act to provide financing for transportation infrastructure redirected a small portion of the Fed's assets and some of its net profit into the Highway Trust Fund. The Fed did not protest the way this budgetary "sleight of hand" procedure inappropriately used monetary policy for fiscal purposes.

In light of the magnitude of federal debt outstanding (currently $15 trillion and estimated by the CBO to rise to $27 trillion in 2027), budget deficits and debt service costs are very sensitive to interest rates. The CBO (2017) estimates that a 1 percentage point increase in interest rates from its baseline assumptions over the 10-year projection period would add $1.6 trillion to the budget deficit. Such interest-rate risk must be taken seriously. The Fed's forecasts of higher policy rates, sustained economic growth, and a rise in inflation to 2 percent point toward higher bond yields. Prior experiences of positive carry strategies often end badly. Witness the failures of many private financial companies, as well as Fannie Mae and Freddie Mac, which required government bailouts. The Fed's efforts to be more transparent should include a clear and honest assessment of the government's budgetary risks of its sustained outsized balance sheet.

Fiscal Policy Influences on Monetary Policy

To date the basic thrust of the Fed's monetary policy has not been materially influenced by budget deficit considerations, although the Fed takes into account fiscal policy deliberations and is sensitive to the impact some of its extraordinary actions have had on the federal budget. But these have been relatively low-level concerns. A much larger concern centers on projections of dramatically rising government debt and the lack of impetus of fiscal policymakers to address the issue, which raise the prospects that the government's finances may exert burdens on the Fed and impinge on monetary policy.

Sound monetary policy ultimately relies on sound government finances (Leeper 2010). In the extreme, unsustainably high government debt service burdens may dominate monetary policy and require the Fed to accommodate fiscal policy by reducing the real value of the debt or, in an extreme case, ensuring the government's solvency. Such a prospect of fiscal dominance of monetary policy seems remote and far off. However, it may not be so distant, particularly if fiscal policymakers ignore the longer-term budget debt realities. Moreover, nobody really knows when the level of debt becomes "unsustainable" or when or how government finances may unhinge inflationary expectations (Weidmann 2013).

In this context, the current fiscal debate about tax policy should be focusing on reforms that increase productive capacity by reducing inefficiencies and distortions and reducing the disincentives to invest, rather than temporary fiscal stimulus that involves more deficit spending. This is particularly true with the economy in its ninth consecutive year of expansion and clearly displaying signs of self-sustaining growth.

Congress faces several alternative fiscal policy paths. It may continue to avoid reforming current spending programs and the tax structure. This would reinforce disappointing economic performance, and downside risks would rise. Economic growth would remain slow, large pockets of underperformance in labor markets and slow wage growth would persist, reliance on income support would mount and government programs would become increasingly strained, and government debt would continue to rise rapidly. Alternatively, Congress may reform current spending programs, particularly entitlements, by improving their structures while maintaining their intent. Congress also needs to address the sources of the rising government debt and overhaul the tax system. The latter requires reducing marginal tax rates, particularly corporate taxes; broadening the tax base through eliminating the array of deductions, deferrals, exemptions and credits; and simplifying the tax code. Those efforts would lift sustainable economic growth, improve productivity, increase wages and economic well-being of underperformers in labor markets, ease burdens on income support systems, and improve government finances. Future concerns are quickly becoming current realities.

Conclusion

Is it appropriate to be critical of macroeconomic policies amid sustainable economic expansion and low inflation? Yes. Debt projections and the current tax code cry out for reform. The current corporate tax reform initiative is promising. But addressing the government's deficit spending and rising debt is a thorny challenge. How can current fiscal policymakers be expected to make necessary strategic changes to entitlement programs when doing so may involve short-term political fallout? There is no easy answer, but a good starting point would involve members of Congress learning the basic structures and key details of the biggest government spending programs—beneficiary requirements and benefit structures, the magnitude and distribution of benefits, and how they are financed. Such programmatic knowledge could become a healthy basis for a more economically rational policy debate and replace the current tendency of fiscal policymakers to make superficial statements on key programs that only serve to polarize the debate.

Redirecting monetary policy is simpler. The Fed must change its mindset. It should purposely narrow the objective of monetary policy to maintain low inflation and inflationary expectations and be more circumspect about the proper role of monetary policy as an input to sustainable healthy economic performance. This would lead the Fed to redirect itself from its recent thrust of "managing the real economy" and excessive fine-tuning, and acknowledge that some challenges facing the economy are better addressed through other economic, fiscal, and regulatory policy tools. This would steer the Fed away from its harmful roles in fiscal and credit policies.

References

Bernanke, B. (2008) "Federal Reserve Policies in the Financial Crisis." Speech at the Greater Austin Chamber of Commerce, Austin, Texas (December 1).

Calomiris, C. W. (2017) "The Microeconomic Perils of Monetary Policy Experimentation." *Cato Journal* 37 (1): 1–15.

CBO (Congressional Budget Office) (2017) *An Update to the Budget and Economic Outlook: 2017 to 2027* (June 29).

Ireland, P., and Levy, M. (2017) "A Strategy for Normalizing Monetary Policy." Shadow Open Market Committee (April 21): http://shadowfed.org/wp-content/uploads/2017.pdf.

Leeper, E. (2010) "Monetary Science, Fiscal Alchemy." Federal Reserve Bank of Kansas City, Jackson Hole Symposium (August 26–28).

Levy, M. (2017) "Why Have the Fed's Policies Failed to Stimulate the Economy?" *Cato Journal* 37 (1): 39–45.

Levy, M., and Reid, R. (2016) "How Much Can Wages Rise?" *Berenberg Capital Markets* (October 26).

Selgin, G. (2016) "Interest on Reserves and the Fed's Balance Sheet." Testimony before the U.S. House of Representatives Committee on Financial Services, Monetary Policy and Trade Subcommittee (May 17). Available at www.cato.org/publications/testimony/interest-reserves-feds-balance-sheet.

Weidmann, J. (2013) "Who Calls the Shots? The Problem of Fiscal Dominance." Speech to the BdF-BBk Macroeconomics and Finance Conference, Paris (May 24).

Yellen, J. (2017) "From Adding Accommodation to Scaling It Back." Speech to the Executives' Club of Chicago (March 3).

3

LEARNING THE RIGHT LESSONS FROM THE FINANCIAL CRISIS

Kevin Dowd and Martin Hutchinson

More than eight years after the onset of the global financial crisis, there is one thing that ought to be clear to everyone: unconventional monetary policies are not working. We have had three rounds of quantitative easing (QE) and the Fed's balance sheet has increased nearly fivefold from $825 million in August 2007 to just over $4 trillion today; the federal funds rate fell from 5.25 percent to almost zero by December 2008 and has remained there until the 25 basis point increase in December 2015; federal debt has more than doubled to just over $18 trillion, rising from 61 percent to 101 percent of GDP; vast amounts of public money have been thrown at the banks to keep them afloat; and there has been a huge expansion in financial regulation. To say that the results have been disappointing would be an understatement: output has been sluggish, unemployment has been persistent, bank lending has flatlined, productivity has risen at an unprecedentedly slow rate since 2011, and poverty and inequality have greatly increased.[1] For their part, the banks are still much weaker

Kevin Dowd is Professor of Finance and Economics at Durham University in the United Kingdom, a partner at Cobden Partners, and an Adjunct Scholar at the Cato Institute. Martin Hutchinson is a journalist and author of the Bear's Lair column (http://tbwns.com/category/the-bears-lair). This article is reprinted from the *Cato Journal*, Vol. 36, No. 2 (Spring/Summer 2016). The authors thank Anat Admati, Roger Brown, John Butler, Gordon Kerr, Alasdair Macleod, Alberto Mingardi, and Kevin Villani for helpful comments.

[1]Going further, these policies have even managed to defy the Zarnowitz rule—

than they should be, and major banking problems—especially, "too big to fail"—are still unresolved and continue to pose major threats to future financial stability. Seven years of extreme Keynesian policies have failed to produce their intended results. We see similar results in Europe and in Japan. In the latter, this comes after 25 years of such policies.

It is curious that in every discipline except Keynesian macroeconomics, practitioners first consider what caused a problem and then seek a treatment that addressed the cause. If the cause of a medical condition is excess, then the remedy would be moderation or abstinence. However, in Keynesian economics, if the cause is excess spending, then the standard treatment is *even more* spending. Keynesians then wonder why their treatments don't work. To give one example, former U.S. Treasury secretary Larry Summers (2014: 67) recently observed: "It is fair to say that critiques of [recent] macroeconomic policy . . . , almost without exception, suggest that prudential policy was insufficiently prudent, that fiscal policy was excessively expansive, and that monetary policy was excessively loose." Summers is correct, but he fails to note the irony: that the majority of policymakers *still* advocate insufficiently prudent prudential policy, excessively expansionary fiscal policy, and excessively loose monetary policy. One can only wonder what these policymakers expect to achieve, other than the same result those policies produced last time, on a grander scale.

It is therefore important that we return to first principles and rethink monetary and banking policy. Instead of mindlessly throwing more money and stimulus around, we should consider what caused our current problems and then address those root causes. We would suggest that the causes of our malaise are activist monetary policies on the one hand, and a plethora of government-created incentives for bank risk taking on the other. Both causes are themselves the product of earlier state interventions.

---

that sharp recessions are followed by sharp recoveries (Zarnowitz 1992). This suggests that these policies have been not so much ineffective as counterproductive, and that the economy would have recovered faster had the policy response been less aggressive.

This diagnosis suggests the following reform program: (1) recommoditize the dollar, (2) recapitalize banks, (3) restore strong governance in banking, and (4) roll back government interventions in banking. The first two reforms directly address the causes just mentioned—monetary meddling and government-subsidized risk taking—and are intended to get the financial system functioning normally again. The two remaining reforms serve to eradicate the root causes and strengthen the system long term by protecting it against future state intervention.

Recommoditizing the Dollar

The key to monetary reform at the most fundamental level is to establish a robust monetary constitution that would have no place for institutions with the power to undermine the currency; thus, there would be no central bank. However, before we can end the Fed, we must first put the U.S. dollar on a firm footing. The natural way to do that is to recommoditize it—that is, anchor the value of the dollar to a commodity or commodity bundle.

The obvious reform is to restore the gold standard. In its purest form, a gold standard involves a legal definition of the currency unit as a specified amount of gold. For example, the Gold Standard Act of 1900 defined the dollar as "twenty-five and eight-tenths grains of gold nine-tenths fine." This definition implies a fixed equilibrium gold price of just over $20.67 per troy ounce.

The gold standard has much to commend it: it imposes a discipline against the overissue of currency, restrains monetary meddlers, and has a fairly good track record. The main problem, however, is that it makes the price level hostage to the gold market. If the demand for gold rises, then the only way in which the gold market can equilibrate is through a rise in the relative price of gold—that is, a rise in the price of gold against goods and services generally—and this requires a fall in the price level (i.e., deflation). Conversely, if the demand for gold falls or the supply rises, the price level must rise (i.e., inflation must occur) to equilibrate the gold market. The stability of the price level under the gold standard, therefore, depends on the stability of the factors that drive demand and supply in the gold market. Historical evidence suggests that the price level under the gold standard was fairly volatile in the short term but much more stable over the longer term.

We might then ask whether we can improve on the gold standard. Over the years there have been many proposals to do so. Perhaps the most promising—and one of the least known—is the "fixed value of bullion" standard proposed by Aneurin Williams in 1892:

> In a country having a circulation . . . made up of paper, and where the government was always prepared to buy or sell bullion for notes at a price, the standard of value might be kept constant by varying from time to time this price, since this would be in effect to vary the number of grains of gold in the standard unit of money. . . . If gold appreciated [relative to the price level], the number of grains given or taken for a unit of paper money would be reduced: the mint-price of gold bullion raised. If gold depreciated, the number of grains given or taken for the note would be increased: the mint-price of gold bullion lowered [Williams 1892: 280].

Thus, the proposal, which admittedly lacks operational details, is that the system respond to shocks in the relative price of gold by changing the gold content of the dollar, instead of letting the whole adjustment fall on the price level, as would occur under a true gold standard. The gold content of the dollar becomes a shock absorber.

We would emphasize, too, that the Williams system is only one example from a broader family of similar systems.[2] We can imagine even better systems that would deliver greater price-level stability.

Having thus restored the convertibility of currency, the next step is to liberalize its issue by removing any Federal Reserve privileges. Any bank would be allowed to issue its own currency, including banknotes. The main restriction would be one designed to guard against counterfeit: any notes should be clearly distinguishable from those issued by other banks. Commercial banks would be free to issue notes denominated in U.S. dollars if they wished but those notes would only be receipts against U.S. dollars as legally defined. In other words, a commercial bank one-dollar note might state, "I promise to pay the bearer the sum of one dollar," as per the conditions governing the redeemability of the dollar note, and respecting the *legal definition of the U.S. dollar as a given amount of gold* at any particular time. There would be no restrictions against the issue of currency denominated in other

---

[2]See, for example, Irving Fisher's "compensated dollar" plan (Fisher 1913).

units of account, nor any restrictions on private currencies. The law would also be changed to allow U.S. courts to enforce contracts made in any currencies freely chosen by those involved.

By this point, the door would be open to private banknotes that would start to circulate at par with Federal Reserve notes. Over time, their market share would rise, as note-issuing banks would be incentivized to promote their own notes over those of rivals, and the Fed's share of the currency market would gradually diminish.

Recapitalize the Banks

Turning now to banking, the first point to appreciate is that the banks are still massively undercapitalized. The root causes of this undercapitalization are the incentives toward excessive risk taking created by various government interventions, including the limited liability statutes, government deposit insurance, the central bank lender of last resort function, and the general expectation that banks can count on being bailed out if they get themselves into trouble. With the exception of limited liability, these interventions are specifically designed to protect the banking system. In fact, however, they are seriously counterproductive: by protecting the banks against the downside consequences of their own decisions, these interventions subsidize risk taking, and the downside is passed on to the taxpayer. Naturally, banks respond to this regime by maximizing the value of the risk-taking subsidy: they increase their leverage and become far too big, with the biggest ones becoming *too big to fail*.

This trend toward weaker banks can be seen in the history of bank capital ratios. In the late 19th century, it was common for banks to have capital ratios of 40 to 50 percent. By the beginning of the recent financial crisis, however, the capital-to-asset ratios of the 10 biggest banks in the United States had fallen to less than 3 percent. The banks were thus chronically weakened, and the authorities—the Federal Reserve, the Federal Deposit Insurance Corporate (FDIC), and even the federal government—became hostage to them. The authorities dared not let weak banks fail for fear of the consequences. It is essential, therefore, that this dependence be ended, with viable banks made to stand on their own feet, and weak ones eliminated.

Accordingly, the most pressing task is to recapitalize the banking system: the required minimum capital standards need to be much higher and much less gameable than they currently are. To this end, we suggest that the United States impose a minimum bank capital ratio of 20 percent, with a further 10 percentage points on top (i.e., a 30 percent minimum) for systemically important financial institutions (SIFIs). We suggest that the numerator and the denominator of the capital ratio be defined as conservatively as possible:

- The numerator should be Common Equity Tier 1 (CET1), defined as tangible common equity plus retained earnings. CET1 capital gives us a conservative measure of the buffer available to absorb losses in a crisis. Broader definitions of capital are not appropriate because they include items such as deferred tax assets, goodwill, and other intangible assets that cannot be deployed in a crisis.
- The denominator should be the bank's total exposure or total amount at risk. This consists of total assets plus the additional exposures buried in off-balance-sheet positions—including securitizations, guarantees, and other commitments. It is important that these be estimated prudently, with no allowances made for hedging or correlation offsets, as these can be unreliable. The objective is to estimate the total amount that can be lost under worst-case assumptions.

Note that this capital ratio makes no use of risk weights or even risk models, both of which are essentially useless (Dowd 2014). It is precisely these features that undermine the Basel bank capital regulations, which, despite their stated intent to the contrary, have long since become means by which bankers decapitalize their own banks and pass much of the cost of their risk taking onto the taxpayer. One might add that the Basel system is insanely wedded to risk weights and risk models, because it is captured by the banking industry, which uses it to game the system. There is therefore no point in the United States arguing the issue as a topic for future Basel reform. Instead, the United States should simply withdraw from the Basel system and impose the above rules unilaterally on banks operating within its own territory.

A high capital requirement would have a number of beneficial effects:

- First, by forcing banks to bear the downside consequences of their actions, it would greatly reduce moral hazard, significantly curb risk taking, and thereby make the financial system much stronger. We can also think of higher capital requirements as greatly reducing the value of the government-created risk-taking subsidy.

- Second, shareholders would be more exposed to downside risks, which would strengthen the incentive of bank shareholders to ensure that senior management—who ultimately account to them—behave more responsibly. This, in turn, would help strengthen the governance structures of banks.

- Third, since the new capital regime would dispense with the arbitrary risk weights that permeate the Basel system, it would help correct the distorted lending incentives that Basel has created. Most notably, Basel attaches a zero risk weight to sovereign debt, a 50 percent risk weight to mortgage debt, and a 100 percent risk weight to corporate debt. Those risk weights artificially encourage banks to buy government, and to a lesser extent mortgage, debt in preference to corporate debt. Abandoning risk weights would remove those distortions and lead to more balanced bank portfolios with a greater emphasis on corporate lending. The distortions created by the very low risk weights attached to securitizations and model-based risk estimates would also be removed.

- Fourth, the use of the total exposure measure in the denominator of the capital ratio would mean that different positions would attract different capital requirements in proportion to the amounts at risk. This would serve to penalize risky positions and help drive out much of the toxicity that still exists in banks' on- and off-balance-sheet positions.

For its part, the supplementary SIFI capital requirement would provide additional insurance against the possibility of a big bank failure, as well as reducing the damage when such an event does occur. Big banks would have an incentive to slim down or break themselves up in order to avoid the higher SIFI capital requirement; smaller banks would be discouraged from becoming megabanks themselves. The bankers concerned might object that this additional requirement would help to make their banks uncompetitive. They would be right: the underlying objective here is precisely to make the antisocial, too-big-to-fail business model unsustainable. We want to squeeze the megabanks so that they shrink, get rid of their toxic positions, simplify themselves, and become manageable again. That way, they cease to be threats to the financial system and taxpayers.

We would also emphasize that high capital requirements should be imposed as soon as possible. As Admati and Hellwig (2013a: 169) point out:

> It is actually best for the financial system and for the economy if problems in banking are addressed speedily and forcefully. If bank equity is low, it is important to rebuild that equity quickly. It is also important to recognize hidden insolvencies and to close zombie banks. If handled properly, the quick strengthening of banks is possible and beneficial, and the unintended consequences are much less costly than the unintended consequences of delay. This is true even if the economy is hurting.

The need for speed arises in part because zombie banks would have both the opportunity and the incentive to waste even more public money, but also because their ongoing weakness would continue to hamper economic recovery.[3]

A natural question is why have a 20–30 percent minimum capital requirement? There are no magic numbers, but we want a minimum capital requirement that is high enough to remove the overwhelming part of the moral hazard that currently infects the banking system. We also want a requirement that is much higher than what we have at present. As John Cochrane (2013) put it: the capital requirement should be high enough that banks will never be bailed out again.

In this context, many experts have recommended minimum capital-to-total asset ratios that are much greater than those called for under current Basel rules. In an important letter to the *Financial Times* in 2010, no less than 20 experts recommended a minimum ratio of equity-to-total assets of at least 15 percent (Admati et al. 2010), and some of these wanted minimum requirements that are much higher. In addition, John Allison (2014) and Allan Meltzer (2012) have called for minimum capital-to-asset ratios of at least 15 percent; Admati and Hellwig recommended a minimum "at least of the order of 20–30 percent"; Eugene Fama and Simon Johnson recommended a minimum of 40–50 percent (see Admati and

---

[3]The damage caused by excessive regulatory forbearance has been a recurring theme in U.S. history (see, e.g., Salsman 1990) and is also a key factor in Japan's poor economic performance since the Japanese asset bubble burst in 1990.

Hellwig 2013a: 179, 308, 311); and Cochrane (2013) and Thomas Mayer[4] have advocated 100 percent.

The minimum capital requirement would be enforced by a simple rule: banks would not be permitted to make any distributions of dividends, or to pay any bonuses, until they met the above capital requirements.[5]

All banks with capital ratios below the minimum would then be pressured to produce credible capital plans so that they could resume distributions. They would have three ways to rebuild their capital: increase retained earnings, shrink assets, and/or issue more equity. The first two options, which banks would be forced to do anyway, would be slow, and given the pressure to resume distributions as soon as possible, it is difficult to see how most banks could avoid the need for a share issue to speed up the recapitalization process. The stock market would value a bank's shares in line with its perception of each bank's future profitability. A bank that is perceived to have good prospects would obtain good prices for its shares and should be able to recapitalize easily and quickly. On the other hand, a bank that is perceived to have poor prospects would experience difficulty selling its shares. At best, they would trade for low prices and recapitalization would be a slow process dependent on the accumulation of retained earnings and asset sales. At worst, the market might perceive the bank to be insolvent, in which case it would not be able to raise any new capital at all. The stock market reaction to a bank's share offering would provide a very useful signal of the bank's financial health.

Strong banks would be revealed to be strong and could recapitalize quickly; weak banks would be revealed to be weak, and the weakest would head toward extinction via takeover or failure. In the interim period, there would be a mass sale of banking assets and superfluous operations, which would depress the market for those

---

[4]Personal discussion.

[5]In the period since the onset of the financial crisis, the Federal Reserve has caved to bank pressure in allowing the banks to make dividend payments and stock repurchases, which undermine the Fed's own attempts to recapitalize the banking system. The amounts involved have been very substantial. For example, from the third quarter of 2007 through the height of the crisis, the largest 19 U.S. banks paid shareholders almost $80 billion; in fact, about half the money the government invested in the banks during the crisis went straight out the back door to shareholders (Admati 2012).

things and ensure that bank managements repositioned themselves with the most rigorous regard for what was actually profitable. In particular, capital- and risk- thirsty investment banking operations would be closed down or sold to brokerage operations without banking licenses or deposits from the public.

There then arises the delicate question of what to do if some banks are revealed to be very weak, even insolvent. This is very likely to occur: some of the big banks (e.g., Bank of America, Citi, and Deutsche) have high leverage, major problems, and vast off-balance-sheet positions. Indeed, we cannot rule out the possibility that imposing higher capital standards would reveal the hitherto hidden weakness of major banks, thereby triggering a major crisis. However, we can also well imagine a renewed financial crisis being triggered by other factors, such as a rise in interest rates.

So what should be done in such circumstances? It would make no sense to keep weak banks afloat at public expense; nor should the authorities respond as they did in 2007–08, with a series of panicked late-night deals of (at best) dubious legality. Instead, the authorities should be required by law to close distressed banks in an orderly fashion—possibly after a temporary period of public ownership to preserve orderly markets—with losses allocated according to existing seniority structures and viable units sold off to competitors. It should also be mandatory that senior management prepare living wills[6] and be made personally liable for any losses that might fall on taxpayers, which would almost certainly bankrupt them if their banks failed. Criminal investigations should also be opened so that any criminal behavior can be uncovered and punished. Ultimately, we need to give bankers the right incentives. By way of contrast, the current system imposes vast, random fines upon the banks, in some cases for minor violations that were not illegal at the time they were "committed." This is a scam that punishes the wrong people: bank managements make it through unscathed, but shareholders don't get the returns they have earned.

---

[6] The downside with existing provisions for living wills is that bankers might be tempted to booby-trap them in order to blackmail the authorities in the heat of a crisis. To make living wills useful, it is therefore essential that bankers be suitably incentivized: they should be made strictly (and potentially criminally) liable for any losses that might arise if something nasty "unexpectedly" crawls out of the woodwork.

Naturally, the imposition of higher capital requirements would cause the bankers to howl like hyenas, as it would greatly diminish their pay. Indeed, bankers have been very effective in fighting off attempts to impose serious increases in capital requirements by spreading a number of self-serving misconceptions—the real purpose of which is to defend their subsidized risk taking. This suggests that even the modest increases mandated under Basel III would be an enormous imposition to be resisted at all costs (Admati and Hellwig 2013a, 2013b). These misconceptions have seriously distorted public discussion and done much to block the reforms needed to get the banking system working properly again. We should consider a few of them.

The first misconception is that the banks are already adequately capitalized as they have capital ratios higher than Basel requires: the eight biggest SIFI banks, the ones that really matter, had an average ratio of capital to risk-weighted assets of almost 13 percent at the end of 2014. However, these capital ratios are meaningless; their Basel adequacy only serves to demonstrate the inadequacy of Basel itself. The ratios that matter are the *leverage ratios*, which for the same banks, at the same time, were 7.26 percent using U.S. Generally Accepted Accounting Principles (GAAP), and just over 5 percent using International Financial Reporting Standards (IFRS) (FDIC 2015). The latter are more reliable because of stricter rules applied to netting, but IFRS also has many problems and is far from perfect, not least because of its vulnerability to gaming. What's more, no current accounting standards even remotely address the issues raised by enormous off-balance-sheet positions or allow you to determine whether a bank is really solvent or not. The much-lauded rebuilding of American banks' balance sheets is greatly exaggerated.

The second misconception is that higher capital requirements would increase banks' costs. However, if this argument were correct, it would apply to nonbank corporations as well, and we would expect them to be equally highly leveraged in order to take advantage of the "cheapness" of debt. Instead, most nonbank corporations have capital ratios of over 50 percent. Some don't borrow at all. In reality, equity actually helps reduce the costs associated with potential distress and bankruptcy, and the same benefits apply to banks as to other corporations.

There is, nonetheless, one case where higher capital is costly—at least to bank shareholders. When the government intervenes to cover banks' downside risk, capital becomes expensive to the bank's shareholders: the higher the bank's capital level, the more of the risk subsidy they forgo, because higher capital reduces the cost to third parties of their risk-taking excesses. When bankers complain that capital is expensive, they consider only the costs to shareholders and themselves and do not take into account the costs of their risk taking to the economy.

In fact, the social cost of higher equity is *zero*. To quote Admati and Hellwig (2013a: 130):

> A bank exposing the public to risks is similar to an oil tanker going close to the coast or a chemical company exposing the environment to the risk that toxic fluid might contaminate the soil and groundwater or an adjacent river. Like oil companies or chemical companies that take too much risk, banks that are far too fragile endanger and potentially harm the public.

But unlike the case of safety risks posed by oil or chemical companies, higher bank safety standards can be achieved at no social cost, merely by requiring that banks issue more equity. This, in turn, can be achieved by reshuffling paper claims between banks and their investors.

Another of the banks' false, scaremongering arguments is that high minimum capital requirements would restrict bank lending and hinder economic growth. To give just one example: Josef Ackermann, the then-CEO of Deutsche Bank, claimed in 2009 that higher capital requirements "would restrict [banks'] ability to provide loans to the rest of the economy" and that "this reduces growth and has negative effects for all" (quoted in Admati et al. 2014: 42). The nonsense of such claims can be seen by noting that they imply that further increasing banks' leverage must be a good thing, notwithstanding the fact that excessive leverage was a key contributing factor to the financial crisis, and that ongoing bank weakness—weakness associated with too much leverage—is still impeding economic recovery.

One also encounters claims, based on a confusion of capital with reserves that mixes up the two sides of a bank's balance sheet, that higher capital requirements would restrict bank lending. To give two examples:

> Think of [capital] as an expanded rainy day fund. When used efficiently, a dollar of capital on reserve allows a bank to put ten dollars to work as expanded economic activity. The new

> Basel rules would demand that banks would maintain more dollars on reserve for the same amount of business, or more capital for no new economic work [Abernathy 2012].

> Higher capital requirements would require the building up of a buffer of idle resources that are not otherwise engaged in the production of goods and services [Greenspan 2011].

These statements come from experts who should know better. Such statements would be correct if they applied to requirements for higher cash reserves, but are false as they apply to requirements for higher equity capital. Capital requirements constrain how banks *obtain* their funds but do not constrain how they *use* them, whereas reserve requirements constrain how banks use their funds but do not constrain how they obtain them.

In fact, evidence suggests that high levels of capital actually support lending. To quote former Bank of England Governor Mervyn King (2013):

> Those who argue that requiring higher levels of capital will necessarily restrict lending are wrong. The reverse is true. It is insufficient capital that restricts lending. That is why some of our weaker banks are shrinking their balance sheets. Capital supports lending and provides resilience. And, without a resilient banking system, it will be difficult to sustain a recovery.

Then there is the "the time is not right" bugbear, which is merely an excuse to kick the can down the road:

> From the bankers' perspective, the time is never ripe to increase equity requirements or to impose any other regulation. As for the regulators, when the industry is doing poorly, they worry that an increase in equity requirements might cause a credit crunch and harm the economy [and never mind that excessive forbearance only makes the problem worse]. When the industry is doing well, no one sees a need to do anything [Admati and Hellwig 2013a: 171].

Last but not least, there is the "level playing field" excuse—a claim that higher capital requirements would disadvantage "our" banking industry relative to overseas competition. U.S. bankers make this claim against competition from Europe; British bankers make it against competition from the United States and Europe; and European bankers make it against competition from the United States and Britain. In other words, everyone makes it against everyone else. This argument is false because it presumes that higher capital is costly, and we know that it is not. It is also false because it ignores the point that higher capital supports a more resilient banking sector. On the other hand, the "level playing field" excuse is a good one to give impressionable local politicians who don't know any better.

Restore Strong Governance in Banking

We need to restore strong governance in banking. The key to achieving this is to reestablish strong personal liability on the part of the major decisionmakers with the bank—namely, senior bank management, including board members. More precisely, bank directors should be subject to unlimited strict personal liability for any losses that lead their banks to become bankrupt. This would effectively mean that the bankruptcy of the bank would entail the personal bankruptcy of its senior management. The strict liability provision would strip them of any excuses: if it happened on their watch, they would be automatically liable, without any need to prove dereliction of duty on the part of any particular director. These liability rules would encourage senior bankers to take a much greater interest in risk management and shut down high risk operations that could redound on them personally.

There is also the question of whether there should be extended liability for bank shareholders. In the United States, double liability for bank shareholders was common until the 1930s and made for conservative banking and low bank leverage. Extended liability provided reassurance to clients—both depositors and borrowers—and greatly reduced the moral hazards associated with the separation of ownership and control. The net effect was to greatly strengthen corporate governance in banking and ensure a tight grip on risk taking. It didn't always work: even under unlimited liability, the unfortunate Overend and Gurney shareholders of 1866 subscribed £10 toward their £100 shares—and were then called upon to put up the other £90 after the bank defaulted.

Going further, the default liability structure for bank shareholders should be *unlimited* liability. Recall that American investment banks were all unlimited liability partnerships a generation ago. The last to convert into a limited liability company was Goldman Sachs in 1986.

It is also worth noting that just over a century ago, J. P. Morgan preferred to use the unlimited liability model despite the fact that he could have incorporated—precisely because of the reassurance that unlimited liability gave his clients. With each deal he made, he put all his personal wealth on the line.

It is also widely recognized that the conversion of the unlimited liability investment bank partnerships into corporations was a major factor promoting greater risk taking and leverage. Describing the first such conversion—that of Salomon Brothers—Michael Lewis writes:

> John Gutfreund [Saloman's CEO] had done violence to the Wall Street social order—and got himself dubbed the King of Wall Street—when, in 1981, he'd turned Salomon Brothers from a private partnership into Wall Street's first public corporation. He ignored the outrage of Salomon's retired partners. . . . He and the other partners not only made a quick killing; they transferred the ultimate financial risk from themselves to their shareholders. . . . But from that moment, the Wall Street firm became a black box. The shareholders who financed the risk taking had no real understanding of what the risk takers were doing, and, as the risk taking grew ever more complex, their understanding diminished [Lewis 2010: 257–58].

These conversions then led to an increased focus on return on equity, much greater risk taking, and a major deterioration in the quality of corporate governance—all of which were highly predictable.

Of course, unlimited liability has its downsides: if a bank goes bankrupt, it can ruin its shareholders; it also discourages investors at the margin, who would expose themselves to losses beyond their investment; and it makes share trading difficult, because other shareholders would want to verify and approve new shareholders. However, one could argue that this is all to the good, because unlimited liability creates exactly the right incentives: if we want the guardians of our money to guard it as carefully as if it were their own, then unlimited liability is the natural choice. Recall, also, that Adam Smith ([1776] 1976: 741) was famously critical of the limited liability company: "The directors of such companies . . . being the managers of other people's money than their own, it cannot well be expected that they should watch over it with the same anxious vigilance. . . . Negligence and profusion must always prevail . . . in the management of such a company."

Moreover, limited liability is not a natural market outcome, but rather the product of government intervention after a vexed controversy—during which the free-market advocates of the time raised exactly the points that we are making here (see Campbell and Griffin 2006: 61–62).

Roll Back Government Interventions in Banking

The costs of financial regulation cannot be reliably quantified, but one thing is for sure: they are truly enormous. John Allison likes to point out that if you asked bankers whether they would prefer to eliminate taxes or eliminate regulation, the answer would be a no-brainer: regulation. He also notes that about 25 percent of a bank's personnel cost relates to regulations alone (Allison 2014: 351).

Crews (2014) estimates the cost of federal regulation to be just over $1.8 trillion, or 11 percent of GDP. Of that, the cost of economic and financial regulation makes up the thick end of half a trillion dollars. There can therefore be no doubt that regulation is a huge and growing drag on the economy. Most of it should simply be swept away: in the banking area, this would entail the repeal of a whole range of legislation, including Dodd-Frank, Sarbanes-Oxley, the Community Reinvestment Act, and Truth in Lending.

We also need to eliminate the various government-sponsored enterprises (GSEs) set up to interfere with the banking system, which have each promoted excessive risk taking. The first target would be Fannie Mae and Freddie Mac. These entities have absolutely no useful role to play in the economy, have done enormous damage to the U.S. housing market, and were key contributors to the global financial crisis. They should be shut down forthwith before they do any more damage.

The next target would be the FDIC, the very existence of which serves to encourage excessive risk taking by protecting bankers against many of the adverse consequences of bank failure. In particular, the FDIC removes any incentive depositors have to monitor their banks as they otherwise would; bankers respond by lowering their lending standards, taking more aggressive risks, and running down their capital. Reforms here would entail:

- The establishment of a program to phase out deposit insurance: this might involve a gradual reduction in the amounts covered—currently $250,000 in standard cases—combined with the introduction of and gradual increase in depositor coin-surance, up to the point where FDIC insurance is eliminated.

- A gradual reduction and eventual phasing out of the FDIC's role in examining and supervising banks: such functions would no longer be necessary once strong governance structures had been reestablished, and banks had been recapitalized and then adjusted their business models to root out excessive risk taking.

- Reforms to provide for low-cost means of enforcing consumer protection: these might involve private arbitration mechanisms or ombudsmen procedures, as are used in many other countries.

- Reforms to privatize decisions about when banks should go into bankruptcy and how such institutions should be resolved: such issues should be left to the private sector as is standard in other industries. A major benefit of such reforms is that they would eliminate the current biases—the incentives toward excessive forbearance—that exist when such decisions are left with regu-latory agencies that are subject to capture by political or indus-try interests.

The third and most difficult reform is to roll back the most trou-blesome GSE of all—the Federal Reserve. The initial steps would entail implementation planning for the reforms suggested here (e.g., to recommoditize the dollar), as well as contingency planning for plausible adverse events such as a rise in interest rates, the failure of a SIFI, or a renewed financial crisis.[7] We then need a series of pro-grams to carry out the following important tasks:[8]

- Roll back and ultimately abolish the Fed's supervisory and reg-ulatory roles, and eliminate ancillary programs such as the Fed's Comprehensive Capital Assessment Review "stress tests."

- Privatize the Fed's payment system, FedWire.

---

[7]This contingency planning should consider the possibility of another financial emergency and should include a program to keep the banking system as a whole operating at a basic level to prevent widespread economic collapse, fast-track bankruptcy processes to resolve problem banks and, where possible, return them to operation as quickly as possible, a prohibition of cronyist "sweetheart deals" for individual banks, and provisions to hold senior bankers to account.

[8]There are other tasks of lesser importance, which nevertheless still need doing. These include, for example, transferring the Fed's statistical operations to the U.S. Bureau of Statistics.

- End the Fed's lender of last resort function, and close down its discount window: last resort and discount window lending would then be left to the private sector.
- Close down the Fed's foreign exchange desk and the New York Fed's open market operations.
- Close the Consumer Financial Protection Bureau, or, failing that, transfer it to the Commerce Department where Congress can oversee it.
- Transfer the Fed's government debt management responsibilities to the Treasury.
- End the Fed's role as a bankers' bank by, for example, spinning off the Fed's deposit-taking functions to a separate voluntary-membership bankers' bank entity whose only function would be to hold and manage banks' deposits.
- Wind down and eventually phase out Federal Reserve currency: the only currency in circulation would then be that issued by regular commercial banks.
- Clean up and wind down the Fed's balance sheet: this task is probably best carried out by spinning off the Fed's asset portfolio into a separate runoff company, whose sole purpose would be to run down its asset portfolio at minimum cost to the taxpayer. Given the size of the Fed's balance sheet, this process would likely take a considerable amount of time and lead to a prolonged period of depressed asset prices and associated higher interest rates. It is likely to end up being very costly to the taxpayer whatever happens.
- Shut down the Federal Reserve Board. Individual Federal Reserve banks would then be free to continue to operate but would be stripped of any privileges or public policy responsibilities. It would be up to their member banks to decide upon their future.

The final regulatory rollback would be to phase out capital adequacy regulation. Such regulation would no longer be necessary once government-created incentives to excessive risk taking had been eliminated. The determination of banks' capital ratios could then be left to the banks themselves operating under the discipline of the free market. Banks that ran their capital ratios too low would then be subject to punishment by the market: they would lose confidence and market share, and so forth; *in extremis*, they would eventually be run out of business and should be allowed to fail as would be the case with badly run firms in any free market.

Conclusion

Central bankers have printed trillions in new base money, brought interest rates to zero (or even below), and thrown trillions at banks in subsidies with no noticeable positive effects. Yet, central bankers are considering more monetary stimulus. It appears that they have learned all the wrong lessons from the crisis. The central lesson they drew was that if a policy doesn't have the desired effects, then they should keep trying it again and again but on ever-greater scales. The lessons they should have drawn are that "stimulus"—whether in the form of QE, ZIRP, or NIRP—is counterproductive.

As far as the banking system is concerned, they convinced themselves that they had no choice but to bail the banks out; instead, they failed to realize that what was needed was a major structuring in which the zombies would have been shut down, the remaining banks recapitalized (and *not* at public expense), and the banks' governance structures overhauled to make the bankers personally liable for any losses they make.

The task ahead is to get both groups to unlearn these lessons: central bankers need to return to their senses, and commercial bankers need to be made to understand that the ongoing party of excessive risk taking at public expense is over; and, in turn, will only happen when the party *really* is over.

The four reforms discussed in this article—recommoditizing the dollar, recapitalizing the banks, restoring strong governance in banking, and rolling back government interventions in banking—can lead the way to a more robust financial system and strong economic growth. To implement a positive reform program, however, will require leaders who have both an understanding of the lessons learned from the financial crisis and the courage to act on them.

References

Abernathy, W. A. (2012) "Shrinking Banks Will Drag Down the Economy." *American Banker* (August 27).

Admati, A. (2012) "Why the Bank Dividends Are a Bad Idea." *Reuters* (March 14).

Admati, A.; Allen, F.; Brealey, R.; Brennan, M.; Boot, A.; Brunnermeier, M.; Cochrane, J.; DeMarzo, P.; Fama, E.; Fishman, M.; Goodhart, C.; Hellwig, M.; Leland, H.; Myers, S.; Pfleiderer, P.; Rochet, J.-C.; Ross, S.; Sharpe, W.; Spatt, S.; and Thakor, A. (2010) "Health Banking System Is the Goal, Not Profitable Banks." *Financial Times* (November 9).

Admati, A.; DeMarzo, P. M.; Hellwig, M. F.; and Pfleiderer, P. (2014) "Fallacies and Irrelevant Facts in the Discussion of Capital Regulation." In C. Goodhart, D. Gabor, J. Vestergaard, and I. Ertürk (eds.), *Central Banking at a Crossroads: Europe and Beyond*, chap. 3. New York: Anthem Press.

Admati, A., and Hellwig, M. (2013a) *The Bankers' New Clothes: What's Wrong with Banking and What to Do About It*. Princeton, N.J.: Princeton University Press.

——————— (2013b) "The Parade of the Bankers' New Clothes Continues: 23 Flawed Claims Debunked." Unpublished manuscript, Stanford Graduate School of Business.

Allison, J. A. (2014) "Market Discipline Beats Regulatory Discipline." *Cato Journal* 34 (2): 345–52.

Campbell, D., and Griffin, S. (2006) "Enron and the End of Corporate Governance." In S. MacLeod (ed.), *Global Governance and the Quest for Justice*, 47–52. Oxford, U.K.: Hart Publishing.

Cochrane, J. (2013) "Running on Empty." *Wall Street Journal* (March 1).

Crews, C. W. Jr. (2014) "Ten Thousand Commandments 2014." Washington: Competitive Enterprise Institute.

Dowd, K. (2014) "Math Gone Mad: Regulatory Risk Modeling by the Federal Reserve." Cato Institute Policy Analysis No. 754. Washington: Cato Institute.

Federal Deposit Insurance Corporation (2015) "Global Capital Index Capitalization Ratios for Global Systemically Important Banks (GSIBs)." Data as of December 31, 2014. Washington: Federal Deposit Insurance Corporation.

Fisher, I. (1913) "A Compensated Dollar." *Quarterly Journal of Economics* 27 (2): 213–35.

Greenspan, A. (2011) "Regulators Must Risk More to Push Growth." *Financial Times* (July 27).

Kerr, G. (2011) *The Law of Opposites: Illusory Profits in the Financial Sector*. London: Adam Smith Institute.

King, M. (2013) "A Governor Looks Back—and Forward." Speech given at the Lord Mayor's Banquet for Bankers and Merchants of the City of London (June 19).

Lewis, M. (2010) *The Big Short: Inside the Doomsday Machine*. New York: W. W. Norton.

Meltzer, A. H. (2012) "Banks Need More Capital, Not More Rules." *Wall Street Journal* (May 16).

Salsman, R. M. (1990) "Breaking the Banks: Central Banking Problems and Free Banking Solutions." *Economic Education Bulletin* 30 (6): 1–171.

Smith, A. ([1776] 1976) *The Wealth of Nations*. Oxford, U.K.: Oxford University Press.

Summers, L. H. (2014) "U.S. Economic Prospects: Secular Stagnation, Hysteresis, and the Zero Lower Bound." *Business Economics* 2 (2): 65–73.

Williams, A. (1892) "A 'Fixed Value of Bullion' Standard: A Proposal for Preventing General Fluctuations of Trade." *Economic Journal* 2 (6): 280–89.

Zarnowitz, V. (1992) *Business Cycles: Theory, History, Indicators, and Forecasting*. Chicago: University of Chicago Press for the NBER.

4

THE NEW MONETARY FRAMEWORK

Jerry L. Jordan

Do the policy actions of monetary authorities actually affect economic activity? We know that time and other resources are expended, but what can we observe about the results of such efforts?

In answering this question, it is helpful to begin with an account of how monetary authorities in discretionary, fiat currency regimes are traditionally thought to influence economic activity. Here, every college course in intermediate monetary theory tells essentially the same story. A nation's money supply comprises two distinct components: paper currency and deposits at banking organizations. The former was the largest component in earlier times, but the latter has come to dominate in recent decades—at least in most countries. The deposits in banks are subject to minimum reserve requirements, and the total deposit liabilities of banks constitute some multiple of reserve balances (that is, vault cash plus deposits at the central bank). The banking system as a whole is thus "reserve constrained," which means that, unless the central bank provides more reserves, there is an upper limit to the total deposits that may be held by individuals and businesses. By extension, if currency outstanding increases, and the central bank fails to add to the total supply of reserves available to private banks, then there has to be a corresponding contraction of deposit money. These reserve constraints have historically meant that, for better or worse, monetary authorities have the power to control the nation's money supply, and, in so doing, affect economic activity.

Jerry L. Jordan is former President of the Federal Reserve Bank of Cleveland. He served on President Reagan's Council of Economic Advisers and was a member of the U.S. Gold Commission. This article is reprinted from the *Cato Journal*, Vol. 36, No. 2 (Spring/Summer 2016).

However, this traditional account no longer holds true. The commercial banking system has ceased to be reserve constrained, and this means that *monetary authority actions to change the size of the central bank balance sheet do not affect the nation's money supply*. Now, instead of being constrained by the amount of reserves supplied by central banks, banking companies are constrained by the supply of earning assets that are available to them. And it is the supply of these earning assets that, subject to capital constraints, determines banks' aggregate deposit liabilities.

What implications does this shift have? Brunner and Meltzer (1972: 973) suggested that while it was possible for inflation or deflation to occur without changes in the monetary base, most inflations were, in practice, the result of base money expansion. That conclusion reflected the fact that the banking system was reserve constrained, so that increases in the stock of money were limited in the absence of expansion of the central bank balance sheet. However, in today's world of massive excess reserves in the banking system, the same model used by Brunner and Meltzer suggests that money creation has become a function of loan demand and the securities on offer to banks.

The new college textbook for intermediate monetary theory explaining all this has not yet been written, but when it is, it will not say that the monetary authorities control the "supply of money" and estimate the "demand for money," the objective being to prevent either an excess supply (which would cause inflation), or an excess demand (which would trigger a recession). That theoretical framework is broken—at least for now—in such a way that the monetary authorities can no longer formulate policy actions intended to influence aggregate economic activity by expanding or contracting the central bank balance sheet.

Interest Rates and Monetary Stimulus

The intermediate college course on monetary theory also offers an alternative theoretical avenue for influencing the economy—the level of *nominal* market interest rates. The basic idea is that when interest rates are lower, people borrow more to consume and invest, and when interest rates are higher, people will borrow less for consumption and investment. The big economic debate—and empirical contest—has been about the degree to which people understand the inflation premium in nominal interest rates, as well as the before- and after-tax interest expense they will bear. The economic argument is that if people think in terms of interest rates that are adjusted for anticipated inflation and/or taxation, observed market interest rates are higher than the "real" interest that affects consumer and investor decisions.

One hypothesis is that central bank "zero-interest-rate-policy" (ZIRP) works by pushing down bond yields so that investors are driven into equities in search of higher returns. Consequently higher valuations in equity markets then create a "wealth effect," wherein stockholders decide to increase consumption spending. Presumably, greater consumption demand will, in turn, give potential investors more confidence to forge ahead with capacity expansions and new projects.

However, this model only makes sense in a closed economy. In an open, global economic system, there is no reason to expect that increased investment and output will be domestic—even if aggregate consumer spending does respond to stock prices. This is especially so in a context of tax and regulatory policies hostile to capital formation. And surely no policymaker would argue that the best way to promote prosperity via monetary policy is to drive the trade deficit ever higher as imports outpace export growth.

Whatever the theoretical arguments, and regardless of the evidence of most of the past century, the near-zero interest rates we have seen in recent years have shown no correlation with domestically produced consumption by households, or with domestic investment activity in the private sector. In fact, an argument can be made that the low interest rate environment has reduced the demand for bank credit while increasing the demand for earning assets by non-bank lenders such as mutual funds, pension funds, and insurance companies (Jordan 2014). Hence, the liabilities of banks (i.e., demand deposits) have grown more slowly than they otherwise might have. In other words, the "low interest rates are expansionary" view conflicts with the "slow money growth is contractionary" view of the channels by which monetary authorities influence the economy.

Central Banks and Economic Growth

Another contribution to this debate about the influence of monetary authorities on the economy comes from the "market monetarists," who argue that central banks should focus their policy actions on achieving a target growth rate for nominal GDP that is consistent with their objectives for inflation and real economic growth. This claim, however, is the "assume we have a can opener" approach to economics. Monetary authorities once had several tools in their policy bag—reserve requirements, discount rates, interest ceilings, open market purchases and sales—that might be employed to achieve any objective they chose. But what tools do they have today to influence the pace of nominal GDP growth? What instructions can the monetary authorities give to their trading desk to achieve a faster or slower growth of nominal GDP? None!

The notions behind monetary and fiscal stimulus are, first, that that economic growth comes from getting consumers to spend or businesses to invest, and, second, that this can be brought about by government actions designed to "stimulate demand." But that is not how growth happens. A couple of hundred years ago, Adam Smith would have laughed at the idea that consumers' wants are satiated and must be "stimulated" by government, or that investors don't foresee opportunities to enhance profit without the government hyping demand for something—and rightly so.

In fact, growth (i.e., rising standards of living) happens when there are opportunities for real cost reductions. Put simply, when innovations cause the information and transactions costs of doing something to decline, people do more of the now-lower-priced thing. The demand was always there. It was never necessary for either monetary or fiscal authorities of government to "promote demand" for something. Wants are insatiable. If the cost of a weekend fly-around-Mars drops dramatically, the amount demanded will rise. The notion that government can or should do something to stimulate demand is, at best, obsolete.

Monetary Policy and the Politics of Wealth Sharing

Economic progress comes from reducing the sand in the gears. Often that sand is natural—information and transaction costs, for example. In modern societies, however, many such costs are artificial, created by collusive behavior between private interests, who want to protect their turf, and government officials, who want campaign contributions. Erecting and maintaining barriers to entry from potential competitors generates more political contributions than do promises to reduce such barriers. During the last half of the 20th century, burgeoning licensing and certification requirements created new obstacles to competition, so that innovations, new business startups, and real cost reductions slowed in many industries and sectors.

Meanwhile, political parties competed to build coalitions of voters by promising to transfer to them part of someone else's paychecks—either now or in the future. Eventually, even highly efficient and effective tax systems are no longer able to generate the collections necessary to fulfill all such promises, and political choices become unavoidable. In this dynamic, modern central banks have been part of the problem, not part of any lasting solution.

In the United States in the 1960s, promises made to individuals and households, together with rising government expenditures for the military, began to outrun tax revenues at an accelerating rate. Instead of reining in spending, the Johnson administration and then the Nixon administration cut the U.S. central bank loose from its specie anchor in three steps. First, the "London Gold Pool" was suspended; then the "gold window" was closed while the "gold cover" of U.S. currency was removed by Congress; finally, the commitment to redeem foreign-held dollars for gold was eliminated in 1973. These steps freed the central bank from any institutionalized discipline in the creation of new currency and bank reserves, and in turn removed any need for fiscal discipline. The result was accelerating inflation—the form of taxation favored by politicians for at least a couple of thousand years.

In this respect, the U.S. experience in the 1960s and 1970s was no different from that of other developed and developing countries with central banks and a monopoly national currency. Political promises of other people's money eventually added up to more than the tax system could generate, central banks were called upon to make up the difference with additional new money creation, and the ensuing inflation resulted in devaluation or depreciation of the currency. In the end, voters had been suckered into accepting nominal money units in exchange for their votes, but found the money they received did not buy as much as it had previously. They were the victims of an unholy alliance between fiscal and monetary authorities under the sway of politicians.

The recent experience of Greece is instructive. Even with a booming economy in the 1950s and 1960s, the Greek tax system did not collect enough revenue to fund all the promises politicians were making to voters. So the country's national currency was devalued in the early 1970s and depreciated continuously for a couple more decades until the drachma was replaced by the euro. Once Greek politicians realized they could sell euro-denominated bonds to foreign investors in order to fund the promises they had made to voters, a frenzy of vote buying led to a national debt much larger than any tax system could service. Because inflation and devaluation were not possible once the Greek central bank was deprived of its power to create new money, default on the foreign-owned Greek government bonds became unavoidable.

Ironically, the absence of a national currency—and a central bank able to create more of it—had in Greece's case allowed politicians to dig a debt hole much larger than had previously been possible. This was because foreign buyers of Greek euro bonds knew that the creator of euros—the European Central Bank (ECB)—would be pressured by governments of lender countries in the eurozone to create the additional euros needed by the Greek treasury to make the interest payments to the non-Greek banks and other lenders that owned the Greek debt.

Of course, the holders of Greek government bonds do not care whether the euros necessary to pay them back with interest come from the ECB or loans from other governments to the Greek government. However, some of those other countries have very large debts of their own, so issuing even more bonds in order to finance loans (or gifts) to the Greek government was a nonstarter. The moral of this story is that effective discipline in the fiscal decisions made by politicians cannot and will not be achieved as long as there are central banks empowered to create more of the money that politicians have promised to deliver.

All bonds issued by governments and all "entitlement" promises made by governments to voters are claims on future tax collections. Historical experience has been that such government-created claims on the tax system will always grow to exceed potential future tax receipts. Yet this experience of central banking and monopoly currency appears to have had no lasting effect on the propensities of politicians to promise potential voters that, if elected/reelected, he/she will vote to transfer other taxpayers' money to his/her supporters. In almost all democracies, the "politics of wealth sharing" has come to dominate the "politics of wealth creation." The reason is simple. No single elected representative or group of elected representatives has much, if any, influence over the pace at which an economy creates wealth. Any promise that newly created national wealth will benefit any one voter or even group of voters is simply not credible. However, even a single elected representative can facilitate a transfer of existing wealth to particular voters or constituents. A group of politicians, organized as a coalition or political party, can arrange this transfer of wealth on a much larger scale.

When it inevitably turns out that the aggregate of such promises exceeds the amount available for redistribution, no recipient group will voluntarily forgo their claims to other people's money. There are, of course, those rare politicians who campaign on promises to reduce some beneficiary groups' payments from government, but they are rarely elected (or reelected). And even in office, they often find themselves powerless to actually carry out their agenda.

All of this was understood very well by James Madison as he drafted the U.S. Constitution to replace the failed Articles of Confederation. The decision that the country's money should be backed by gold and silver was deliberately intended to impose fiscal discipline; since the amount of money in circulation was limited by available precious metals to back the currency, current expenditures of government, and promises of payments in the future, had to be limited to tax collections. Even when the Federal Reserve banks were created in 1914, the currency issued by these new "bankers' banks" was defined in terms of a weight of gold. *There was no provision in the Federal Reserve Act for discretionary monetary policy.*

Sadly, the United States' on-again/off-again efforts to anchor the value of the dollar to a specified weight of gold came to an end as the first six decades of U.S. central banking drew to a close. The next phase included efforts to achieve monetary discipline within the decisionmaking bodies of the monetary authority, sometimes under pressure from congressional oversight.

Learning and Unlearning from Experience

The past four decades of discretionary monetary management have been mixed, to say the least. The first decade saw soaring inflation and simultaneous increases in unemployment—contrary to widespread economic opinion at that time, there was no apparent tradeoff to exploit. With politicians and central bankers mugged by this unfortunate reality, cold-turkey monetary policy was accompanied by tax reductions and regulatory reforms, which in turn unleashed unexploited supply-side opportunities. Prosperity flourished without monetary actions to stimulate consumption and investment demand.

The second and third of the past four decades supported the view that monetary discipline was a necessary condition—and perhaps even a sufficient condition—for fiscal discipline. The era of the "bond-market vigilantes" dissuaded politicians from incurring budgetary deficits to fund their promises to voters, and the alternative of raising tax rates was constrained by the political process.

Meanwhile, the explosion of e-commerce and the surprisingly large productivity increases throughout the economy in the 1990s helped to continuously drive the measured unemployment rate below the level at which trade-off theorists claimed that inflation would begin to surface. Instead of questioning the validity of their model, these theorists simply kept revising down where they thought the noninflationary rate of unemployment might be encountered. The puncturing of the dot-com bubble cut short this experiment, so the model was not successfully rejected by actual experience.

By the fourth decade of managing a purely fiat currency, politicians were gaining experience in the use of mandates and government guarantees to compete for voter support. There were few dissents from the view that it was the government's job to promote home ownership. The credit standards for obtaining mortgages and other qualifications for purchasing houses were lowered, and government agencies guaranteed that investors in securities backed by home mortgages would not face losses. In that episode, the stated objectives included promoting home ownership as a good thing in itself, with any wealth effects caused by rising house prices a secondary objective. Nevertheless, the phenomenon of "mortgage equity withdrawals"—refinancing as house prices rose—generated a few trillion dollars for households to spend on consumption, driving the consumption-spending share of national output to historic record levels.

The ensuing collapse of house prices would ordinarily have been accompanied by an associated drop in the consumption share of GDP. However, the political process kicked in, and government issued massive amounts of debt in an effort to sustain aggregate demand at the "bubblenomics" levels. Any notion of fiscal discipline was abandoned quite quickly, and with little political objection. Decades of shrinking the outstanding national debt relative to the productive potential of the economy were reversed in just a few years of political panic. The decoupling of fiscal actions from the monetary regime raised concerns that the "fiscal dominance hypothesis"—namely, that monetary policy is ultimately a fiscal instrument in a world of unanchored fiat currency—had reemerged.

Given the inability of the political process to rapidly reestablish fiscal discipline and begin to reverse the excesses of 2008–09, the widely held view was that it was only a matter of *when* the subordination of monetary to fiscal policy would show up in the form of taxation by way of inflation. For their part, monetary managers began to publicly lament that the inflation rates in the United States and other major economies were *too low*, and that policy should aim to create higher inflation. Two decades earlier, no central banker or minister of finance would have dared to suggest that inflation rates were too low and needed to be nudged higher. However, the bond market vigilantes of the 1990s were, by now, nowhere in sight. As the first decade of the new millennium drew to a close, monetary authorities around the world vowed to take strong actions in pursuit of the faster erosion of their currencies. It wasn't just fiscal discipline that had been abandoned; ideas and theories about monetary discipline were shoved into a corner too.

Two lines of thinking drove this rush to monetary pump priming. The first was that the Great Depression of the 1930s could have been prevented if only the central bank had expanded its balance sheet sufficiently. Contemporary monetary authorities vowed not to make that mistake again. Second, the idea that there was a tradeoff between inflation and employment, which could be exploited by policymakers, reemerged. While such notions had been badly damaged by the experience of the 1990s, they returned as the dominant view among policymakers only a decade later. "Pedal-to-the-metal" monetary actions were defended on the grounds that there would be plenty of time to ease off of monetary stimulus as the rate of unemployment moved down toward the nonaccelerating-inflation threshold.

An unanticipated development was that while the unemployment rate did in fact decline, this was not because of stronger labor demand and rising employment, but rather because of an unprecedented decline in the labor force participation rate. Even adherents to the trade-off model struggled to explain how they would know when a low reported unemployment rate would trigger higher inflation, given that any increase in the demand for labor could be met by several million people *returning* to the labor market. Clearly, the tradeoff theory holds that if labor force participation rates were already high, and monetary stimulus promoted even more demand for labor, wages would rise more rapidly, and that would be one component of faster inflation. However, with the labor force participation rate falling to a 38-year low, even if monetary actions succeeded in promoting greater labor demand, wouldn't the response simply be increases in labor supply? How can rising "wage-push" be expected to emerge and help produce higher consumer inflation if there is no excess demand for labor? Ultimately, the tradeoff model proved to be unreliable when the labor force participation rate was high; why should policymakers rely on it when the participation rate is severely depressed?

A companion theory about *economic slack* as a factor in assessing potential inflationary pressures suffers similar weaknesses. The idea is that an economy has a long-run sustainable potential output that derives from working age population, labor productivity, the pace of technological innovation, and other factors. If current actual output is below the estimated potential, according to this theory, inflationary price and wage pressures are expected to be minimal. It is therefore safe for policymakers to stimulate consumption and investment demand so as to drive actual output closer to potential. Of course, the actual pursuit of such a strategy raises all kinds of knowledge problems, even in the best of circumstances. Moreover, in a global economy, the notion that there can be economy-wide capacity constraints does not fit reality. Except for some nontradable goods and services, sourcing of both final goods and inputs to production occurs in a global marketplace. Any estimate of *domestic* capacity is therefore useless in assessing potential price pressures.

Monetary Decoupling

One thing central banks *can* control is the size of their balance sheets. However, as we have already seen, recent efforts to increase the pace of consumer inflation have not been successful. Some, no doubt, will argue that an even larger bond-buying program is called for in order to get the job done. An alternative conjecture is that the central bank balance sheet is simply unconnected to economic activity in the national economy. Quite obviously, the various measures of the nation's money supply have not responded to the enormous increase in the volume of central bank money. Moreover, the prevailing (worldwide) low interest rates can be explained by factors other than central bank bond buying (Walker 2016).

Superficially, it seems that central bank purchases of large quantities of any asset ought to bid up the price and (in the case of bonds) lower the current yield. However, a central bank is not like other portfolio managers. Central banks acquire additional financial assets by creating liabilities (more fundamentally, by creating money out of thin air)—not by selling other assets. In an important sense, large-scale asset purchases (LSAP) by central banks involve a form of liability swap within consolidated government accounts—the duration, or maturity structure, of outstanding government liabilities is shortened by LSAP.

It is important to be clear that central bank purchases of government bonds have different effects than purchases of private assets such as mortgage-backed securities. While both reduce the outstanding stock of earning assets available to commercial banks and other investors, only the acquisition of private assets shifts potential default risk to taxpayers. Central bank acquisition of Treasury bonds can be thought of as merely "early retirement" of one form of outstanding national debt. Suppose, by way of illustration, that U.S. Treasury bonds were "callable," as many corporate bonds are. Let's assume that the Treasury chose to issue $1 trillion of very short-term securities at near zero interest rates and then "called" for early redemption a corresponding amount of long-term debt. While total debt would remain unchanged, both the duration and the interest burden of the debt would be altered; lower-cost, short-term liabilities were issued in order to redeem higher-cost, longer-term debt.

Because (net) interest income earned by Federal Reserve Banks on their holdings of securities is returned to the Treasury, the effect of central bank purchases of Treasury bonds—matched by interest-bearing liabilities (that is, interest paid on reserve deposits)—is not different, analytically, from what would happen if a bureau of the Treasury financed the purchase of long-term bonds by issuing short-term bills.[1] Consolidation of the Treasury and central bank's balance sheets would cancel out the bonds held as assets by Federal Reserve Banks, while the interest-bearing liabilities of the Federal Reserve Banks would show up as part of the government's outstanding debt. The composition of government debt is altered in exactly the same way as would be the case if the longer-term bonds had been retired via issuance of short-term bills.

This transformation is important in modern financial markets, which use "riskless" government debt as collateral for many types of transactions. When the availability of securities that can be used for collateral declines, there is a "tightening" of conditions in the greater financial intermediary system. In other words, LSAP by a central bank emits a contractionary impulse through the financial system.[2]

Williamson (2015) argues that the use of high-quality "riskless" securities as collateral in financial markets declined for several reasons following the financial crisis of 2008. Prior to that time, U.S. government and European sovereign debt were viewed as riskless, as were the obligations of U.S. government-sponsored enterprises (GSEs) such as Fannie Mae and Freddie Mac. Some privately issued mortgage-backed securities (MBS) were also considered safe enough to use as collateral. Of course, it turned out that the GSEs failed and had to be nationalized, that the MBS market seized up, and that some European countries found themselves on the brink of default.

---

[1]A peculiarity of U.S. national income accounting is that in the government's budget, the line for interest expense on the national debt includes the amount paid to the Federal Reserve Banks as interest on the bonds held in the central bank's portfolio. When the central bank returns the net interest earned to the Treasury, it is reported as part of "corporate profits." The reason is that the Federal Reserve Banks are technically private corporations. The effect of these accounting entries is to overstate the net interest expense on the national debt and to overstate corporate profits. In 2014, the Federal Reserve Banks' income (and the amount returned to the Treasury) exceeded $100 billion.

[2]See Williamson (2015:10): "A Taylor-rule central banker may be convinced that lowering the central bank's nominal interest rate target will increase inflation. This can lead to a situation in which the central banker becomes permanently trapped in ZIRP. With the nominal interest rate at zero for a long period of time, inflation is low, and the central banker reasons that maintaining ZIRP will eventually increase the inflation rate. But this never happens and, as long as the central banker adheres to a sufficiently aggressive Taylor rule, ZIRP will continue forever, and the central bank will fall short of its inflation target indefinitely. This idea seems to fit nicely with the recent observed behavior of the world's central banks."

Those developments resulted in a sharp decline in the stock of assets deemed to be of sufficiently high quality to serve as collateral in financial transactions. Taken in combination with these developments, the large-scale purchase of U.S. Treasury securities by the central bank, while intended to inject a form of monetary stimulus, had the unintended effect of further tightening the functioning of capital markets. For this reason alone, quantitative easing (QE) was a mistake.

Unfortunately, reversing QE at this point would also have adverse effects. So what can the Federal Reserve do? For one thing, the current portfolio of mortgage-backed securities can be held to maturity and not replaced. That would gradually shrink the central bank balance sheet by over $1.7 trillion. This would still leave a very large quantity of excess reserve balances on which the depositors are earning interest, but much more needs to be understood about the demand for such interest-bearing deposits before we conclude that they should shrink back to pre-crisis levels.

Much attention has been paid to the size and composition of the Federal Reserve's $4.5 trillion of assets—and with good reason. But not nearly enough focus has been placed on the liabilities. In recent years, the cash assets of foreign banks have exceeded the cash assets of large domestic banks. By some estimates, approximately half of the interest-bearing reserve balances at Federal Reserve banks are held by foreign banking entities (including branches and subsidiaries) operating in the United States. These cash assets have constituted as much as half of the total dollar assets of these foreign companies. The current large amount of foreign-owned, dollar-denominated deposits held by banking companies may partly reflect foreign governments' supervisory requirements for liquidity. To some extent, they also reflect the very large increase in these foreign companies' dollar liabilities. Compared with 2007, for example, the deposits of foreign banking companies operating in the United States were up by almost 50 percent in 2014.

It is important to note that increased demand for Federal Reserve deposits does not appear to reflect the availability of interest on reserves (IOR). After an initial jump in deposits during the crisis period of 2008–09, dollar deposits in 2011 were not much different than they had been in 2007. What's more, we know that the foreign owners of U.S. currency—the other major liability of the U.S. central bank—do not receive interest. It is estimated that more than half of the $1.3 trillion of Federal Reserve notes outstanding are foreign held. That means that a majority of each of the two major categories of Federal Reserve Bank liabilities—deposits and currency—are owned by foreigners. These estimates do not count foreign individual and business holdings of dollar-denominated deposits at commercial banks and money market funds, and of course do not count other holdings of dollar-denominated financial assets and real properties. Nevertheless, the fact that foreign banks' U.S. currency holdings, as well as deposits at Federal Reserve Banks, total almost $2 trillion reveals an enormous global demand for high-quality money.

At present, it would not be possible to assert the existence of either an excess supply of, or an excess demand for, dollars. Of course, dollar currency held by foreigners, like currency held by domestic residents, constitutes an interest-free loan to the U.S. Treasury. Since late 2008, the deposits held by foreign banks at the Federal Reserve have been earning 25 basis points, so that "loan" is no longer interest free.[3] However, because the assets acquired by the Federal Reserve banks have all been longer term and higher yielding, the net interest expense of the U.S. Treasury has gone down as a result of this large amount of foreign-owned dollar deposits.

Some countries have formally "dollarized," but far more people around the world have "spontaneously dollarized." Clearly, where it is not effectively prohibited and punished, people choose currency competition. They want high-confidence money, especially during times of political turmoil. One conclusion has to be that the United States has provided a public benefit to the rest of the world. At the same time, U.S. taxpayers have benefited from very large foreign holding of dollars—and here we are referring only to currency and to dollar deposits of foreign banks at the Federal Reserve.

No Exit

Any analysis, however preliminary, suggesting that LSAP actually had a contractionary effect during the period of quantitative easing must be taken seriously. Certainly, the cessation of such transactions was desirable; the principle of "do no harm" applies to central banks as well as to doctors. Nevertheless, the problem of formulating an "exit

---

[3]In December 2016, the monetary authorities announced an increase in the interest on reserve balances to 50 basis points.

strategy" remains. Some believe that the central bank balance sheet should shrink back to pre-QE levels, and that reserve requirements should once again become binding on commercial bank deposit creation. But that is simply not going to happen. The past practice of conducting daily open market operations in order to closely control the overnight interbank lending rate—the federal funds rate—is not going to resume. Central bank purchases and sales of securities in the "open market" can no longer be policymakers' primary tool.

Their new tools—administering the interest rate paid on reserve deposits and auctioning "reverse repurchase agreements" (RRP)—have not been tested in an accelerating inflation environment. No matter how aggressively utilized, neither has any direct effect on money creation. The former (IOR) can be viewed simply as central bank borrowing *from* private banks, while the latter (RRP) is central bank borrowing from GSEs and money market firms. In theory, market interest rates would be influenced by the rate the central bank offers for such borrowings. If higher rates paid by monetary authorities cause other interest rates to be higher, businesses and households will curtail some credit-financed purchases, aggregate demand for output will be moderated, and inflationary pressures will be mitigated—or so the theory goes.

This theory depends on several assumptions, however. Monetary policymakers must have considerable knowledge about the impact of their actions on other interest rates; about the lags involved before businesses and households respond to rising rates; and about whether and how much *real* interest rates—rather than just nominal rates—are changing. As there is no historical experience employing these tools, there is no basis for assessing their effectiveness. Central banks have demonstrably failed to achieve their objective of higher inflation during the past five years; their tools to contain any inflation that emerges are untested.

The risk posed by the enormous central bank balance sheet is that the willingness of commercial banks to hold idle balances (even those earning some administered rate of interest) will decline. Of course, while any individual commercial bank can take actions to reduce its holdings of "excess" reserves, the banking system as a whole cannot do so. Without a corresponding reduction in the securities held by the central bank as assets, "excess" reserves can decline only if they become "required" reserves. This suggests two possibilities: *either* Congress can authorize a substantial increase in administered reserve requirement ratios; *or* an extraordinary increase in reservable deposit liabilities of commercial banks absorbs the excess. The second option would certainly involve a hyperinflationary increase in the money supply. What are the odds of that?

Commercial bank deposit liabilities are now a function of the supply of earning assets—both domestic and foreign—offered to commercial banks. In other words, the quantity of "inside money" created by the banking system depends on the demand for bank loans and the aggregate supply of government bonds, mortgage-backed-securities, and other suitable instruments available for acquisition by banks. A forecast of deposit growth—and the money supply—must be derived from a forecast of the supply of (and yields on) earning assets offered to the banking system. That includes forecasts of government budget deficits that must be financed, as well as the prices of commercial and residential real estate against which mortgage securities can be created. The knowledge necessary to make confident forecasts cannot be obtained from historical experience.

Conclusion

For several years, major central banks have pronounced that the objective of massive quantitative easing was to raise the inflation rate. That objective has not been achieved despite the quadrupling (in the case of the United States) of the central bank balance sheet. Because commercial banks are no longer reserve constrained, the historical linkage between the central bank balance sheet (the monetary base) and the outstanding money supply has been broken. Changes in the size and composition of the central bank's assets and liabilities are thus unrelated to the amount of money in circulation. Without the ability to influence the supply of money, central bank open market operations have no influence on the rate of inflation. Announced changes in the federal funds rate therefore have no implications for economic activity, or the rate of inflation.

If inflation should emerge, central banks will have no tools for countering the pace at which the purchasing power of money declines. In the early stages of past periods of accelerating inflation, central banks mistakenly expanded their balance sheets as they "leaned against" the trend of rising nominal interest rates, failing to see that an "inflation premium" was being incorporated by both lenders and borrowers. In other words, monetary authorities' policy actions were "accommodative" of rising prices. For the foreseeable future, however, no such accommodation will be necessary. Ballooning central bank balance sheets are more than sufficient to fuel extreme rates of inflation without further debt monetization. This is not a forecast that inflation will in fact occur. It simply is a statement of the new reality: whether or not there is inflation is unrelated to anything central banks do or do not do.

References

Brunner, K. and Meltzer, A. H. (1972) "Money, Debt, and Economic Activity." *Journal of Political Economy* 80 (5): 951–77.

Jordan, J. L. (2014) "A Century of Central Banking: What Have We Learned?" *Cato Journal* 34 (2): 213–27.

Walker, M. (2016) "Why Are Interest Rates So Low? A Framework for Modeling Current Global Financial Developments." Vancouver B.C.: Fraser Institute.

Williamson, S. D. (2015) "Current Federal Reserve Policy under the Lens of Economic History: A Review Essay." Federal Reserve Bank of St. Louis Working Paper No. 2015-015A. Available at https://research.stlouisfed.org/wp/2015/2015-015.pdf.

5

LIQUIDITY RISK AFTER THE CRISIS
Allan M. Malz

The state of liquidity after the global financial crisis presents paradoxes. The money markets are awash in liquidity provided by central banks in most advanced countries. Yet by some indicators, liquidity appears to be impaired compared with precrisis conditions. By some market indicators, risk taking appears to be vibrant. By others, risk aversion and caution are dominant.

Also puzzling—and troubling—is a proliferation of market anomalies and oddities that have persisted or even grown more pronounced as the crisis itself recedes further into the past. These range from the failure of some basic near-arbitrage relationships to hold, to sporadic market "tantrums" and "flash crashes."

Much criticism of postcrisis financial regulation has argued that it has made basic intermediary functions—lending and facilitating trades—costlier. The market paradoxes and anomalies indicate that something more is happening. They may be related to a more general impairment of market functioning, or to a rebuilding of precrisis levels of leverage, partly in hard-to-discern forms.

A reduction in liquidity compared with precrisis may not be unambiguously harmful. Liquidity is closely related to leverage, and ample liquidity before the crisis reflected the extensive leverage some market participants took on, enabled in large part by explicit or implicit public-sector repayment guarantees.

Allan M. Malz teaches graduate courses in risk management at Columbia University. He has served as a risk manager at several financial firms and is a former Vice President at the Federal Reserve Bank of New York. This article is reprinted from the *Cato Journal*, Vol. 38, No. 1 (Winter 2018).

Liquidity is affected not only by regulations directly addressing liquidity, but also by policy measures affecting short-term funding markets, and the supply of and demand for liquidity in various forms. The impact on liquidity is not one to one with any particular change in policy. Frictions and tensions have been introduced that are hard to attribute to specific policies or trends. There is generally an identification problem in associating specific changes in the economy with specific policy changes. It is far more challenging when so many policy changes and changes in the overall economic environment have been taking place simultaneously.

But the results are potentially ominous. The still-highly leveraged financial system has a good chance of being subjected to unusual stresses soon as monetary policy normalizes in a low-growth environment and with high political risks. Will relatively modest reductions in central bank securities purchases or holdings be disruptive? Will the tensions be resolved "peacefully" or otherwise? The risk of disruptions emanating from surprising corners of the financial system is high.

What Is Liquidity Risk?

Liquidity is a difficult concept to pin down. It can refer to phenomena that seem quite disparate but are closely related: how easy it is to buy and sell assets, ease of access to credit, and the amount and forms of money in the financial system. Liquidity is intertwined with other phenomena, especially leverage and risk taking.

Market or transactions liquidity risk is the risk of moving an asset price against oneself while buying or selling, or covering a position, and thus being locked into it. It arises from the cost of searching for a counterparty and the cost of inducing someone else to hold a position. Market liquidity depends on participants' positions, on institutions such as exchanges and dealer firms that aid search and make markets, and above all on the risk appetites of market participants.[1]

Funding liquidity risk is the risk to market participants of being unable to maintain debt financing, and having as a result to liquidate a position at a loss that they otherwise would keep. Funding liquidity risk events typically involve short-term debt, which rolls over more frequently than long-term. Financial firms are most susceptible, since they are often in the business of using short-term debt to finance longer-term financial assets, which are harder to sell

[1]Foucault, Pagano, and Roell (2013) is a general introduction to market liquidity risk.

without loss. The yield curve is generally upward-sloping, making maturity mismatches attractive.

Funding liquidity depends on both the reality and perceptions of borrowers' creditworthiness and is more fragile when borrowers are highly leveraged. This fragility can be even greater when there is uncertainty about how leveraged the borrowers are; large banks' balance sheets, for example, are notoriously opaque. Short-term credit is granted in part based on public-sector guarantees, adding to fragility.

Liquidity is closely connected to risk appetites. Higher risk aversion renders liquidity fragile; perceptions about creditworthiness or the solidity of guarantees may suddenly seem less well-founded. When risk aversion is high, dealers are more reluctant to make markets in size and lenders, including short-term lenders on collateral, are less eager to extend credit and to put up with sparse information on creditworthiness.

Funding liquidity is also closely linked to market liquidity, since they interact, and since both suffer when risk aversion is high. Banks, dealers, and traders depend on funding liquidity, either to finance inventories or provide collateral, in order to make markets. Short-term lenders depend on market liquidity to support borrowers' ability to repay and the value of the collateral they hold. If many borrowers experience a liquidity risk event at the same time, or market liquidity for the assets being financed is poor, forced unwinding or positions may result in a "fire sale," with prices driven far from any notion of fair value.

Financial crises are often triggered by liquidity events coinciding with abrupt changes in sentiment. Liquidity risk events in financial markets are apt to affect many market participants at the same time. The withdrawal of short-term lenders may be effected through higher interest rates, but as often through nonprice rationing, such as increases in "haircuts" on collateral, refusal to accept some collateral, or simple refusal to lend. The onset of a crisis is often described as a liquidity crunch, but could as easily be described as a sudden spike in risk aversion, expressed in part as aversion to some types of privately created liquidity. It is often marked by a run or run-like behavior, in which short-term lenders suddenly converge on a borrower.[2]

---

[2]Shleifer and Vishny (2011) is an overview and Acharya and Schnabl (2010) a case study of the role of funding liquidity risk in crises and its relation to market liquidity risk.

The financial system creates most of what is used as money, in the form of assets corresponding to some short-term debt. Most of the narrowly defined money supply consists of bank deposits. Other short-term assets included in standard definitions of monetary aggregates also carry out at least some of the functions of money, such as availability at par or at least a highly predictable value to buy other assets. A large volume of assets with these characteristics, but not necessarily included in monetary aggregates as defined by central banks, is created by financial intermediaries in wholesale short-term funding markets, in which larger financial and nonfinancial firms participate. Also known as shadow banking, they have grown rapidly over the past four decades.

The spread between short-term rates with terms of a few days or weeks and longer money market rates is generally particularly wide. Part of the term spread at the very short end of the yield curve is a money premium, the interest forgone in exchange for money services. The money premium makes short-term wholesale funding even more attractive (Greenwood, Hanson, and Stein 2015).

Two important mechanisms of private money creation outside banking are repurchase agreement or repo markets and money market mutual funds (MMMFs). Repo is a form of short-term collateralized lending in which the lender of cash receives bonds as collateral from the borrower. Repo is legally framed as a pair of bond purchases and sales, one now and the other in the future, both at prices that are determined now and imply a lending rate. Repo adds to the supply of liquidity because holders of repo-eligible securities can use them to quickly obtain a predictable amount of liquidity at a predictable rate. It has become a large part of short-term wholesale lending, particularly since a regulatory change in the 1980s exempting repo from the automatic stay in bankruptcy, thus permitting repo cash lenders to immediately sell collateral if their counterparty defaults.[3]

MMMFs first arose in 1971 and grew rapidly from the mid-1970s, a time of high and rising interest rates, as a means of evading the regulatory ceiling on bank deposit rates. From 1983, the Securities and Exchange Commission (SEC) set credit standards for MMMFs' asset pools and permitted them to use a fixed $1 par value for share transactions. Growth of so-called institutional MMMFs serving

---

[3]Baklanova, Copeland, and McCaughrin (2015) is an introduction to repo.

nonfinancial firms, used less as ready cash than as liquidity reserves, was even faster than that of retail MMMFs. MMMF assets reached nearly $4 trillion before the crisis, the bulk initially in commercial paper, but displaced in part over time by short-term municipal and corporate bonds, and increasingly, repo.

Policy Changes and Interest Rates Since the Crisis

Market behavior has been affected by major changes in monetary and regulatory policies. Policy has in some respects added tremendously to both the supply of and demand for liquidity. Liquidity is also affected by nonpolicy trends that began before the crisis, but have been transformed in its wake, mostly associated with low interest rates. We'll summarize these developments to help understand recent market behavior.

The identification problem makes it difficult to say which policy or economic change has led to which impact on liquidity. But, in some cases, some direction of influence can be stated.[4]

Monetary and Debt Management Policies

The Federal Reserve initially responded to the crisis with conventional monetary easing and emergency programs that combined liquidity support for the financial system as a whole with targeted credit support for specific firms and types of intermediation. For most of the past decade, the main policy tool in the major industrial countries has been variants of quantitative easing, the purchase of bonds in large volumes on the open market. It is intended to further reduce the long-term rates most relevant for investment by reducing term and risk premiums once short-term rates have been brought near zero.[5]

Forward guidance through public statements, on which the Fed has placed far greater reliance since the crisis, is intended to support easing by committing the Fed to keep short-term rates near zero in the future and thus lowering the expected future rates component of the long-term rate. Forward guidance adds to

---

[4]The identification problem also makes it difficult to estimate the compliance cost of new and revised regulation, which often leads to different ways of conducting business, not just additional staff and systems.

[5]Ihrig, Meade, and Weinbach (2015) is an overview of the Fed's new policy tools and its choices for an exit from crisis policies.

liquidity in the same way that interest-rate smoothing did prior to the crisis, by making market participants confident that financing rates will stay steady.

Quantitative easing is intended to work through different channels from conventional monetary policy, which relies on managing overnight liquidity to set the overnight federal funds rate, focusing on central bank assets rather than liabilities. But by creating a large volume of central bank reserves, it has a strong impact on the markets in which the funds rate is determined. The most direct impact is to flood markets with safe overnight liquidity and vastly reduce banks' need to trade them.

Several new policy tools have been introduced in the United States to manage that impact and preserve the fed funds market for a future return to conventional policy. Interest on reserves was introduced in late 2008 to keep the funds rate near the target rate or within the target range once the Fed permitted its balance sheet to expand to accommodate the emergency programs. Overnight reverse repurchase agreements (ON RRPs) were introduced as a floor on the funds rate once the bottom of the target range was raised above zero. Policymakers have expressed concern that, by providing a flight destination from private forms of liquidity, ON RRPs could be destabilizing in times of financial stress. While lower limits have at times been placed on ON RRP volume, it is currently limited only by the size of the Fed's portfolio of Treasury bonds.

U.S. Treasury cash management practices were adapted early in the crisis to support the Fed's efforts, and more recently have been an independent factor influencing markets. All these changes have affected all money markets, not only that for fed funds.

Regulatory Policies

Regulatory policies have changed substantially since the crisis. Many new rules, a number ordained by the 2010 Dodd-Frank Act, have been adopted in the United States, though the compliance deadlines for some have not yet arrived.[6]

---

[6]See Aaron, Demers, and Durr (2015) for an overview of the leverage and liquidity rules and the likely direction of their impact. The Basel capital and liquidity standards are stated in Basel Committee on Banking Supervision (2011, 2013), among other standards documents.

The Basel minimum capital standards have been revised and increased in a several ways. The minimum common equity ratio is now higher. Criteria for the recognition of nonequity capital have been tightened, but most of the additional capital required can be funded in nonequity forms. Dividends and other payouts are to be slowed or halted if additional capital buffers are breached. Some apply to the largest banks, including a requirement to issue non-equity capital that is intended to be zeroed out and thus limit the need to apply public funds in the event of insolvency.

The revised Basel and U.S. capital standards retain the precrisis reliance on risk-weighted assets, and the minimum ratios remain low compared with previous eras; but a capital ratio based on the size of the bank's balance sheet has been introduced. Banks must satisfy the higher of the two, so either can become a binding constraint. The size-based capital ratios also have a more stringent version for certain very large U.S. bank holding companies, insured bank subsidiaries of which are subject to an enhanced Supplementary Leverage Ratio (SLR) of 6 percent.

Leverage ratios endeavor to address two drawbacks of risk-weighted ratios. Whether based on a table of weights supplied by the regulator or on internal models, weights designed to be risk-sensitive may be drastically inaccurate and induce banks to shift to higher-risk assets. Two classic precrisis examples are the zero or near-zero weights on sovereign debt and on senior securitization tranches with low-quality underlying asset pools. The second drawback is that risk-weighting systems, if they are to be accurate and comprehensive, must also be complex in design, on top of the complexities of the composition of regulatory capital. Together with the presence of public-sector guarantees, these problems enable banks to take risk beyond what their capital funding can appropriately bear without external guarantees.

The advantages of a regulatory leverage ratio in countering these problems, however, have the inverse consequence of disincentivizing transparent low-risk activities that "use a lot of balance sheet," that is, add large positions counted as assets in the denominator of the ratio. The U.S. deposit insurance program now imposes fees based on total assets rather than insured deposits, with a similar effect. Criteria for inclusion or exclusion of on- and off-balance sheet positions in the denominator are themselves complex, in addition to the complexities of the capital numerator.

One of the goals of postcrisis regulatory reform has been to reduce short-term wholesale funding. Higher capital standards work in that direction, but new liquidity regulations have also been introduced. Banks' thin capital cushions and funding liquidity risk are treated as requiring distinct regulatory approaches, rather than viewing short-term wholesale funding as a form of leverage that is particularly attractive to large banks with stronger implicit guarantees.

To that end, two new minimum ratios have been introduced. The Liquidity Coverage Ratio (LCR) can be thought of as a 30-day liquidity stress test, requiring banks to keep enough liquid assets to meet a specific scenario of a run on their short-term funding. The Net Stable Funding Ratio (NSFR) limits maturity mismatch on banks' balance sheets. Both rely on complex rules for inclusion, weighting and exclusion of assets, liabilities, and off-balance sheet items. The ratios penalize short-term funding not secured by low-risk collateral (i.e., government bonds) and reward short-term lending, and would *ceteris paribus* increase the money premium.

There is a tension between the liquidity and capital standards as they now stand. Deposits with central banks—primarily excess reserves in the United States—are near-riskless. But they lengthen the balance sheet and raise minimum capital if the SLR is binding and are thus costly to finance relative to their risk and return. But these excess reserves can be used to satisfy the new liquidity regulations, so banks reap a regulatory compliance reward, in addition to interest on reserves.

The so-called Volcker Rule prohibits proprietary trading, as well as ownership by banks, which benefit from deposit insurance and lender of last resort support, of hedge funds, private equity funds, and loan securitizations. Because of the difficulty of discriminating between positions held in anticipation of price changes and those held to facilitate market-making, hedging, and other permitted activities, the Volcker Rule is accompanied by extensive recordkeeping requirements, and its implementation will depend on regulators' interpretation even more than for other postcrisis rules.

Changes in the rules affecting MMMFs include permitting a fixed net asset value (NAV) only for funds that invest in U.S. government-issued securities and repo, or serve exclusively retail investors. Other MMMF types must mark their NAV to market daily. Moreover, if there are substantial redemptions in a short time from a nongovernment fund, it is obliged to restrict or impose fees on further redemptions.

The revised rules shift demand from corporate, and to a lesser extent municipal securities, to U.S. issues. The share of government-only funds in total MMMF assets has grown from about one-third in mid-2015 to about three-quarters. The share of U.S. government securities and repo in the assets of all MMMFs has also risen. The shift in allocation enlarged the market for the Fed's floor-setting ON RRPs.[7]

Some changes have been introduced through persuasion more than regulation. Repo trading is carried out in different trading venues. Some repo trades are focused on financing long or short positions in specific bonds used as collateral. These repo trades between dealers and their customers are usually cleared bilaterally, a process called delivery versus payment. Dealers themselves want to have matched books, that is, facilitate trades for customers, but limit their own net risk, and interdealer trading that achieves this has been moving to a facility called the General Collateral Financing (GCF) Repo Service. Repo trading focused on lending or borrowing money, rather than on specific securities, including GCF repo, settles on the triparty repo platform, a service that has been provided by two large U.S. banks, JP Morgan and BNY Mellon.

A major supervisory concern has been the extremely large exposure of the two triparty clearing banks during regular business hours. The banks, one of which is exiting the business, fund repo dealers between the time expiring contracts roll off and the dealers return cash to their counterparties in the morning, and the time they enter into new contracts in the afternoon. The Federal Reserve has been pressuring the banks to reduce this intraday exposure and dealers to use GCF repo. The intraday exposure has in fact been greatly reduced. The effort is consistent with the regulatory effort to channel derivatives trading from bilateral to multilateral clearing platforms.

A relatively new and still diffuse regulatory effort addresses financial stability through a so-called macroprudential approach to regulation, which views regulation from the point of view of the

---

[7]The shift in demand was also reflected in a widening of spreads between commercial paper and Treasury bills, and of term spreads in the unsecured interbank lending market, which have since been reversed.

stability of the financial system as a whole, in addition to the traditional microprudential focus on the safety and soundness of individual financial firms. The approach focuses on externalities and systemic risk in finance, that is, profitable activities of individual intermediaries that are said to impose uncompensated risks on others. While not yet well articulated, it has motivated liquidity regulation, as well as supervisory guidance restrictions on riskier loans by banks.[8]

The macroprudential approach creates tensions with monetary policy. The approach could aim to crack down on symptoms of excessive credit expansion through regulatory measures. This would insulate monetary policy from financial stability considerations and permit longer periods of ease. Or it might add countercyclical regulatory measures to a generally tight monetary stance that is wary of credit expansion. In the past, this debate was known as "lean or clean." Today, it is related to the debate on the pace of normalization in the absence of rising inflation.[9]

Low Interest Rates and Demand for Safe Assets

Some precrisis trends have continued since the crisis. Interest rates, particularly long-term rates, had fallen steadily in the years leading up to the crisis. The real interest rate is not directly observable, econometric estimates have wide confidence bands, and market-based estimates are bundled with unobservable risk premiums. But the estimates agree that the real rate has been falling steadily, worldwide. The U.S. real rate has fallen about an additional 200 basis points since the onset of the global financial crisis.

The demand for "safe assets," including highly rated sovereign bonds and the short-term assets resulting from private liquidity creation described earlier, is closely related to low rates. Before the crisis, the two phenomena met in the "conundrum," the unusually

---

[8]Kim, Plosser, and Santos (2017) describe some of the problems arising from reliance on guidance in supervision.

[9]An inverse argument is presented by Greenwood, Hanson, and Stein (2016), who propose the Fed maintain a large balance sheet for the foreseeable future. Its liabilities would substitute for private-sector money-like assets that are vulnerable to runs. The authors argue this would be a better-aimed method for averting such runs than the SLR. They address the concern about flight into Fed liabilities by limiting expansion during stress periods.

flat term structure of interest rates, reflecting high demand for longer-term bonds. It was attributed to demand for low-risk fixed-income assets by an aging, wealthier world population. More recently, attention has focused on the ability of such assets to serve liquidity functions, as described above. The crisis is said to have eliminated some asset classes from the supply of safe assets by exposing their credit risk, adding to the downward pressure on interest rates.[10]

The demand for safe assets contributes to strong demand for U.S. dollar-denominated assets. The demand for U.S. dollar intermediation, including high volumes of both dollar funding and dollar-denominated assets, was seen prior to the crisis and continues after. Much dollar funding is raised directly by non-U.S. issuers of dollar-denominated bonds, and much of that in recent years has been in emerging markets. But a great deal of dollar funding is raised by U.S. offices of foreign banks (FBOs) and lent both within and outside the United States.

Is Liquidity Impaired Now?

Financial markets are displaying many unusual behaviors: conflicting indicators of market and funding liquidity, anomalies and impairments of normal market functioning, and conflicting indicators of risk appetite. These behaviors are related to one another, and how the conflicting evidence is resolved will influence how well the economy can respond to shocks and how disruptive will be central bank efforts to return to more normal monetary policies.

Market liquidity, the ability to alter holdings quickly and cheaply, is very hard to measure. Observable phenomena such as trading volumes and bid-ask spreads are only indirectly related to the cost of buying and selling, and to how much a large securities order changes the market price, and for how long. Even data on observable characteristics are hard to obtain and summarize across asset markets.

Concerns have been raised that higher capital and new liquidity requirements and the Volcker Rule have inhibited market liquidity

---

[10]Caballero, Farhi, and Gourinchas (2017) is a recent survey. The authors take the view that the effective lower bound in interest rates can prevent the market for safe assets from clearing, leading to elevated risk premiums and forcing the market to clear via a reduction in economic activity.

since the crisis, particularly in the U.S. corporate bond market. But the evidence isn't robust. Market structure has also been changing, for example the growing prevalence of electronic trading, so identification of the cause of change is difficult.

Trading volume of U.S. bonds overall and dealer balance sheets have declined since the crisis (Figure 1), although trading in corporate bonds, a small fraction of the total, has increased a bit. Much of that may be due to the increased issuance of corporate bonds. Turnover of corporate bonds, the frequency with which the bonds are traded, appears to have declined over the postcrisis decade.

Bid-ask spreads, however, don't appear to have greatly changed. That would be consistent with the shrinking of dealer balance sheets and a shift from market makers acting as principals and taking long and short positions, to agency trading. It would also be consistent with a shift away from low-risk intermediation requiring balance sheet, and thus debt or equity funding. But entering or exiting a position may now take longer and require more, smaller transactions. All in all, the upfront cost of trading may be steady or even

FIGURE 1
U.S. DEALER ASSETS AND BOND MARKET TRADING VOLUME, 1996–2017

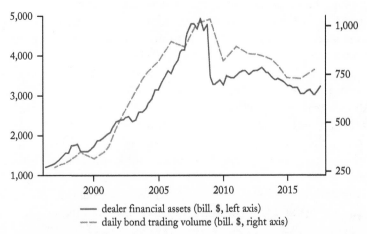

— dealer financial assets (bill. $, left axis)
--- daily bond trading volume (bill. $, right axis)

SOURCES: Total financial assets of security brokers and dealers, $bill. Federal Reserve Board, Financial Accounts of the United States (Z.1), Table L.130. Average daily trading volume of U.S. bonds, $bill. Securities Industry and Financial Markets Association (SIFMA).

declining, but less immediacy in trades imposes additional implicit costs.[11]

Since the crisis, transactions liquidity in specific markets has suddenly become not just impaired but has virtually disappeared for periods of a few minutes to a few days. These episodes are loosely referred to as "tantrums" and "flash crashes," and have occurred in a range of markets and market types. An early such episode took place on May 6, 2010, in the U.S. equity market. Others have occurred in U.S. Treasury and German Bund markets, as well as in the sterling markets. A recent episode in the silver markets is typical of the intraday variety. On July 6, 2017, silver futures fell about 10 percent early in the Pacific trading day, and recovered within a few minutes.

Market as well as funding liquidity may appear ample if demand to use it is low, but disappears if uncertainty and risk aversion abruptly rise. The experience during tantrums suggests that market liquidity may become much less reliable if there is a sustained change in sentiment from the current low volatility regime. The concern about liquidity in a stressed market is strengthened by evidence from the U.S. corporate bond market that market liquidity of specific issues is badly affected by downgrades.[12] The tantrums also suggest that market liquidity can't be assessed on its own but only in the context of the other unusual market behaviors we're describing.

Risk Appetite

Evidence on risk appetites is also in conflict, with evidence of both risk seeking and risk avoidance. Concerns had been raised prior to the crisis about "reaching for yield," the propensity of unleveraged long-term investors such as pension funds and insurance companies with fixed future retirement or claim liabilities to shift allocations to higher-risk assets to compensate for low interest rates. It may also be driven by regulatory constraints and public guarantees enjoyed by some intermediaries. For example, regulatory capital requirements on U.S. and European insurers are lower if they hold bonds rather

---

[11]See, for example, Mizrach (2015), Adrian et al. (2017), and International Organization of Securities Commissions (2017). Anecdotal evidence from portfolio managers, as well as a report on European corporate bond market liquidity (European Commission 2017), is decidedly more negative on the state of corporate bond market liquidity.

[12] See Bao, O'Hara, and Zhou (2016).

than equities as investments, and regulatory and accounting rules constrain pension plans to hold bonds rather than equities against some liabilities. But within those constraints, long-term investors may increase the duration or credit risk of loan and bond portfolios, select the riskiest bonds within a regulatory category, or deploy their equity allocations in riskier forms such as hedge funds and private investments. Bond investors, before the crisis, pressured rating agencies to inflate ratings by assigning a higher fraction of securitization pools to the most senior bonds (Calomiris 2009).

The precrisis patterns of reaching for yield and demand for safe assets have continued barely interrupted after the crisis. For example, the allocation to lower-quality bonds (BBB-rated and speculative grade) in U.S. property and casualty insurance fixed income sector portfolios has risen from about 7 percent in 2007 to about 21 percent in 2016 (New England Asset Management 2017).

Implied and realized asset return volatility have been extremely low in recent years. Implied volatility is expressed through option prices, and it is low when market participants expect future realized volatility to be low, but also when they are eager to take the risk of selling puts and reluctant to pay for the corresponding protection, even at relatively low prices. Figure 2 illustrates with the VIX, a well-known index of equity implied volatility, and the MOVE index of U.S. interest rate volatility. Both are at the lowest levels of their quarter-century history.

Implied volatility is generally close to, but somewhat higher than, expected volatility, measured using recent realized volatility. The difference, or variance risk premium, is a measure of the pure reward to supplying protection against volatility, and has been substantially lower in the post- than in the precrisis years.[13]

Like low interest rates, low volatility is a precrisis phenomenon that has reached new extremes. It is related to reaching for yield, as both express an increased supply of implicit liquidity puts at given prices. Stress conditions have a similar impact on option sellers and investors

---

[13]See Bollerslev, Tauchen, and Zhou (2009) and subsequent literature. A simple measure of the variance premium is the difference between the VIX and an exponentially weighted moving average measure of S&P 500 index return volatility (using a decay factor of 0.94). The average daily difference in annualized volatilities from January 1990 to the onset of the crisis at the end of February 2007 was about 4.25 percentage points. The average difference from late September 2011, when the "hot" phase of the crisis can be said to have calmed down, to present was about 2.75 percentage points.

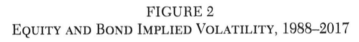

FIGURE 2
EQUITY AND BOND IMPLIED VOLATILITY, 1988–2017

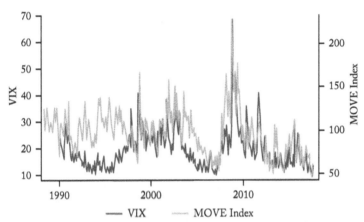

SOURCES: CBOE Volatility Index (VIX), weighted average of prices of options on the S&P 500 Index with approximately one month to expiry and with a range of strike prices. Merrill Lynch Option Volatility Estimate (MOVE) Index of implied normal volatilities of at-the-money options with approximately one month to expiry on U.S. Treasury notes and bonds. Bloomberg LP.

in down-in-credit bonds: both find themselves locked into positions that can only be exited at prices that have just changed sharply for the worse. Both volatility selling and reaching for yield can lead to discontinuous, "tantrum" behavior of markets.

Leverage, finally, remains very high, just below precrisis levels. The financial sector has reduced debt levels, and households modestly, while the nonfinancial business and public sectors have increased borrowing (Figure 3). But the rapid increase in debt levels of the post-stagflation era hasn't been reversed.

Yet there is also countervailing evidence on risk appetites. One indicator of high risk aversion is the same low real interest rates said to motivate reaching for yield. The flat yield curve, the strong demand for 100-year bonds, and the implied volatilities discussed above suggest strong expectations that nominal rates will remain low for the foreseeable future. Some of the factors that could be causing this decline are consistent with or point to risk aversion: a decline in growth and anticipated future real returns, and higher demand for safe assets.

FIGURE 3
U.S. DEBT-TO-GDP RATIO BY SECTOR, 1946–2017

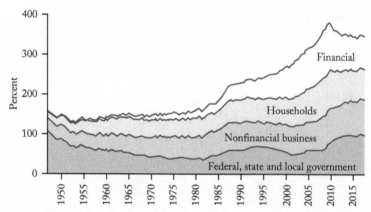

SOURCES: Ratio of total debt outstanding (debt securities and loans) to GDP, current dollars, percent, quarterly, Q4 1946 to Q2 2017. Federal Reserve Board, Financial Accounts of the United States (Z.1), Tables D.3 and F.2.

Lower prospective growth and returns are consistent with a range of other observations. Rates of capital investment, the growth of labor productivity, new business formation, and growth of bank loans and leases, for example, are lower than before the crisis. There are alternative explanations for them (e.g., the shift to a service economy, measurement issues, and the role of technology), but these data are also quite consistent with low prospective returns.[14]

The demand for safe assets may also have increased in recent decades due to factors other than risk aversion, such as increased wealth and aging populations in both developed and developing countries. Some observers have also argued that the supply of safe assets has declined due to central bank purchases and the

---

[14]Two examples: The entry rate of new establishments—places of business—in the United States fell from an average of 12 percent in the decade before the crisis to 10 percent since the crisis, at times below the exit rate (U.S. Census Bureau, Business Dynamics Statistics). Loans and leases in bank credit have grown about 5 percent annually over the past 5 years, a period starting 3 years after the last NBER business cycle trough, compared to about 8 percent over the entire postwar era and over the 20 years prior to 2007 (Federal Reserve H.8 release).

disqualification of securitized products considered low-risk prior to the crisis. The effect on collateral supply of central bank purchases is only partially offset by adding short-term safe assets in the form of reserves.

The persistence of risk aversion can be seen in corporate bond spreads over risk-free rates, which have tightened massively since the crisis, but are not at record lows. Similarly, Libor remains at a wider spread to overnight interest rate swap rates than before the crisis. Money-market credit spreads may also be kept wider by the combined impact of the LCR and MMMF reform, which has made banks less eager to receive deposits of corporate cash balances not intended for daily transactions, pushing them to government-only funds, and has made government paper relatively attractive. Issuance of commercial paper by U.S. banks other than FBOs has also declined.[15]

Risk aversion can be seen even in equity prices. Although some commonly cited measures, such as the Shiller CAPE, are high, they are in part an artifact of low interest rates.[16] An alternative measure takes low rates into account by subtracting an estimate of the real interest rate from the current dividend yield. Both are real, rather than nominal rates, and the spread is a simple measure of the real equity excess return or risk premium, in effect treating equity as a bond that has both credit and cash-flow risk. The dividend-real yield spread is very high by historical standards, higher even than during the bear market of the late 1970s (Figure 4).[17]

But low interest rates may not be due only to low growth and pessimism about future returns. Persistent and surprisingly low inflation and inflation expectations are a large part of surprisingly low nominal rates. There is wide agreement that low inflation is a result of past

[15]The lows in the BofA Merrill Lynch U.S. Corporate Master Option-Adjusted Spread (OAS) data are in 1997, and a substantially higher precrisis low was reached in March 2005. As of early October 2017, OAS for all ratings, as well as the BBB-AAA quality spread, were higher than their March 11, 2005, levels. Astonishingly, even in the eurozone, where the quantitative easing policy has included large-scale purchases of corporate bonds, the Bloomberg Barclays Euro-Aggregate Corporates OAS is three times as high as in March 2005. The BofA Merrill Lynch Euro High Yield Index OAS is also materially higher than its mid-2007 low.

[16]The Shiller CAPE is currently over 30, its highest value since the decline in 2000–01.

[17]This observation is another way of seeing the safe asset shortage.

FIGURE 4
Dividend–Real Rate Yield Spread, 1970–2017

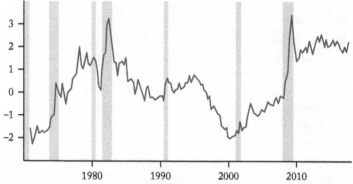

SOURCES: Twelve-month trailing dividend yield of the S&P 500 index (Bloomberg LP) minus Laubach-Williams estimate of the short-term natural rate (available at http://www.frbsf.org/economic-research/files/Laubach_Williams_updated_estimates.xlsx), percent, Q4 1970–Q2 2017.

success in anchoring expectation inflations and current low growth rates.[18] But while different approaches to the relationship between low inflation and real rates point in the same direction for monetary policy, they point in opposite directions for an understanding of risk appetites.

In one view, the market rate is generally near the equilibrium real rate. Inflation is suppressed because both the real and nominal rates are near zero. Rather than inflation expectations dictating the gap between real and nominal rates, the low nominal rate, together with a real rate immune from longer-term policy influence, dictates low inflation expectations. In this view, pessimism and risk aversion are ascendant. In another view, and despite the evidence to the contrary provided by dormant inflation, the current market rate may be below the real rate. The relatively low market rate may then be an incentive to risk taking. Both views imply a similar policy conclusion: raise nominal rates. But the motivations are quite different: on the one

[18]Apart from survey data and yields on inflation-indexed U.S. Treasury securities, the anchoring of inflation expectations can be seen in the strongly positive correlation between stock market returns and changes in government bond yields. The correlation had been negative during the 1970s, turned positive around 2000, and increased sharply during the crisis.

hand, to provide room for inflation to rise, and thus permit at least a transitory rise in growth, and, on the other, to equalize the market to the real rate and tamp down financial excesses.[19] The debate is related to the paradox of volatility, the likelihood that periods of unusually buoyant risk appetite, ample liquidity, and low volatility tend toward instability.

Arbitrage Failures and Other Anomalies

Many anomalies have appeared, primarily in the money markets, in which near-riskless arbitrage opportunities fail to disappear over time. Banks are apparently unwilling to lend at a virtually risk-free spread in these cases. These anomalies persist either because banks and other intermediaries aren't devoting sufficient capital to exploiting them, or because of market frictions that are new or worse since the crisis.

Persistent arbitrage opportunities are not a new phenomenon. The arbitrage process is almost never entirely free of risk, and takes place slowly and incompletely due to various market frictions.[20] Some arbitrage opportunities are astonishingly large and persistent, and preceded the crisis, such as the difference between estimates of future inflation rates expressed in nominal and indexed U.S. Treasury securities, and fixed rates of inflation swaps (see Fleckenstein, Longstaff, and Lustig 2014).

But the phenomenon of unexploited arbitrage has become more widespread and pronounced since the crisis, and derivatives markets are not always involved. We'll examine a set of anomalies in the Eurodollar, fed funds, repo, and swap markets.

One prominent example has been occurring in foreign exchange markets. The cross-currency basis is the spread between the cost of borrowing U.S. dollars directly versus indirectly, by borrowing in local currency and engaging in a foreign exchange swap. Many non-U.S. entities, such as non-U.S. banks lending dollars to their own customers, want to fund in dollars, and may even be providing dollar

---

[19]These views can be compared in a recent issue of the *Cato Journal*. The so-called neo-Fisherian view that inflation may be suppressed by low nominal rates is summarized in Bullard (2016); the view that the equilibrium real rate may be higher than a low inflation rate might lead one to believe in Borio (2016).

[20]See Shleifer and Vishny (1997) and a more recent survey, Gromb and Vayanos (2010).

FIGURE 5
CROSS-CURRENCY BASIS OF EUR-USD, 2006–17

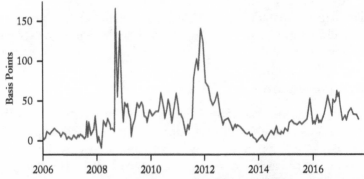

SOURCES: Spread between three-month USD Libor and USD borrowing rates implied by foreign exchange spot and swap markets, euro-dollar rate. Daily, smoothed using two-week moving average, in basis points. Market data from Bloomberg LP.

funding to their own customers. However, they have less access to the U.S. money markets than U.S. banks, particularly to privileged funding sources such as insured deposits, and face transaction costs in obtaining dollar funding via the foreign exchange markets, so the cross-currency basis is generally positive, but small. The basis spiked at the onset of the global financial crisis and has been unusually wide since, though it should be reduced through a low-risk near-arbitrage carried out by U.S. banks with natural access to dollar deposits. Figure 5 displays the basis for the U.S. dollar against the euro, but it has appeared for a range of major exchange rates against the dollar.[21]

Another anomaly arose almost immediately after the Fed's introduction of interest on reserves. Reserve balances at the Fed are free of credit risk, but federal funds transactions are unsecured. Banks should be unwilling to lend in the interbank market at an interest rate below that on reserves, which should therefore act, as originally intended, as a floor on the funds rate. With the money markets awash in liquidity, the fed funds rate has generally been well below IOER.

Some nondepository institutions, the housing-related government-sponsored enterprises (GSEs) Fannie Mae and Freddie Mac, and the

[21]See Du, Tepper, and Verdelhan (2017) and Borio et al. (2016).

Federal Home Loan Banks (FHLBs) may keep balances at the Fed, but may not earn interest on reserves. Currently, the limited activity in the fed funds market involves lending by the FHLBs of their large mortgage interest inflows until they are reinvested in new mortgages. The banks could borrow from the FHLBs in the funds market and receive interest on reserves at the Fed, earning a near-riskless spread.

The persistence of the spread has been attributed to regulatory changes, particularly those related to leverage, liquidity, and deposit insurance, as well as the potential stigmatization of banks seen to be borrowing heavily in the funds market. The asset-based deposit insurance fee adds costs to holding balances at the Fed for those banks subject to it. Most of the arbitrage activity is therefore carried out by FBOs, which are subject to different regulatory and accounting rules from U.S. banks, and now hold half of all reserve balances.

Another postcrisis anomaly is the prevalence of negative swap spreads. Interest-rate swap fixed rates are generally at least somewhat higher than on-the-run U.S. Treasury yields, since swaps have counterparty and liquidity risk premiums absent from the bond yields. Since the crisis, the 30-year spread has been negative, and more recently the 10-year spread has turned negative as well. The swap rates are driven lower in part by institutional investors' strong demand for duration risk, part of the reaching for yield phenomenon discussed earlier.[22]

An arbitrage in which banks pay the fixed rate on swaps and establish government bond short positions in the repo market would bring a low-risk net positive cash flow from two sources, the spread between the swap rate and bond yield and the spread between the Libor floating rate paid on the swap and the repo financing rate of the bond short position (Figure 6).

U.S. repo markets are heavily impacted by many of the recent regulatory changes. The repo markets are also at the crux of efforts to normalize monetary policy without disruption. With the fed funds rate essentially disabled as a policy tool, the Federal Reserve has relied increasingly on repo markets to recreate scarcity in the money markets and signal and enforce its target money market rate.

---

[22]The excess of credit default swap premiums over corporate bond spreads to plain-vanilla swap rates, described in Boyarchenko et al. (2016), is a similar phenomenon.

FIGURE 6
SWAP SPREADS, 1994–2017

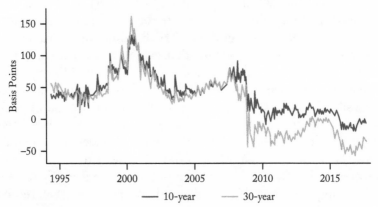

SOURCES: Spread of plain-vanilla interest-rate swaps over yield of Treasury of like maturity, basis points, daily. Bloomberg LP.

The target market-adjusted rate increasingly appears to be the GCF repo rate. The evolution dovetails with regulators' desire to replace Libor, a set of indexes prepared by banks of interbank rates of different terms to maturity for different currencies, with a more purely market-based index. GCF repo rates have been suggested as replacements for both the fed funds rate as a policy rate and for Libor as a loan and derivative benchmark.[23]

Repo markets have displayed several anomalies in recent years. Repo lending is secured, and should therefore be executed at lower rates than funds trades. Repo rates have instead generally been above the funds rate in recent years, although the spread has diminished since the end of 2016 (Figure 7). Repo rates have also been quite volatile. Accounting and regulatory reporting constraints have long induced month- and quarter-end "window dressing" spikes in money market rates. These have grown more pronounced for GCF repo. European banks are subject to quarter-end rather than daily average

[23]See Committee on the Global Financial System (2015) for an overview of anomalies in money markets in relation to the implementation of monetary policy in several advanced economies. Federal Reserve Bank of New York (2017) provides an update for the U.S. as part of its discussion of the effectiveness with which policy rate increases have been passed through to money markets generally.

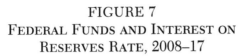

FIGURE 7
FEDERAL FUNDS AND INTEREST ON RESERVES RATE, 2008–17

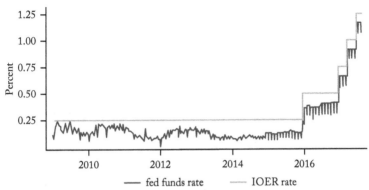

SOURCES: Federal funds effective rate and interest rate on reserve balances at Federal Reserve Banks. Daily, percent, from Decemer 18, 2008. Bloomberg LP.

reporting, and are particularly inclined to withdraw from lending on reporting dates. Quantitative restrictions, in which intermediaries show reluctance to accept investors' cash near reporting dates, are reportedly also appearing.

GCF repo trades at a persistent spread above triparty repo. Triparty repo can be viewed as the marketplace in which the dealers seek funding for this business from MMMFs and other providers of short-term wholesale funding, while GCF repo can be viewed as the marketplace in which dealers trade among themselves and offer repo to hedge funds and other market participants taking positions in securities. In this sense, the GCF-triparty repo spread has been likened to the bid-ask spread of the repo market. This spread is wide and fluctuates quite a bit, particularly at month-end. It ought to be contained by arbitrage, since the trades through which the spread is earned are low in risk (Figure 8).[24]

Since the crisis, the incidence of fails in the repo market has greatly increased (Figure 9).[25] Fails occur when borrowers of securities don't

[24]Greenwood, Hanson, and Stein (2016) attribute negative swap and the wide GCF-triparty spread to the SLR.
[25]The figure omits the extremely large increase in fails during the worst part of the crisis in 2008 and 2009.

FIGURE 8
TRIPARTY AND GCF REPO RATES, 2012–17

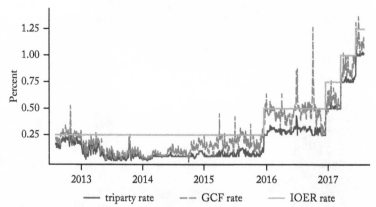

SOURCES: Triparty: BNY Mellon Treasury Tri-Party Repo Index (Bank of New York Mellon). GCF: DTCC GCF Repo Index for Treasury (Bloomberg LP).

return them to the lenders and take back the cash they lent, therefore forgoing interest on it. They can occur for operational reasons, or because there are large short positions in the specific securities borrowed, among other reasons, and are a longstanding phenomenon in repo markets. The incentive to fail to deliver is greater with low

FIGURE 9
TREASURY FAILS, 2009–17

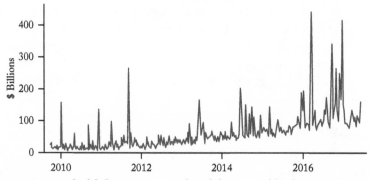

SOURCES: Total of fails to receive and to deliver, weekly, from September 30, 2009, $ bill. Federal Reserve Bank of New York, Primary Dealer Statistics.

interest rates, since the interest forgone on the cash lent is small. A fails penalty was introduced in 2010, but fails have increased greatly nonetheless. Occasionally, they spike briefly to extreme levels. The increase may be due not only to low interest rates but also to the large share of Treasury securities now held on the Fed's balance sheet and thus out of the market.

Some of the anomalies we've looked at have become somewhat attenuated during 2017, though they haven't disappeared or returned to the precrisis state. One possible reason may be a decline in the Treasury's General Account deposit balances as the federal debt limit nears. Since the asset side of the balance sheet is being held constant as a matter of policy until the pace of reinvestment is slowed as part of normalization, another Fed liability position must rise. Banks' reserve balances, which had been declining since 2014, have increased moderately, adding to the supply of liquidity (Figure 10).

Arbitraging these anomalies requires considerable balance sheet and in the presence of a potentially binding leverage ratio, it has been argued, additional balance sheet has a high cost of capital. But the arbitrage is quite low in risk, so the hurdle rates should not be assumed frozen at high levels. Adding very low-risk activities should

FIGURE 10
FEDERAL RESERVE LIABILITIES, 2007–17

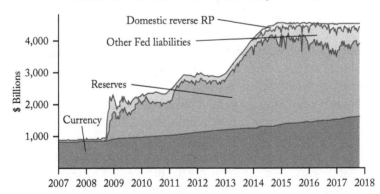

NOTES: Currency includes other liabilities and capital. Other Fed liabilities include foreign official reverse repos, deposits other than reserves, and Treasury cash.
SOURCE: Federal Reserve Board, H.4.1 release, Table 1.

lower them.[26] Rates of return bank equity investors currently seek are based on current equity levels and asset mix. Just as relying more on equity funding would induce a lower market-clearing return on equity, so also would a lower-risk asset mix. The argument that the regulatory capital and liquidity constraints raise the required return on capital above the hurdle rate doesn't therefore fully explain the phenomenon. One explanation may be debt overhang, a situation in which firms are so highly levered that at least part of the return to profitable equity-financed activities accrues to debt holders.

Conclusion

"Inadequate liquidity" may not be the best way to describe the phenomena we currently see. The anomalies and conflicts we've described indicate a larger underlying disfunction. Each anomaly is hard to trace back to a specific regulatory change. Not only have there been major regulatory changes, but the monetary policy response to the crisis, the crisis itself, the continuation of precrisis trends, and the financial industry's adaptation to these also influence market functioning. But taken as a whole, they indicate a general decline in market responsiveness.

Liquidity currently seems ample, but perhaps only because market participants don't urgently need it right now. The market appears persistently less able to withstand large shocks. Disruptive shocks are likely in the years to come, especially sudden changes in expectations that increase the desire for liquidity, but also cause it to disappear. There are many potential sources that have been of concern for some time: policy normalization, conflict risks, and problems in a number of specific large countries. Overseas reliance on U.S. dollar funding is as great as ever, while the intermediation channels by which it is obtained remain as fragile as ever.

The slowness and difficulty of arbitrage is important. While slow arbitrage is normal, and exceptionally slow arbitrage was part of the crisis, arbitrage is a key mechanism through which shocks and surprises are absorbed. If it's impaired, the ability to adjust is impaired, and disruptions are more likely to take the form of large price swings, reductions in credit, and other typical crisis phenomena. The banking

---

[26]The argument is analogous to that in favor of much higher equity ratios (see Admati et al. 2013).

system remains at the core of the arbitrage process, but is still highly leveraged and dependent on public-sector support in severe stress.

One potential source of shocks and surprises is the anticipated normalization of monetary policy and gradual reduction in central bank balance sheets or in the pace of new purchases. There are potential disruptions if normalization goes forward as expected, and others that might result from much faster or slower normalization than expected. Even in the absence of major surprises in the pace of normalization, the Fed's new tools for raising rates might not work as expected, resulting for example in money market rates failing to rise with higher targets, or opening wider spreads among money markets. This has not been the case for the first 75 basis points of hiking: market rates have risen in tandem with policy rates, and the ON RRP floor has held, albeit with larger volumes than initially anticipated. But it remains a risk.

The contrast between market expectations of future rates and the expectations reported by Federal Reserve officials parallels the contrast between indicators of risk aversion and risk appetite. Figure 11

FIGURE 11
FEDERAL RESERVE AND MARKET VIEWS OF FUTURE INTEREST RATES

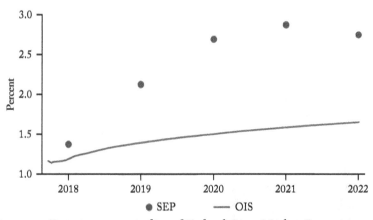

SOURCES: Dots represent median of Federal Open Market Committee participants' projections of future fed funds rate from the September 20, 2017, Summary of Economic Projections (SEP). Solid plot represents rates on overnight interest swap (OIS) settling on different future dates, as of September 20, 2017. Horizontal axis displays horizon of SEP rate projections and OIS settlement dates. Both from Bloomberg LP.

displays future overnight rates from a recent Summary of Economic Projections (SEP), alongside an implied forecast of the overnight rate drawn from money market derivatives markets. Several years out, the gap between market expectations and Fed projections is well over 200 basis points. The projected pace of increases and longer-term market rates have both fallen since the SEP was introduced, but the size of the gap has been remarkably persistent.

This tension will have to be resolved somehow, and it may not be resolved without market disruption. Normalization is needed, but itself poses risks. Future rates closer to Fed projections would surprise markets, while future rates closer to those implied in markets would validate their pessimism. Surprises in either direction could result from the use of new operational tools in drastically transformed markets. Low interest rates may also move discontinuously, amplifying the extensive revaluations that can be expected to accompany a rise in rates.

Low interest rates and volatility, sustained over a long period time, are apt to contribute to a further tightening of financial conditions in response to adverse shocks. The paradox of volatility suggests that hard-to-detect imbalances are growing that are apt to correct themselves disruptively, perhaps as pockets of leveraged investing turn sour. Microeconomic anomalies and evidence of market fragility increase the likelihood of disruptive market events with surprising loci and timing, exacerbating the effects of rising rates and volatility.

References

Aaron, M.; Demers, A.; and Durr, S. (2015) "The Effect of Regulatory Changes on Monetary Policy Implementation Frameworks." *Bank of Canada Review* (Autumn): 39–49.

Acharya, V. V., and Schnabl, P. (2010) "Do Global Banks Spread Global Imbalances? Asset-Backed Commercial Paper during the Financial Crisis of 2007–09." *IMF Economic Review* 58 (1): 37–73.

Admati, A. R.; DeMarzo, P. M.; Hellwig, M. F.; and Pfleiderer, P. (2013) "Fallacies, Irrelevant Facts, and Myths in the Discussion of Capital Regulation: Why Bank Equity Is Not Socially Expensive." Working Paper No. 2065 (October), Stanford Graduate School of Business.

Adrian, T.; Fleming, M.; Shachar, O.; and Vogt, E. (2017) "Market Liquidity after the Financial Crisis." Staff Report No. 796 (June), Federal Reserve Bank of New York.

Baklanova, V.; Copeland, A.; and McCaughrin, R. (2015) "Reference Guide to U.S. Repo and Securities Lending Markets." Staff Report No. 740 (December), Federal Reserve Bank of New York.

Bao, J.; O'Hara, M.; and Zhou, A. (2016) "The Volcker Rule and Market-Making in Times of Stress." Finance and Economics Discussion Series No. 2016–102, Board of Governors of the Federal Reserve System.

Basel Committee on Banking Supervision (2011) *Basel III: A Global Regulatory Framework for More Resilient Banks and Banking Systems* (June), Bank for International Settlements.

_____ (2013) *Basel III: The Liquidity Coverage Ratio and Liquidity Risk Monitoring Tools* (January), Bank for International Settlements.

Bollerslev, T.; Tauchen, G.; and Zhou, H. (2009) "Expected Stock Returns and Variance Risk Premia." *Review of Financial Studies* 22 (11): 4463–92.

Borio, C. (2016) "Revisiting Three Intellectual Pillars of Monetary Policy." *Cato Journal* 36 (2): 213–38.

Borio, C.; McCauley, R.; McGuire P.; and Sushko, V. (2016) "Covered Interest Parity Lost: Understanding the Cross-Currency Basis." *BIS Quarterly Review* (September): 29–41.

Boyarchenko, N.; Gupta, P.; Steele, N.; and Yen, J. (2016) "Trends in Credit Market Arbitrage." Staff Report No. 784 (July), Federal Reserve Bank of New York.

Bullard, J. (2016) "Permazero." *Cato Journal* 36 (2): 415–29.

Caballero, R. J.; Farhi, E.; and Gourinchas, P. (2017) "The Safe Assets Shortage Conundrum." *Journal of Economic Perspectives* 31 (4): 29–46.

Calomiris, C. W. (2009) "A Recipe for Ratings Reform." *The Economists' Voice* 6 (11): 1–4.

Committee on the Global Financial System (2015) "Regulatory Change and Monetary Policy." CGFS Paper No. 54 (May), Bank for International Settlements.

European Commission (2017) *Drivers of Corporate Bond Market Liquidity in the European Union*. Available at https://ec.europa.eu/info/sites/info/files/171120-corporate-bonds-study_en.pdf.

Federal Reserve Bank of New York (2017) *Domestic Open Market Operations during 2016*. Available at www.newyorkfed.org/medialibrary/media/markets/omo/omo2016-pdf.

Fleckenstein, M.; Longstaff, F. A.; and Lustig, H. (2014) "The TIPS-Treasury Bond Puzzle." *Journal of Finance* 69 (5): 2151–97.

Foucault, T.; Pagano, M.; and Roell, A. (2013) *Market Liquidity: Theory, Evidence, and Policy*. New York: Oxford University Press.

Greenwood, R.; Hanson, S. G.; and Stein, J. C. (2015) "A Comparative-Advantage Approach to Government Debt Maturity." *Journal of Finance* 70 (4): 1683–1722.

_____ (2016) "The Federal Reserve's Balance Sheet as a Financial-Stability Tool." Economic Policy Symposium Proceedings, Federal Reserve Bank of Kansas City: 335–97.

Gromb, D., and Vayanos, D. (2010) "Limits of Arbitrage." *Annual Review of Financial Economics* 2: 251–75.

Ihrig, J. E.; Meade, E. E.; and Weinbach, G. C. (2015) "Rewriting Monetary Policy 101: What's the Fed's Preferred Post-Crisis Approach to Raising Interest Rates?" *Journal of Economic Perspectives* 29 (4): 177–98.

International Organization of Securities Commissions (2017) "Examination of Liquidity of The Secondary Corporate Bond Markets." Available at www.iosco.org/library/pubdocs/pdf/IOSCOPD537.pdf.

Kim, S.; Plosser, M. C.; and Santos, J. A. C. (2017) "Macroprudential Policy and the Revolving Door of Risk: Lessons from Leveraged Lending Guidance." Staff Report No. 815 (May), Federal Reserve Bank of New York.

Mizrach, B. (2015) "Analysis of Corporate Bond Liquidity." Research Note, FINRA Office of the Chief Economist. Available at www.finra.org/sites/default/files/OCE_researchnote_liquidity_2015_12.pdf.

New England Asset Management (2017) "2016 Investment Highlights: Historic and Future." *Perspectives* (July).

Shleifer, A., and Vishny, R. W. (1997) "The Limits of Arbitrage." *Journal of Finance* 52 (1): 737–83.

_____ (2011) "Fire Sales in Finance and Macroeconomics." *Journal of Economic Perspectives* 25 (1): 29–48.

PART 2

EXIT STRATEGY AND NORMALIZATION

6

EXIT STRATEGIES FROM MONETARY EXPANSION AND FINANCIAL REPRESSION
Gunther Schnabl

The world has moved into a low-interest rate trap. Since the mid-1980s, asymmetric monetary policy patterns—that is, sharp interest rate cuts during crises and hesitant interest rate increases during the post-crisis recoveries—have pushed interest rates toward zero (Hoffmann and Schnabl 2011) (see Figure 1).[1] With short-term interest rates having reached the zero bound, unconventional monetary policies (i.e., extensive government and corporate bond purchases) have nudged long-term interest rates further downward.

The ultra-low interest rate policies encouraged financial market exuberance, which led to painful financial meltdowns, during which exploding debt of financial institutions was transformed into public debt to ensure financial stability. By pushing long-term interest rates downward, central banks are keeping growing general government debt levels (see Figure 1) sustainable and are discouraging efforts to reduce government spending. Inflated central bank balance sheets,

Gunther Schnabl is Professor of Economics at the University of Leipzig, Institute for Economic Policy. This article is reprinted from the *Cato Journal*, Vol. 38, No. 2 (Spring/Summer 2018).

[1]In Figure 1, unconventional monetary policy measures are converted into implied interest rate cuts. This leads to negative "shadow" interest rates in a close-to-zero interest rate environment. Implied ("shadow") interest rates come from Leo Krippner. See www.rbnz.govt.nz/research-and-publications/research-programme/additional-research/measures-of-the-stance-of-united-states-monetary-policy/comparison-of-international-monetary-policy-measures.

which contain growing amounts of government bonds, erode the credibility of central banks.

Meanwhile, the exit from the low, zero, and negative interest rate policies is strongly dependent on the public debt levels, because every increase in interest rates threatens to cause a meltdown in the financial system and (thereby) to block the budgets of highly indebted countries (see Figure 1). For this very reason—while pretending to pursue inflation targets—the central banks in the core of the international monetary system either continue their extensive bond purchase programs (Bank of Japan, European Central Bank) or have moved very hesitantly toward the exit from ultra-loose monetary policies and financial repression (U.S. Fed, Bank of England).

The literature on the exit from the low interest rate environment is scarce. Summers (2014) argues that, given aging societies and a

FIGURE 1
CENTRAL BANK INTEREST RATES AND GENERAL GOVERNMENT DEBT IN G4 COUNTRIES

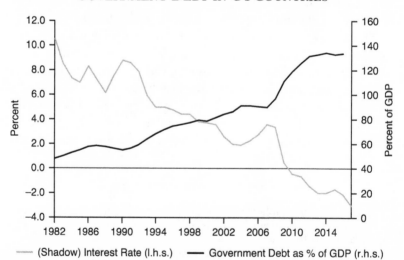

—— (Shadow) Interest Rate (l.h.s.)　—— Government Debt as % of GDP (r.h.s.)

NOTES: Arithmetic average for United States, Japan, Germany/eurozone, and United Kingdom. Debt on the right axis equals the arithmetic averages of the euro area (represented by Germany, France, Spain, and Italy), Japan, United Kingdom, and United States.
SOURCES: Thomson Reuters Datastream, Federal Reserve Bank of St. Louis, IMF, and Krippner (see footnote 1).

declining marginal efficiency of investment, the key interest rates set by the central banks reflect the gradual decline of the equilibrium interest rate in the industrialized countries. Given these assumptions an exit from the ultra-expansionary monetary policies is not necessary.

Reinhart and Sbrancia (2015) argue on the basis of historical experience that low nominal interest rates help to contain debt servicing costs and to reduce the real value of government debt. Thus, financial repression is seen as a pre-step for the exit from excessive monetary expansion. McKinnon (1993) has developed a blueprint for the exit from financial repression in emerging market economies based on the reconstitution of market forces, which has proven to be highly successful in many East Asian as well as Central and Eastern European countries, and in particular in China.

Low-Growth Effects of Financial Repression

McKinnon (1973) showed the negative growth effects of the financial repression imposed on the capital markets of emerging market economies in the 1950s and 1960s.[2] Uncontrolled government expenditure financed by the expansion of the real stock of money undermined via repressed financial markets the efficiency of investment. With state-controlled interest rates the allocation of capital had become disconnected from market principles.[3] Similarly, since the mid-1980s the asymmetric monetary policy patterns of the large central banks have disturbed the allocation function of capital markets by driving a wedge between the returns of financial assets and physical capital stock.

Since the mid-1980s asymmetric monetary policies have subsidized investment in financial assets. During upswings, low central bank interest rates have inflated asset prices, whereas during crises the decline of asset prices has been countered with even further

---

[2]See also Shaw (1973). Financial repression was defined as a set of policy measures that constitute the transfer of wealth from the private to the public sector. The measures include interest rate controls, including low government bond yields, other price controls, state control of banks, and restrictions to international goods and capital flows.

[3]Whereas neoclassical theory regards real money balances and physical capital as substitutes, McKinnon (1973) stressed the complementarity.

FIGURE 2
DEVELOPMENT OF STOCK AND CONSUMER PRICES IN
G4 COUNTRIES

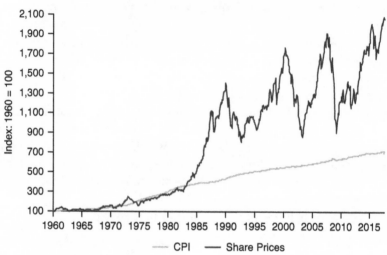

SOURCES: IMF and OECD.

NOTES: Arithmetic averages for the United States, United Kingdom, Japan, and Germany. After 1999, the CPI for the euro area replaces Germany.

interest rate cuts and unconventional monetary policy measures (Hoffmann and Schnabl 2011).[4] As a result, since the mid-1980s asset prices—as represented in Figure 2 by the share prices in the four largest industrialized countries—have increased dramatically, leading to substantial speculation gains. Since 1985—despite

---

[4]The increasing cyclicality of financial markets can be explained using the monetary overinvestment theories of Mises (1912) and Hayek (1931), which attribute overinvestment and exuberance in financial markets during the upswing to too low central bank interest rates. In crisis, central banks keep interest rates too high, thereby aggravating the crisis. In contrast to the monetary overinvestment theories, the monetary policy mistakes during the last three decades tended to be asymmetric: interest rates tended to be kept too low during the upswing, but were kept too high during the downswing. In Hayek (1931) the economy is in equilibrium when the central bank sets the central bank interest rate close to the natural interest rate. The natural interest rate is the interest rate that aligns saving and consumption preferences with the production structure over time. A fall in the central bank interest rate (capital market interest rate) below the natural interest rate causes a cumulative inflationary process, creating distortions in the production structure that later make an adjustment necessary (unless the central bank keeps on inflating credit at an ever-increasing pace and thereby artificially prolongs the credit boom). See also Hoffmann and Schnabl (2011).

substantial swings—the average increase in share prices per year has been close to 7 percent.

In contrast, investment in physical capital was discouraged because no public insurance mechanism was provided for risk linked to investment in innovation and attempts to increase the efficiency of the production process. The ultra-expansionary monetary policies have disturbed—like in the emerging market economies formerly plagued by financial repression—the adoption of best-practice technologies[5] by undermining the allocation function of interest rates, which separates between investment projects with high and low expected returns. This has clouded growth perspectives and therefore profit opportunities of most enterprises.

Whereas interest rate cuts during boom phases encouraged investment projects with lower returns, during the crisis further interest rate cuts prevented the dismantling of investment projects with low marginal efficiency.[6] On the global level, this resulted in an increasing number of zombie enterprises and zombie banks, which are kept alive by the low-cost liquidity provision of central banks (see Peek and Rosengreen 2005 as well as Cabellero, Hoshi, and Kashyap 2008 on Japan).[7] Kornai (1986) dubbed this phenomenon "soft budget constraints" for the former centrally planned economies of central and eastern Europe. Unemployment was regarded as politically undesirable; thus, state-owned enterprises were subsidized with costless credit by state-controlled banks. The banks were kept alive with the help of the printing press of the central bank.

With resources remaining bound in low-return investment projects, a restraint has been put on efficiency-increasing innovation. In the neoclassical growth model, given a declining marginal efficiency of investment, output converges toward a steady state (Solow 1956, Swan 1956). Beyond that point, growth is only possible, if innovation takes place (Solow 1957). If, however, financial

---

[5]See Hayek (1968) on competition as a discovery procedure.

[6]The overinvestment theories by Mises (1912) and Hayek (1931) assume that central bank interest rates above the natural interest during the downturn trigger a dismantling of investment projects with low returns. Schumpeter (1934) dubbed this process cleansing effect: resources bound in investment projects with low or negative returns are freed and can be shifted into projects with higher returns. See also White (2015).

[7]Hayek (1976) would characterize this process as a gradual shift from a spontaneous to a planned order.

FIGURE 3
LABOR PRODUCTIVITY GROWTH IN G4 COUNTRIES

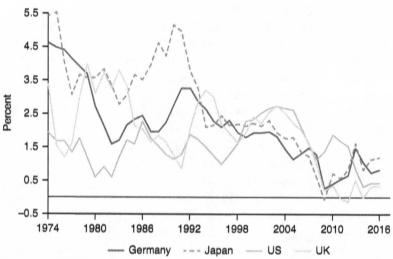

SOURCE: OECD.

repression undermines the innovation process by binding resources in inefficient investment projects and reducing the incentive for household savings,[8] then investments, productivity gains, and growth will slow. This is shown in Figures 3 and 4 for the United States, United Kingdom, Japan, and Germany.

Distribution Effects and Political Instability

The negative growth effects have been paired with far-reaching redistribution effects of the very expansionary monetary policies.[9] First, if central banks depress government bond yields, the public sector gains at the cost of the private sector, which holds these assets. Second, the financial sector gains relative to the rest of the economy because currency units newly issued by the central bank are transferred first to the financial institutions, which can spend

[8]Since the mid-1980s household savings rates have trended downward in all major industrialized countries, which puts into question the savings glut hypothesis (Summers 2014).

[9]For details see Hoffmann and Schnabl (2016) and Duarte and Schnabl (2017).

FIGURE 4
INVESTMENT AS PERCENT OF GDP AND REAL GROWTH IN G4 COUNTRIES

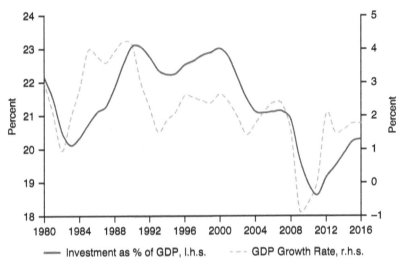

NOTE: Each line is the arithmetic average of the values for United States, Japan, Germany, and United Kingdom.
SOURCE: IMF.

the newly issued currency units first. Each previously created currency unit held by other economic agents can purchase a smaller portion of goods, services, or assets (such as stocks and real estate) (Cantillon 1931).

Third, the higher income class (which owns the largest share of stocks and real estate) gains relative to the middle class (which tends to save in low-risk asset classes) because the excessive money creation inflates asset prices (see Figure 3), while it depresses returns on bank deposits and government bonds.

Fourth, young people lose relative to older people because productivity gains converging toward zero put a restriction on real wage increases. This burden is overproportionally shifted to newcomers in the labor markets, because older contracts allow for a stronger wage negotiation power. Given productivity gains close to zero, the wage level (and the social security benefits) of the younger generation declines compared to former generations. The real wage level of the younger generation declines even more when deflated by real estate prices. The acquisition of real estate has become increasingly difficult for young people in the economic centers.

Fifth, as financing conditions for bank-based lending deteriorate while financing conditions on capital markets improve, large banks and enterprises (which have direct access to capital markets) gain relative to small and medium banks and enterprises. A concentration process in both the financial and enterprise sector evolves.[10] Sixth, if large enterprises and financial institutions are clustered in specific regions, regional economic disparity grows. Young people are forced to move from the peripheries to the centers to find employment.

All in all, the redistribution effects of ultra-loose monetary policies and financial repression lead to growing wealth and income inequality. According to Hayek (1976) people regard the granting of privileges to specific groups—such as investment bankers, managers of large enterprises, and real estate owners—as unjust. Even if in the short-term it is rational to ignore the impact of monetary policies for increasing inequality,[11] in the longer term more and more people will call for change.

People who want to stress the need for more redistribution will tend to vote for very left parties or candidates. Others will move to the extreme right, as they see the solution to the problem in more economic (and thereby political) nationalism. The rise of nationalism is particularly favored when growing inequality is attributed in the public to globalization (see, e.g., Rodrik 2017). Figure 5 shows for the EU28 the average share of votes for the established parties in the EU, which has been declining together with "shadow" interest rates in the eurozone.[12]

The causality between increasingly loose monetary conditions and political destabilization goes in both directions. First, the preceding monetary expansion increases inequality and therefore the likelihood of political dissatisfaction. Second, the resulting loss of votes for the established parties triggers additional redistribution efforts by the

---

[10]For details on the concentration process in the financial sector of Japan, see Gerstenberger and Schnabl (2017).

[11]On the rational ignorance, see Caplan (2001).

[12]The support for established parties is defined as one minus the share of votes for extreme left and extreme right parties in parliamentary elections. For detailed information on the data see Schnabl and Müller (2017).

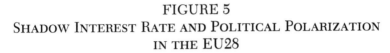

FIGURE 5
SHADOW INTEREST RATE AND POLITICAL POLARIZATION
IN THE EU28

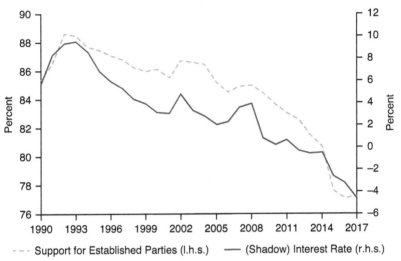

SOURCE: Krippner (see footnote 1) and Institute for Economic Policy.

governments, which aim to restore political stability (e.g., by increasing retirement benefits and providing more financial support for young families and periphery regions). To finance the additional government expenditure, additional government bond purchases (quantitative easing) of central banks become necessary, which initiates a new round of adverse redistribution effects of monetary expansion.[13]

Because growing political instability constitutes a severe threat for welfare and peace, a timely exit including an exit strategy from ultra-loose monetary policies is necessary.

Exit Strategies

Debt reduction via financial repression as proposed by Reinhart and Sbrancia (2015) is not a solution. The United States and United Kingdom could reduce their post–World War II debt burden of

---

[13]If the decline of welfare for specific groups is publicly attributed to market forces and globalization, financial market regulation and barriers to international factors flows are encouraged, which puts an additional drag on growth.

more than 100 and 250 percent of the nominal GDP because the postwar reconstruction provided an exogenous source of growth.[14] In sharp contrast, today—by keeping interest rates artificially low—growth and therefore inflationary pressure are undermined by the very factor that has caused high government debt—that is, the extreme monetary expansion.[15]

As Friedman (1967) has noted, in the long run central banks are unable to influence real variables, such as the rate of unemployment, because expectations adjust to any monetary shock. Therefore, as in the emerging markets and the central and eastern European countries since the 1980s, in the industrialized countries a fundamental reconstitution of market principles is necessary to reanimate growth.

McKinnon (1993) shows that many emerging market economies that liberalized their financial markets and economic systems prior to the 1990s were able to achieve impressive economic growth. The most prominent growth miracle since the 1990s has been in China, although the liberalization process has been interrupted by the low interest rate policies of the industrialized countries.[16] Meanwhile, in the most industrialized countries, new unsustainable exuberance

---

[14]According to Reinhart and Sbrancia (2015), debts of 3 to 4 percent of GDP were liquidated annually by the interest rate and inflation effect of financial repression. Rogoff (2017) proposes to abolish cash to make financial repression as a tool to reduce public debt more effective. This would, however, further restrain economic freedom and growth.

[15]The transmission of the monetary expansion to financial markets has been mainly via declining interest rates, which caused—depending on the regulation and the mood of financial markets—inflationary pressure in changing segments of the international financial markets. In the case of the Federal Reserve, increasing deposits of commercial banks since 2008, which were remunerated at a moderate interest rate on required reserve balances and excess balances, cannot be seen as a sterilization tool because the monetary transmission worked via historically low interest rates. In Japan and the euro area, excess balances of commercial banks at the central banks emerged even without being remunerated or even being charged with negative interest rates. From this point of view, the growing balances of commercial banks at the central banks in many industrialized countries are more the consequence of subdued credit growth following the global financial crises rather than an indicator for sterilization.

[16]McKinnon and Schnabl (2014) show how the return of financial repression in China has been imposed from outside by the very low interest rate levels in the industrialized countries. This externally imposed financial repression has undermined the Chinese growth miracle by the build-up of tremendous overcapacities in the enterprise and real estate sectors.

in financial markets is contained by tighter financial supervision and comprehensive macroprudential measures, which have become, however, a main impediment for the efficient allocation of resources.[17]

McKinnon (1993) stressed that fiscal and monetary consolidation has to precede the liberalization of financial markets, otherwise the low-cost liquidity provision of central banks would trigger destabilizing turmoil in financial markets.[18] The focus of fiscal consolidation in industrialized countries would be on curtailing expenditure, as the share of government expenditure as percent of GDP is high in most countries.

The fiscal consolidation process could be facilitated by a debt relief. For instance, postwar Germany and Japan achieved the reduction of public debt by outright default. In Germany in the course of a currency reform, government bonds, cash, and sight deposits were simply devalued. The resulting burdens were partially redistributed by taxing real assets, in particular real estate.[19] As such a redistribution process is vulnerable to the influence of special interest groups, it is likely to further enhance political discontent. Therefore, a market-oriented debt reduction process based on gradual interest rate increases is the superior solution.

To achieve an exit without tears, which avoids major meltdowns in the financial sector and the bankruptcy of highly indebted states, the process has to be simultaneously *credible, slow, transparent, sequenced along the yield curve, and internationally coordinated.* As nominal interest rates at zero and real interest rates below zero can—from a Hayek-Mises perspective—be assumed to be far below the natural interest rate, a sustainable exit strategy would restore the

---

[17]With the financial sector being more tightly controlled, the risks are currently building up in the enterprise sector, represented by sharply increasing volumes of (debt-financed) mergers and acquisitions as well as stock prices.

[18]Before liberalizing financial markets the monetary and fiscal system had to be converted from a passive mode that had simply accommodated the planned government expenditure into a constraint on the ability of enterprises, households and local governments to bid for scarce resources (McKinnon 1993: 3).

[19]The "Law on the Redistribution of Burdens" (Lastenausgleichsgesetz) of 1952 taxed real estate at a rate of up to 50 percent. As the resulting liability could be spread over a period of up to 30 years, the yearly burden could be financed out of the returns of the taxed assets. The real burden was further eased by moderate inflation.

long-term average in the postwar nominal short-term interest rate of about 6 percent.[20] This long-term average before the start of the asymmetric interest rate path can be seen as a rough proxy of Hayek's natural interest rate.

First, as monetary policies have become increasingly expansionary for more than three decades—as represented by the convergence of short-term and long-term interest rates toward zero and the gradual inflation of central bank balance sheets—expectations have become strongly tilted toward the persistence of the ultra-low interest rates. To shift the expectations toward an exit from ultra-low loose policies, a *credible* reversal is necessary. As inflation targeting regimes have contributed to the detrimental persistence of the ultra-loose monetary policies,[21] the credible announcement of a fundamental change in the monetary policy strategy is a prerequisite for a shift in expectations.

For this purpose, consumer price index–based inflation-targeting regimes should be publicly dismissed, as they are mainly serving the perpetuation of government financing by central banks. The new monetary regime should be based on targeting the monetary base in the tradition of the quantity theory of money with base money growth being oriented to output growth.[22] This strategy would minimize the destabilizing effects of monetary policies in financial markets.

Second, the exit from the ultra-low interest rate policies has to be *slow* because the structural distortions, which have been caused by the increasingly expansionary monetary policies, can be assumed to be immense. To avoid major economic disruptions including surging unemployment, the production factors have to be reallocated steadily. A gradual increase of interest rates would force governments to reduce debt by gradually cutting expenditure and streamlining social security systems. This would shift resources from the public sector back to the private sector.

[20]This value is based on the assumption that the long-term average in the inflation is 2 percent and therefore the long-term average in the real interest rates would be 4 percent. In the view of Hayek (1931) and Mises (1949), the real interest rate has to be positive because it represents a positive time preference rate.

[21]Since the mid-1980s, monetary expansion has increasingly become visible on asset rather than goods markets.

[22]Also, nominal GDP targeting may be an alternative (see Meade 1978 and Schumer 2012).

Reducing the liquidity provision to the financial sector would deflate the balance sheets of financial institutions, thereby shifting resources from the financial sector to the enterprise sector. In particular, the financial sectors in the United States and United Kingdom would be consolidated, stimulating industrial production. As speculation would be reduced, investment banking would shrink more than traditional banking (which would be reanimated).

The commercial banks would have to restructure their balance sheets by removing bad loans. By doing so they would have to exert pressure on their debtors in the enterprise sector to increase efficiency. The enterprises would be forced to push forward innovation and efficiency gains in the production process. This would necessitate additional investment in fixed and/or human capital. As the consolidation process in the government, financial, and enterprise sectors would take time, the increase in short-term interest rates should not be more than, say, 0.5 or 0.25 percentage points per year.

Third, to stabilize expectations, the exit process has to be *transparent* by following an exit rule that aims to reconstitute the natural interest rate level.[23] For example, the central bank could be restrained to hold increases in the policy rate to 0.5 or 0.25 percentage points per year for a predefined time period, without any possibility of suspending that rule. The slow, but rule-based interest rate increases would contain financial turbulence as the first move is small and further steps are slow and predictable. The slow speed of interest rate increases would give all involved institutions sufficient time to adjust, so that panic is misplaced. At the earliest, after a period of 12 (0.5) or 24 (0.25) years, the rule should be allowed to be reassessed and to be transformed into a revised monetary policy rule.[24] The respective exit paths are shown in Figure 6.

Fourth, a forward-looking exit strategy should consider the fact that interest rates have become manipulated by central banks both at the short and the long end of the yield curve. Therefore, the exit process has to be *sequenced along the yield curve*. The exit from conventional monetary expansion (targeting the short-term interest rate)

---

[23]This exit rule is not equivalent to a general monetary policy rule, which would be applied once a successful exit has occurred.

[24]With the purchasing power of people being strengthened, inflation would moderately pick up, rendering real interest rate increases smaller than nominal interest rate increases.

FIGURE 6
SIMULATION OF EXIT PATHS

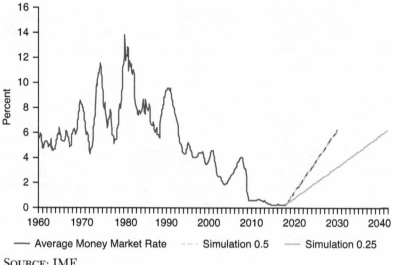

SOURCE: IMF.

should precede the exit from unconventional monetary expansion (targeting the long-term interest rate).

Lifting the short-term interest rate first would stabilize the financial sector. Up to the present, zero- or close-to-zero interest rate policies have paralyzed the money market thereby restricting the lending of banks with liquidity shortages (but good lending opportunities). The conventional and unconventional monetary policies have depressed lending–deposit spreads as the traditional source of commercial banks' income. This has particularly destabilized small and medium banks and their lending activity to small and medium enterprises.

If short-term interest rates increase, potential lenders on the money market would start lending again to banks with liquidity shortages. Both banks with liquidity overhangs and banks with liquidity shortages could generate additional profits. Banks with liquidity overhangs would gain from money market lending. Banks with liquidity shortages would gain, as additional business would be generated and lending-deposit spreads would increase. With growing profits of small and medium banks, lending to small and medium enterprises could grow, thereby supporting small and medium enterprises. The strengthening of the banking sector would contain concerns that banks have to be recapitalized by the governments. This would contribute to the stabilization of the public sectors.

As long-term interest rates would be kept under control via unconventional monetary policies in the first phase of the exit, this would help to stabilize financial institutions and insurance companies, which hold large amounts of government bonds. Sharp fluctuations of long-term interest rates in response to the announcement of the exit would be contained. Governments would gain some time to reduce expenditure and debt levels.

After a year, the restrictions on long-term interest rates should be gradually removed by reducing the stocks of government bond holdings of central banks. The reduction should follow an exit rule as well, specifying a specific amount per month. The rule could mirror inversely the build-up of government bond holdings, with respect to both timing and scale. The target point of the unwinding of government bond holdings should be fixed at the share of GDP as it prevailed before the start of the unconventional monetary policy measures.

Then, long-term interest rates also would be increasingly determined by market forces. Without unconventional purchases of government bonds by the central banks, long-term yields would be set again at the average of expected future short-term rates plus a liquidity premium. The gradual reduction of public debt would help to contain large shifts in risk premiums.

Fifth, the exit from low interest rates has to be *coordinated* among the four largest central banks—Federal Reserve, Bank of Japan, European Central Bank, and Bank of England—to avoid major disruptions in the foreign exchange markets. The recent history of tapering and the exit from low interest rates in the United States has shown that an isolated exit of only one major central bank from the ultra-low interest rate environment causes an appreciation of the domestic currency.

Discontent among export-oriented (i.e., large and politically influential) enterprises and the deflationary pressure of appreciation constitute a restraint on any unilateral exit strategy. A coordinated exit of all major central banks is a way to escape from the current prisoner's dilemma in the international monetary system, which would avoid exchange rate disruptions. The coordination process would also enhance the credibility of the exit in every singly participating country.

Outlook

Many former developing countries and socialist planning economies have shown that the exit from low interest rate policies and financial repression is worthwhile because it nudges companies, banks, and citizens back into a market-oriented, spontaneous order. This boosts productivity gains and growth. Thus, today in the industrialized countries also, the exit from the asymmetric monetary policies would be equivalent to a reanimation of growth, as the hidden nationalization process in the financial and enterprise sector would be reversed.

In the industrialized countries, banks and enterprises still operate based on market principles (although the public sector fundamentally distorts price signals). International trade and capital flows remain widely liberalized, and robust legal frameworks prevail. Therefore, the adjustment to the new environment will be much easier compared to the transformation processes in the formerly financially repressed emerging market economies.

Most financial institutions, enterprises, and governments will be able to adjust. If some banks and enterprises fail, new ones will emerge. Most states would be able to adjust, as huge and inefficient budgets provide ample room for consolidation. Large assets owned by the public sector such as real estate and infrastructure would provide room for debt-equity-swaps. Insolvent states will be forced to restructure.

There are concerns that the exit from low interest rate policies would lead into a global crisis initiated by a meltdown in the financial sector. Yet the opposite is likely to be the case. The gradual decline of interest rates since the mid-1980s has not boosted but has paralyzed growth. It has increased volatility on financial markets, with the resulting uncertainty further depressing investment as a main determinant of growth. Therefore, inverting the process would imply in the medium term accelerating growth supported by growing financial stability.

To achieve an exit without tears, the exit process has to be credible, slow, transparent, sequenced over the yield curve, and internationally coordinated. Neglecting one of these principles would destabilize the exit path. The G7 would provide an appropriate platform for international coordination.

With incentives being restored, resources would be reshuffled from speculative investment toward investment in fixed and human capital. Economic activity would be reshuffled from the public to the private sector and from the financial sector to the enterprise sector. Both are likely to generate substantial productivity gains, which would be the basis for real wage increases. The reduction of financial market speculation would help to reduce wealth and income inequality. This would strengthen private consumption and encourage investment by enterprises, thereby creating better-paid jobs.

As speculation is discouraged, the richer part of the population would contribute more than other parts of the population to the adjustment process via a declining market value of their assets and lower payment for the highly ranked management. The access of low- and middle-income groups to assets such as stocks and real estate would be facilitated. Both factors would be regarded as just among major parts of the population and therefore help to restore political stability. This adjustment would help to promote free markets and free trade, which are the basis of long-run economic growth and welfare in the industrialized countries.

References

Caballero, R.; Hoshi, T.; and Kashyap, A. (2008) "Zombie Lending and Depressed Restructuring in Japan." *American Economic Review* 98 (5): 1943–77.

Cantillon, R. (1931) *Abhandlung über die Natur des Handels im allgemeinen*. Jena, Germany: Fischer.

Caplan, B. (2001) "Rational Ignorance versus Rational Irrationality." *Kyklos* 54 (1): 3–26.

Duarte, P., and Schnabl, G. (2017) "Monetary Policy, Income Inequality and Political Instability." CESifo Working Paper 6734.

Friedman, M. (1967) "The Role of Monetary Policy." *American Economic Review* 58 (1): 1–17.

Gerstenberger, J., and Schnabl, G. (2017) "The Impact of Japanese Monetary Policy Crisis Management on the Japanese Banking Sector." CESifo Working Paper No. 6440.

Hayek, F. A. (1931) *Prices and Production*. New York: August M. Kelly.

_____ (1976) *Law, Legislation, and Liberty. Vol. 2: The Mirage of Social Justice*. Chicago: University of Chicago Press.

Hoffmann, A., and Schnabl, G. (2011) "A Vicious Cycle of Manias, Crises and Asymmetric Policy Responses: An Overinvestment View." *World Economy* 34: 382–403.

_____ (2016) "The Adverse Effects of Ultra-Loose Monetary Policies on Investment, Growth and Income Distribution." *Cato Journal* 36 (3): 449–84.

Kornai, J. (1986) "The Soft Budget Constraint." *Kyklos* 39 (1): 3–30.

McKinnon, R. (1973) *Money and Capital in Economic Development*. Washington: Brookings Institution Press.

_____ (1993) *The Order of Economic Liberalization: Financial Control in the Transition to a Market Economy*. Baltimore: The Johns Hopkins University Press.

McKinnon, R., and Schnabl, G. (2014) "China's Exchange Rate and Financial Repression: The Conflicted Emergence of the Renminbi as an International Currency." *China and World Economy* 22 (3): 1–34.

Meade, J. (1978) "The Meaning of Internal Balance." *Economic Journal* 88 (351): 423–425.

Mises, L. von ([1912] 1980) *The Theory of Money and Credit*. Reprint. Indianapolis: Liberty Classics.

_____ (1949) *Human Action*. New York: Foundation for Economic Education.

Peek, J., and Rosengren, E. (2005) "Unnatural Selection: Perverse Incentives and the Misallocation of Credit in Japan." *American Economic Review* 95 (4): 1144–66.

Reinhart, C., and Sbrancia, M. B. (2015) "The Liquidation of Government Debt." NBER Working Paper No. 16893.

Rodrik, D. (2017) "Populism and the Economics of Globalization." Working Paper, John F. Kennedy School of Government, Harvard University.

Rogoff, K. (2017) *The Curse of Cash*. Princeton, N.J.: Princeton University Press.

Schnabl, G., and Müller, S. (2017) "Die Zukunft der Europäischen Union aus ordnungspolitischer Perspektive." Universität Leipzig Wirtschaftswissenschaftliche Fakultät Working Papers 150.

Schumer, S. (2012) "How Nominal GDP Targeting Could Have Prevented the Crash of 2008." In D. Beckworth (ed.) *Boom and*

Bust Banking: The Causes and Cures of the Great Recession 146–47. Oakland, Calif.: Independent Institute.

Schumpeter, J. (1934) *The Theory of Economic Development.* Cambridge, Mass.: Harvard University Press.

Shaw, E. (1973) *Financial Deepening in Economic Development.* New York: Oxford University Press.

Solow, R. (1956) "A Contribution to the Theory of Economic Growth." *Quarterly Journal of Economics* 70 (1): 65–94.

_____ (1957) "Technical Change and the Aggregate Production Function." *Review of Economics and Statistics* 39 (2): 312–20.

Summers, L. (2014) "U.S. Economic Prospects: Secular Stagnation, Hysteresis, and the Zero Lower Bound." *Business Economics* 49 (2): 65–73.

Swan, T. (1956) "Economic Growth and Capital Accumulation." *Economic Record* 32 (2): 334–61.

White, L. H. (2015) "Hayek and Modern Macroeconomics." George Mason University Working Paper in Economics 15-05.

7

NEEDED: A FEDERAL RESERVE EXIT FROM PREFERENTIAL CREDIT ALLOCATION
Lawrence H. White

In September 2008, the Federal Reserve initiated a series of quantitative easing (QE) programs that dramatically transformed the Fed's balance sheet—in size, liability mix, and asset mix. The "exit strategy" questions now facing the Fed, and the dollar-using public who are its captive customers, are when and how to reverse those transformations.

On the liability side of the Fed's balance sheet, QE swelled the stock of base money (the subset of the Fed's liabilities consisting of currency held by the nonbank public plus depository institutions' reserves) more than four-fold. Contrasting October 2015 to August 2008, the base rose to $4.06 trillion from $0.85 trillion. The mix of Fed liabilities shifted as approximately $2.6 trillion of the $3.2 trillion in new base money was added to the reserve balances of depository institutions (the other $0.6 trillion was added to currency held by the public). Total bank reserves have grown more than 50-fold, to $2.7 trillion from a mere $0.05 trillion. Only a tiny share of the added reserve holdings (about $0.1 trillion) are accounted for by the growth in required reserves accompanying growth in commercial bank deposits held by the public; the bulk are voluntarily held as excess reserves (balances over and above legally required reserves against deposits). Excess reserves have risen to $2.5 trillion and 62 percent

---

Lawrence H. White is Professor of Economics at George Mason University. This article is reprinted from the *Cato Journal*, Vol. 36, No. 2 (Spring/Summer 2016). He thanks Scott Burns for research assistance and Leonidas Zalmanovitz for comments.

FIGURE 1
The Fed Greatly Expanded the Monetary Base (M0) but Kept M2 on Its Pre-Crisis Path

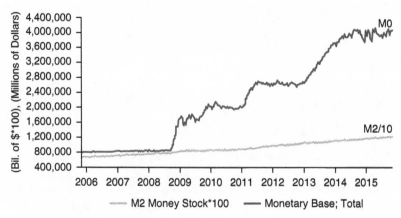

of the monetary base, from only $0.002 trillion and close to zero percent (about two-tenths of 1 percent) pre-QE.[1]

While the QE programs accelerated the monetary base (hereafter M0) at an unprecedented rate, Figure 1 shows that they did not accelerate the quantity of money held by the public as measured by the standard broad-money aggregate M2 (currency in circulation plus all bank deposits). During the pre-QE decade of September 1998–September 2008, the Fed expanded M0 at a compound rate of 5.99 percent per annum. The expansion rate jumped to 23.69 percent per annum during September 2008–September 2015. The growth rate of M2 has fluctuated a bit but hardly changed over the longer term: 6.3 percent per annum in the pre-QE decade and 6.6 percent since the beginning of QE. The fact that M2 has hardly budged from its established long-term path indicates that *quantitative easing was not a change in monetary policy*, in the sense that it was not used to alter the path of the standard broad monetary aggregate in a sustained way.[2]

---

[1]Figures are from the St. Louis Fed's FRED database, series BOGMBASEM, TOTRESNS, REQRESNS, EXCSRENS, and author's calculations based on those figures.

[2]The growth rate of the alternative broad aggregate MZM meanwhile fell to 6.4 percent from 8.7 percent.

The growth rate of the M1 component of M2 (currency plus only checking deposits) did rise faster, to 11.5 percent per annum from 3.0 percent. But because M2 as a whole did not grow faster, this only indicates that households have reduced the share of their total bank deposits in savings (non-M1) accounts and increased the share in checking accounts. This shift can be explained primarily by households responding to a collapse in the spread between savings and checking account interest rates, both rates falling to near zero. The national average rate on three-month CDs, for example, tumbled to 16 basis points in September 2015 from 359 in September 2008, while the rate on interest checking declined far less, to 4 basis points from 20.[3]

Why didn't M2 grow faster? As money-and-banking textbooks tell us, the growth rate of M2 mirrors the growth of M0 when the commercial banking system sheds excess reserves by banks making loans and securities purchases such that system deposit liabilities grow in proportion to system reserves. After September 2008, however, banks began sitting on the additional reserves the Fed was creating. They did so largely because the Fed almost simultaneously—and not coincidentally—began paying interest on reserves in early October 2008. With a higher reward for holding reserves, banks began holding greater reserves in excess of legal requirements, which meant that the system began creating fewer deposit dollars per reserve dollar. The ratio of excess reserves to deposits rose from a fraction of 1 percent in September 2008, before QE began, to 24 percent today. This enabled M2 to continue along its pre-QE path despite the huge increase in M0.

The initiation of interest on excess reserves (hereafter IOER) and QE at the same time was no accident. The Fed chose to start paying IOER in order to neutralize the flood of excess reserves that QE1 and other Fed lending programs were creating. Fed spokesmen have at times described the rationale for initiating IOER as a move to counteract downward pressure on the federal funds rate (the overnight interest rate at which banks lend reserves to one another) from excess reserves (Dr. Econ 2013). Instead of trying to get rid of excess reserves by lending them and in the process driving the fed funds rate too low, banks would now be happy to hold the reserves.

[3]Figures from FRED and Bankrate.com. See McAndrews, Morgan, and Vickery (2012), who regress M2 and M1 on the one-year Treasury note rate among other variables.

This is a curious account given that the fed funds rate fell to near-zero anyway. A better explanation begins by noting that IOER, by getting banks to hold more reserves, has allowed the Fed to greatly expand its assets and consequently M0, while keeping M2 from ballooning. The combination of QE with IOER enables the Fed to finance a hugely expanded portfolio of assets without inflationary consequences, essentially by borrowing from the banking system. Without IOER, purchasing assets by expanding M0 also expands M2, which has inflationary consequences. At times, the Board of Governors has been almost frank about its policy, as for example in its original press release on October 6, 2008:

> The payment of interest on excess reserves will permit the Federal Reserve to expand its balance sheet as necessary to provide the liquidity necessary to support financial stability while implementing the monetary policy that is appropriate in light of the System's macroeconomic objectives of maximum employment and price stability [Board of Governors 2008].

That is to say, it permits the Fed to expand its balance sheet as desired without corresponding expansion in M2 and the price level.

The Fed has also introduced another policy tool to allow it to keep an expanded balance sheet without corresponding expansion of monetary aggregates. In 2010, it began testing its Term Deposit Facility, whereby the Fed *borrows back* reserve money from commercial banks for 21 days, paying the IOER rate plus 3 basis points. The term deposits are not counted as reserves, so M0 shrinks even though total Fed liabilities and the Fed's asset portfolio do not. In tests of the facility, the Fed has sterilized up to $400 billion this way.

If not for monetary expansion, for what purpose did the Fed deem base expansion desirable? Why was the Fed so keen on purchasing trillions in assets? The reference in the above-quoted statement to providing liquidity is a red herring. The Fed could have provided all the liquidity it wanted simply by acquiring more of the same assets it already held, short- and medium-term Treasuries. Instead, as Figure 2 indicates, the Fed purchased and is now holding $1.8 trillion in mortgage-backed securities (MBS) and housing agency debt securities (Fannie Mae, Freddie Mac, and the Federal Home Loan Banks), a drastic change from its near-zero holdings of such securities before 2008. These holdings can be seen only as part

FIGURE 2
FEDERAL RESERVE SYSTEM HOLDINGS OF MBS PLUS FEDERAL AGENCY (FANNIE MAE, FREDDIE MAC, AND FEDERAL HOME LOAN BANKS) DEBT SECURITIES

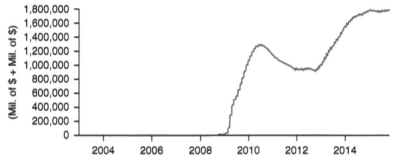

——— Mortgage-backed securities held by the Federal Reserve: All Maturities + Federal agency debt securities held by the Federal Reserve: All Maturities.

of an effort to raise MBS prices and cheapen housing finance relative to finance for other investments.

The bulk of the mortgage-backed securities the Fed holds have maturities of longer than 10 years. The Fed also purchased trillions in longer-term Treasuries (see Figure 3), again discarding its previous policy of concentrating on short- and medium-term Treasuries, in an effort to raise long-term bond prices and lower long-term interest rates relative to short rates, again to favor housing finance. By holding down longer-term Treasury rates, it hopes to hold down 15-year and 30-year mortgage rates. The Board of Governors' own website account of its "maturity extension program" puts it this way:

> By reducing the supply of longer-term Treasury securities in the market, this action should put downward pressure on longer-term interest rates, including rates on financial assets that investors consider to be close substitutes for longer-term Treasury securities. . . . In response to the lower Treasury yields, interest rates on a range of instruments including home mortgages, corporate bonds, and loans to households and businesses will also likely be lower [Board of Governors 2013].[4]

---

[4]Loans to households and businesses, contrary to the suggestion made in the passage quoted, are seldom for 10 or more years at a fixed interest rate, so their rates are *unlikely* to be lowered much.

FIGURE 3
Federal Reserve System Holdings of All Securities and of Securities with Maturities of 10+ Years

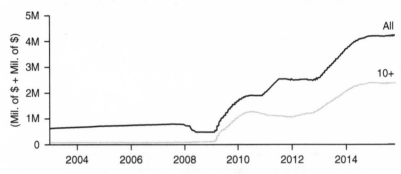

U.S. Treasury securities held by the Federal Reserve: Maturing in over 10 years + Mortgage-backed securities held by the Federal Reserve: Maturing in over 10 years.

U.S. Treasury securities held by the Federal Reserve: All Maturities + Mortgage-backed securities held by the Federal Reserve: All Maturities.

The Fed currently holds $2.4 trillion in securities maturing in 10+ years, more than half of its entire $4.2 trillion portfolio. As Figure 4 shows, using the same data as Figure 3 but in share-of-portfolio terms rather than dollar amounts, the share of the Fed's portfolio in such long-term securities was only about 10 percent at the start of 2008.

There is also an unstated fiscal effect, intended or not, from the Fed's move to longer maturities: the Fed enjoys higher interest earnings at the long end of the yield curve, which benefits the Treasury as the Fed rebates more dollars to the Treasury.[5] For other financial institutions, borrowing short and lending long (without hedging the duration gap) is a risky strategy that endangers solvency, but the Fed's insolvency risk is almost a nonissue. The Fed's "liabilities" never have to be repaid in something it can't create ad lib, and even the interest rate it pays on reserves is discretionary and could be cut to zero tomorrow (although, to be sure, the Fed does not want to cut the IOER rate given the inflationary

---

[5]This was quickly noticed by Willem Buiter (2009), who referred to Ben Bernanke as "the man who allowed the Fed to be turned into an off-budget, off-balance sheet subsidiary of the U.S. Treasury."

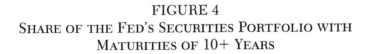

FIGURE 4
SHARE OF THE FED'S SECURITIES PORTFOLIO WITH
MATURITIES OF 10+ YEARS

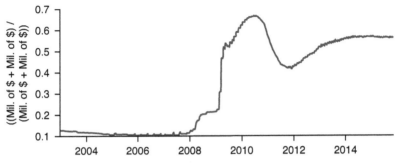

— (U.S. Treasury securities held by the Federal Reserve: Maturing in
over 10 years + Mortgage-backed securities held by the Federal
Reserve: Maturing in over 10 years) / (U.S. Treasury securities held
by the Federal Reserve: All Maturities + Mortgage-backed securities
held by the Federal Reserve: All Maturities).

consequences). The Fed, by enlarging its duration gap, does increase the risk that it would become insolvent on a mark-to-market basis should market interest rate rise sharply, but the Fed does not use mark-to-market accounting. As a San Francisco Fed official (Rudebusch 2011) explained when critics first began raising the concern: "The Fed values its securities at acquisition cost and registers capital gains and losses only when securities are sold. Such historical-cost accounting is . . . consistent with the buy-and-hold securities strategy the Fed has traditionally followed." Even a technically insolvent Fed could easily cover its payroll expenses from its interest income.

The Fed's *Annual Report* shows that it received $116.6 billion in interest income during 2014, for a 2.76 percent return on its $4.22 trillion average asset portfolio. If, instead, the Fed had held its entire portfolio in one-year Treasuries yielding 12 basis points, its interest income would have been only $5.1 billion, not enough to cover its $6.9 billion in interest payments on bank reserves plus its operating expenses of $1.9 billion. Its transfer to the Treasury, instead of $96.9 billion, would have been negative. For five-year Treasuries, the yield during 2014 averaged about 164 basis points. The corresponding interest income from a Fed portfolio entirely of five-year Treasuries would have been $69.2 billion, some $47.4 billion shy of its

FIGURE 5

By Lengthening Its Portfolio after 2009,
the Fed Kept Its Average Yield Above the Declining
Five-year T-Bond Rate

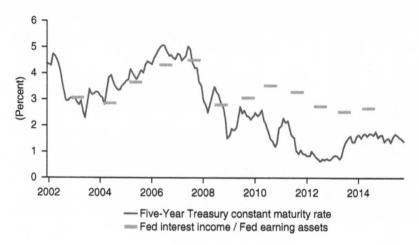

—Five-Year Treasury constant maturity rate
Fed interest income / Fed earning assets

actual interest income.[6] The actual median maturity of the Fed's securities throughout 2014 was more than 10 years.[7] Figure 5 shows how the realized return on the Fed's portfolio roughly tracked the five-year bond rate up to 2008 but has risen well above it since then, indicating that the Fed has moved toward the higher yields available at the long end of the yield curve. Yields on 10-year Treasuries during 2014 were slightly below the 2.76 percent return that the Fed received. The Fed's realized portfolio rate of return matched the yield on a Treasury bond of about 11 years maturity.

The combination of QE + IOER, not a monetary policy, is best understood as a preferential credit allocation policy. Elsewhere (White 2015b), I have tried to spell out why allowing the Fed to conduct a preferential credit allocation policy is a bad idea. To summarize: credit allocation policy is a kind of central planning in which Federal Reserve officials, risking not their own money but that of

[6]The 2014 asset portfolio size is calculated as the simple mean of the figures reported on H.4.1 releases for Reserve Bank Credit at the beginning and end of 2014. The yield figures are the arithmetic means of monthly one-year and five-year Treasury constant maturity rates over the course of the year. Interest income and payments are from the Fed's 2014 Annual Report.
[7]Federal Reserve H.4.1 weekly releases, Table 2.

taxpayers, substitute their judgment for the financial market's about the right prices of various securities and the proper shares of the flow of funds that should go to specific segments of the financial market. When the Fed directs a larger share of credit to one favored sector (like housing), more promising sectors get smaller shares, a waste of scarce loanable funds on lower-payoff investments. Fed-directed allocation of funds to a declining industry throws good resources after bad. An increase in political credit allocation reduces economic growth not only by creating deadweight loss in this way, but by incentivizing socially unproductive lobbying efforts to be among the favored credit recipients.[8] Especially if the Fed allocates funds to rescuing particular firms, it creates tremendous moral hazard and an environment ripe for cronyism.[9]

The importance of an exit strategy from the Fed's currently anomalous balance sheet is not only for the sake of ending an abnormal monetary policy, then, but also for the sake of ending an abnormal, inefficient, and dangerous credit allocation policy.

Monetary Policy Normalization

Seen in this light, the Fed's talk about "normalizing monetary policy" deliberately evades the equally important issue of ending preferential credit allocation. Ben Bernanke declared in June 2013 that "a strong majority now expects that the Committee will not sell agency mortgage-backed securities during the process of normalizing monetary policy."[10] Chairwoman Yellen (2014) has similarly spoken about normalization only in terms of a return to fed funds targeting:

> As was the case before the crisis, the Committee intends to adjust the stance of monetary policy during normalization,

[8]For example, in 2015, lobbyists for the Commonwealth of Puerto Rico promoted the idea that since the Federal Reserve has used its discretion to buy bad assets and save firms in the housing finance industry in the name of systemic stability, it could now use its discretion to buy up Puerto Rican bonds or otherwise extend credit to help Puerto Rico restructure its debt in the name of systemic stability (see Capitol Forum 2015, Jansen 2015).

[9]Thus Buiter (2009) offered a second apt indictment of Ben Bernanke: "He has, however, apparently decided to go down in history as the Federal Reserve chairman who presided over the creation of the biggest moral hazard machine ever."

[10]Quoted by Hummel (2014), who aptly comments that "these developments highlight the extent to which quantitative easing is converting the Fed into a financial central planner."

> primarily through actions that influence the level of the federal funds rate.... The primary tool for moving the federal funds rate in to the target range will be the rate of interest paid on excess reserves or IOER.... The committee intends to use an overnight reverse repurchase agreement facility which ... will help ensure that the federal funds rate remains in the target range.

She affirmed that the Fed's normalization plan does not include an end to the Fed's attempt to favor housing finance: "The Committee does not anticipate selling agency mortgage backed securities as part of the normalization process." The minutes of FOMC meetings during 2015 consistently repeated language to the same effect: "The Committee is maintaining its existing policy of reinvesting principal payments from its holdings of agency debt and agency mortgage-backed securities in agency mortgage-backed securities and of rolling over maturing Treasury securities at auction."

Yellen's reference to the FOMC's intention to use overnight reverse repurchase agreements alludes to a technical problem that the Fed faces in trying to return to pre-2008 fed funds targeting practices without reversing its QE asset purchases. The fed funds market for overnight loans of base money between financial institutions isn't what it was. Commercial banks awash with excess reserves do not need to borrow more for liquidity purposes. And they are not keen to lend reserves at anything less than the interest rate they currently receive from the Fed for holding them. Over the last four years, the effective daily fed funds rate has ranged between 4 and 19 basis points (it was 12 at the end of October 2015), whereas the IOER rate has consistently been above that range at 25 basis points. The volume of fed funds on loan in September and October 2015 was approximately $50 billion, only one-eighth of the $400 billion volume in September 2008.[11] Alfonso, Entz, and LeSueur (2013) find that Federal Home Loan Banks, not eligible for IOER, have done three-fourths to five-sixths of the shrunken volume of lending since IOER began. They speculate that the marginal borrowers hold the borrowed funds in their accounts at the Fed, earning the difference between IOER rate and the fed funds rate. If so, this suggests that the effective fed funds rate tracks below the IOER rate by the transaction cost (10 basis points or so) of carrying out the operation. With

---

[11]FRED series FRPACBW027NBOG, Fed Funds and Reverse RPs with Banks, All Commercial Banks.

a basically horizontal demand curve, the low volume transacted reflects the limited supply from the Home Loan Banks.

In circumstances of excess reserve abundance, it isn't clear that raising the fed funds rate, assuming it can be done just by raising the IOER rate, would be relevant at the margin for broader credit market conditions. The Fed tacitly recognizes this problem when it proposes to conduct reverse repo transactions (selling securities with an agreement to repurchase the next day at a higher price, shrinking M0 overnight), and Term Deposit Facility borrowings from the banks, to make reserves scarcer. It is not known how large these transactions will need to be to make excess reserves scarce enough for commercial banks to start wanting to borrow appreciable sums at the fed funds rate. If they need to be $2 trillion each night, say, that would involve relatively large transaction costs for the Fed.

The Fed's expressed preference for making reserves scarce by borrowing them back in large volumes, rather than simply selling off assets once and for all, shows again how devoted it is to maintaining its swollen portfolio of MBS.

What to Do

As Jeffrey Hummel (2014) notes, there is a "real danger" that the Fed feels "no real need to normalize its balance sheet and therefore may not do so." In that case, to remove the Fed from preferential credit allocation, Congress would have to require it to normalize. Declarations by FOMC officials that they will act according to self-adopted "guidelines" are not time consistent. Fed leadership will find ample good reasons to use preferential credit allocation when the time comes to offset weakening in housing finance or other perceived threats to financial stability. To paraphrase what Buiter (2009) has said about a former Treasury official and moral hazard, Fed officials address the issue of undoing the Fed's huge holdings of mortgage-backed securities only when they feel the need to defend their continued preferential credit allocation by declaring that "now is not the time to worry about it." On the contrary, the moment when sticking to a principle seems difficult is exactly the time to worry about the long-run consequences of breaching it.[12]

A straightforward way to separate the Fed from preferential credit allocation among sectors of the private economy, without major

[12]As I have argued at greater length (White 2010).

changes to the institutional status quo, is to require the Fed to hold only U.S. Treasury obligations on its balance sheet, as recommended by Marvin Goodfriend (2014). An alternative, as discussed by George Selgin (2012: 321), is to allow the Fed to purchase non-Treasury securities only according to prescribed "objective criteria, such as issuers' (risk-adjusted) capital and private-agency security ratings." The Fed's purchases of mortgage-backed securities would have been barred by any reasonable set of such criteria.

A more thoroughgoing reform would be to alter the institutional status quo so as to end the Federal Reserve System and return its useful functions to the private sector. In previous work (White 2011, 2013, 2015a, 2015b), I have made the case for alternative arrangements based on a commodity standard with free banking.

References

Afonso, G.; Entz, A.; and LeSueur, E. (2013) "Who's Lending in the Fed Funds Market?" *Liberty Street Economics* blog, Federal Reserve Bank of New York (December 2): http://libertystreet economics.newyorkfed.org/2013/12/whos-lending-in-the-fed-funds-market.html.

Board of Governors of the Federal Reserve System (2008) "Press Release" (October 6): www.federalreserve.gov/monetarypolicy /20081006a.htm.

_____ (2013) "Maturity Extension Program and Reinvestment Policy" (August 2): www.federalreserve.gov/monetarypolicy/maturity extensionprogram-faqs.htm.

Buiter, W. (2009) "Should Fed Chairmen Go Around Kissing Babies?" *Maverecon* blog (July 28): http://blogs.ft.com/maverecon /2009/07/should-fed-chairmen-go-around-kissing-babies.

Capitol Forum (2015) "Puerto Rico: A Closer Look at Landmark Research Paper's Conclusion that No Legal or Regulatory Impediments Prevent Federal Reserve from Providing Financial Assistance to Puerto Rico" (August 14).

Dr. Econ (2013) "Why Did the Federal Reserve Start Paying Interest on Reserve Balances Held on Deposit at the Fed? Does the Fed Pay Interest on Required Reserves, Excess Reserves, or Both? What Interest Rate Does the Fed Pay?" (March): www.frbsf.org /education/publications/doctor-econ/2013/march/federal-reserve-interest-balances-reserves.

Goodfriend, M. (2014) "The Case for a Treasury-Federal Reserve Accord for Credit Policy." Testimony before the Subcommittee on Monetary Policy and Trade of the Committee on Financial Services, U.S. House of Representatives (March 14).

Hummel, J. R. (2014) "The Federal Reserve's Exit Strategy: Looming Inflation or Controllable Overhang?" Mercatus Center at George Mason University (September): http://mercatus.org/publication/federal-reserve-s-exit-strategy-looming-inflation-or-controllable-overhang.

Jansen, J. (2015) "Can Federal Reserve Buy Puerto Rico Debt?" Across the Curve (June 24): http://acrossthecurve.com/?p=21555.

McAndrews, J.; Morgan, D.; and Vickery, J. (2012) "What's Driving Up Money Growth?" Liberty Street Economics blog (23 May): http://libertystreeteconomics.newyorkfed.org/2012/05/whats-driving-up-money-growth.html.

Rudebusch, G. D. (2011) "The Fed's Interest Rate Risk." Federal Reserve Bank of San Francisco Economic Letter (April 11): www.frbsf.org/economic-research/publications/economic-letter/2011/april/fed-interest-rate-risk.

Selgin, G. (2012) "L Street: Bagehotian Prescriptions for a 21st-Century Money Market." Cato Journal 32 (2): 303–32.

White, L. H. (2010) "The Rule of Law or the Rule of Central Bankers?" Cato Journal 30 (3): 54–63.

_____ (2011) "A Gold Standard with Free Banking Would Have Restrained the Housing Boom, the Bust, and the Bailouts." Cato Journal 31(3): 497–504.

_____ (2013) "Antifragile Banking and Monetary Systems." Cato Journal 33 (3): 471–84.

_____ (2015a) "The Merits and Feasibility of Returning to a Commodity Standard." Journal of Financial Stability 17: 59–64.

_____ (2015b) "The Federal Reserve System's Overreach into Credit Allocation." Journal of Private Enterprise (Winter), forthcoming.

Yellen, J. (2014) Opening statement from Janet Yellen's news conference (September 17): www.marketnews.com/content/yellen-excerpt-exit-strategy-release-not-chg-pol-stance-2.

8

THE OPTIMUM QUANTITY OF MONEY AND THE ZERO LOWER BOUND

J. Huston McCulloch

Since 2008, the monetary base has more than quadrupled through the Federal Reserve's quantitative easing (QE) programs, and yet inflation has shown no signs of accelerating. In fact, inflation has not even met the Fed's announced 2 percent target, despite an essentially zero fed funds rate from 2009 to 2015. This is quite puzzling, both in terms of the traditional quantity theory of money and in terms of the Taylor rule approach to monetary policy.

Before 2008, the Fed could accelerate or decelerate inflation by expanding or contracting the monetary base and therefore bank reserves with open market operations and repo loans to dealers. Since 2008, however, the Fed has paid interest on excess reserves (IOER) equal to or even higher than the effective federal funds rate. As a result, the banks are awash with excess reserves that have zero opportunity cost, and the Fed has lost its primary mode of control over the price level and inflation.

In order to restore the Fed's control over inflation, it is necessary that IOER be abolished. In doing so, however, it is also necessary to undo the post-2008 explosion of the base in order to prevent massive inflation.

Fed economists have recently invoked Milton Friedman's 1969 essay, "The Optimum Quantity of Money" as providing justification

---

J. Huston McCulloch is an Adjunct Professor of Economics at New York University and Professor Emeritus at Ohio State University. This article is reprinted from the *Cato Journal*, Vol. 38, No. 2 (Spring/Summer 2018). It draws on McCulloch (2017a, 2017b).

for the Fed's IOER policy. However, I shall show that strict application of this rule would leave the price level indeterminate in a fiat money world, and hence that it cannot be taken seriously as a monetary policy.

The zero lower bound (ZLB) issue has been used to justify many of the extraordinary measures the Fed has taken since 2008 as well as its interpretation of price stability as 2 percent inflation. This article shows that problem can be solved by temporarily targeting interest rates on loans with maturities longer than the six weeks implicit in the Fed's current operating procedures, even with a 0 percent inflation target.

The Pre-2008 Regime

Prior to October of 2008, bank reserve deposits paid zero interest.[1] Banks normally held only a tiny inventory of excess reserves to meet withdrawals and adverse clearings, typically well under 0.5 percent of checkable deposits. The federal funds market efficiently allowed banks with surplus reserves and no immediate borrowing partner to lend them to banks that were short on reserves or were able to expand loans. The fed funds rate that banks charge one another for one-day use of reserves was typically well below the *average* rate banks got on somewhat risky customer loans that required close supervision, but represented the risk-adjusted opportunity cost to banks of *marginal* excess reserves.

Under this regime, if the Fed expanded the base and therefore excess reserves, banks would scramble to lend out any excess reserves beyond this small inventory to business or consumers who wanted the loans to make purchases they could not otherwise make, thereby driving up prices and at the same time temporarily driving down the fed funds rate.

Similarly, it could decelerate inflation by contracting the base, leaving banks with either precariously small excess reserves or an outright reserve shortfall. As banks contracted loans and thereby

---

[1]The following two sections draw heavily on McCulloch (2017a). See also Selgin (2017).

deposits to restore their reserves, businesses and consumers would spend less. At the same time, banks would temporarily bid the fed funds rate up.

Interest on Excess Reserves since 2008

Since October of 2008, the Fed has paid IOER at or slightly above the fed funds rate. During the same period, the Fed has more than quadrupled the monetary base though its QE I–III acquisitions of mortgage-backed securities (MBS) and Treasury securities. These acquisitions were financed mostly through the creation of new excess reserve balances. Thanks to IOER, however, banks have been in no rush to lend these funds out, and instead are content to just sit on them. The Fed in effect is now acting as a huge financial intermediary, borrowing reserve deposits from the banks at interest and lending them back to homeowners as mortgages or by transforming the maturity of the national debt.

This intermediation activity on the part of the Fed is not without adverse consequences, but has not in itself been inflationary, since IOER ensures that it is being financed with deposits that are savings instruments at the margin, rather than money per se. Thanks to IOER, the Fed is therefore essentially "rudderless" and unable to exert either inflationary or deflationary pressure on the economy.

When banks are awash with interest-bearing excess reserves, as they have been since 2008, there is little if any need for a federal funds market, since banks can earn interest simply by depositing surplus reserves with the Fed, and can obtain funds simply by withdrawing these deposits. To the extent there is a federal funds market, the fed funds rate should be essentially equal to the IOER rate. Indeed, the federal funds market has shrunk from over $300 billion in 2007 to barely $50 or $60 billion in recent years.

From late 2008 through November 2015, the IOER rate was only 0.25 percent and the fed funds rate itself was a little under 0.2 percent, neither of which is much different from zero—recall that the Federal Open Market Committee (FOMC) typically moves its fed funds target in multiples of 0.25 percent, which is therefore its estimate of the smallest perceptible increment to the rate. However, the Fed's IOER policy in fact made a difference for banks' willingness to hold reserves, since they could be confident that when market rates rose, IOER would rise with them, so that there *never* would be an opportunity cost to holding excess reserves. Since late 2015, the IOER and fed funds rate have indeed risen together, to 1.25 percent and 1.16 percent, respectively, by October of 2017.

The Fed's Reckless Maturity Gambles

The Fed's large-scale asset purchases represent financial intermediation rather than central banking—since they are being financed mostly by interest-bearing liabilities of the Fed that provide few if any monetary services at the margin.

Since the national debt is unlikely to be paid off any time soon, the Treasury prudently finances a large portion of it with long-term bonds, so as to lock in current long-term rates and protect taxpayers from even higher future interest rates. Moreover, because the Fed turns the bulk of its profits (or losses) over to the Treasury, its non-monetary liabilities are essentially liabilities of the Treasury. The Fed's purchases of long-term Treasury bonds with interest-bearing zero-maturity excess reserves therefore have essentially second guessed the Treasury's prudent decision to borrow long with its own gamble to finance this substantial portion of the national debt with short-term borrowing instead. This is a decision that properly is the Treasury's, not the Fed's, and in any event the Fed is making the wrong decision.

Furthermore, by financing long-term mortgages with interest-bearing excess reserves, the Fed has taken the same reckless gamble that savings and loan associations (S&Ls) did in the 1960s and 1970s, and that led to the demise of most of the industry, not to mention the Federal Savings and Loan Insurance Corporation, during the 1980s. Long-term mortgages are a sound way to finance durable housing but should be financed by private intermediaries that issue long-term debt of comparable maturity. For all their faults, Fannie Mae and Freddie Mac have at least generally financed their mortgage portfolios with bonds of comparable maturity rather than with zero maturity savings accounts as did the now largely defunct S&Ls, and as now is being done by the Fed. In McCulloch (1981), I show that maturity transformation by financial intermediaries, or "misintermediation" as I call it, can upset the intertemporal equilibrium of the macroeconomy.

Unwinding IOER and the Fed's Balance Sheet

Unfortunately, abruptly restoring IOER to zero would potentially be very inflationary, given the Fed's bloated balance sheet, since it would be equivalent to suddenly quadrupling the base under the pre-2008 regime.

I have no easy solution to this predicament but recommend that the Fed immediately begin reversing its QE I–III acquisitions until the base is approximately back to its 2007 level, adjusted for nominal GDP growth, to approximately $1,130 billion. Treasuries have a very liquid market and can be sold as quickly as the Fed acquired them. Mortgage-backed securities are much less liquid, but at a minimum the Fed should immediately begin allowing them to run down to zero by not reinvesting in mortgages any interest or return of principal it gets from its mortgage portfolio. As it does this, I recommend that it should temporarily hold IOER at its present level, thereby gradually creating an opportunity cost to excess reserves as the base contracts and the fed funds rate eventually lift off above IOER. Then, when it has restored control of the base, it can lower IOER to zero and resume control of the fed funds rate by restoring a $10 billion to $50 billion repo loan balance with dealers as prior to 2008.

So long as currency pays zero interest, it has a clear opportunity cost (at least since early 2016 as nominal rates return to normal positive levels). Ultimately, the price level must equate the demand and supply of every monetary component, including currency. However, when banks are awash with zero-opportunity-cost excess reserves as at present, the Fed has no control over how much base drains from bank reserves into currency in circulation. This currency drain has been lethargic but steady, so that currency in circulation has almost doubled since 2007, while the nominal economy has grown only about 33 percent. While it is undoubtedly true that currency demand has been greatly increased since 2008 as a result of zero or near-zero interest rates, this situation cannot be expected to continue forever. This currency overhang should be cause for great concern.

Interest on Required Reserves

Interest on required reserves (IORR) is an entirely different matter than IOER. Before 2008, when IORR was zero along with IOER, reserve requirements acted as a modest excise tax on transactions deposits, and therefore gave banks a strong incentive to game them through the introduction of negotiable order of withdrawal (NOW) accounts, money market deposit accounts, and retail sweep accounts. These "near money" de facto transactions accounts have left the concept of M1 narrow money hopelessly muddled.

However, there is no particular reason to have a special excise tax on transactions deposits, aside from the Federal Deposit Insurance Corporation's user fee for deposit insurance, since banks already pay income taxes on the income generated by their deposit-creation activities. I therefore recommend retaining IORR, setting it at, say, the average of the fed funds rate over the previous two weeks, or slightly lower.

One beneficial but little-noticed provision of Dodd-Frank is that it rolled back the anti-competitive 1933 prohibition of interest on demand deposits. Retaining IORR would therefore permit the consolidation of NOW accounts and money market deposit accounts, and therefore sweep accounts into a single interest-bearing demand deposit category, thereby greatly simplifying monetary statistics.

In order to give small banks relief from the implicit tax of zero-interest reserve requirements, Congress has mandated a 0 percent reserve requirement for the first $15.5 million of transactions accounts in any one bank, and only 3 percent for further transactions accounts up to $115.1 million. As a result, the average reserve requirement falls short of the 10 percent required for accounts in excess of $115.1 million, and depends on the accidental distribution of deposits between small and large banks. This uncertainty makes the bank expansion multiplier harder to predict than it otherwise would be. IORR makes this wild card in monetary policy obsolete, so that there now can be no objection to abolishing it.

Friedman's Optimum Quantity of Money

Fed economists defending interest on reserves have recently made appeal to an unexpected quarter, namely Milton Friedman's 1969 essay, "The Optimum Quantity of Money."[2] As Ben Bernanke and Don Kohn (2016) put it, "Before the Fed paid interest on reserves, banks engaged in wasteful and inefficient efforts to avoid holding non-interest-bearing reserves instead of interest-bearing assets, such as loans." New York Fed economists Laura Lipscomb, Antoine

---

[2]This section is based on McCulloch (2017b).

Martin, and Heather Wiggins (2017a, 2017b) make essentially the same argument, with explicit reference to Friedman's essay.

This discussion takes me back to my graduate student days at Chicago, when Friedman's essay had just come out, and one witty student had nicknamed it the "optiquan model." "Optiquan" was written shortly after Friedman's December 1967 American Economic Association presidential address, "The Role of Monetary Policy" (1968), in which he had refuted the notion, popularized by the Keynesians Paul Samuelson and Robert Solow, that positive inflation was beneficial to the extent that it reduced unemployment along a stationary Phillips Curve. He had convincingly argued instead that the Phillips Curve shifts up and down with expected inflation, so that the same "natural rate of unemployment" would arise at any sustained inflation rate.

But that left open the question: What inflation rate really is theoretically optimal under a pure fiat money regime in which the central bank is not constrained by a parity to gold or silver? (Recall that 1968–71 was precisely when the U.S. government, with Friedman's approval, finally severed the dollar's external link to gold.)

In "Optiquan," Friedman argued that since fiat money is socially costless to produce, and since optimal inventory management induces money holders to incur real costs to keep down the forgone interest on their money balances, the first best optimum is to pick an inflation rate that drives the opportunity cost of money balances down to zero. One conceivable way this could be achieved would be by paying interest on *all* forms of money—both currency and demand deposits—at the same rate that could be earned on nonmonetary assets. A second conceivable method would be to engineer negative inflation just equal to minus the real interest rate that equated the nonmonetary demand and supply for credit, so that the nominal interest rate would be zero. In either case, agents would in theory hold such large money balances that at the margin they would be savings instruments and provide zero purely monetary services.

However, one big practical problem with the "optiquan model" that bothered me at the time and still does today is that it would leave the price level indeterminate: Friedman's quantity theory of money predicts that the price level will gravitate to the level that equates the real value of the nominal money stock to the economy's real demand for it. This requires (1) that there be a predictable real demand for an appropriately defined monetary aggregate and (2) that the central bank be able to control its quantity.

Friedman recognized that real money demand responds negatively to its opportunity cost, which, assuming money pays zero interest (as was the case for currency and all checking accounts outside New England before the 1980 Depository Institutions Deregulation and Monetary Control Act), would be the nominal interest rate on safe nonmonetary alternatives. He recognized that nominal rates fluctuate because of natural changes in real interest rates and also because of changes in expected inflation. However, inventory models of money demand predict that the money demand schedule is inelastic and therefore relatively steep at moderate nominal interest rates (when i is on the vertical axis and M/P is on the horizontal axis). Real interest rates are normally positive at all maturities, and must be positive at most maturities to prevent the price of land from being infinite. While inflationary finance is always fiscally tempting, deflation is fiscally unattractive, and therefore not an important long-run concern under fiat money, even by accident under a zero-inflation target. The demand for zero-interest money is therefore reasonably predictable as long as nominal rates are positive and inflationary expectations don't drive them excessively high.

However, if the opportunity cost of money actually falls to zero, inventory models such as the famous Allais-Baumol-Tobin model (Baumol and Tobin 1989) predict that real money demand will be literally unbounded. Of course the resources of the economy are finite and money is not entirely costless—due to the risk of theft, loss, bank failures, or unanticipated inflation—so that money demand will never actually reach infinity, but the point remains that it becomes virtually indistinguishable from the horizontal axis over a wide range of values. This implies that an equally wide range of price levels will equate the supply and demand for money, and the quantity theory no longer predicts the price level, within this range.

Figure 1 illustrates the classical quantity theory of money when money pays zero interest, with moderate uncertainty as to the relevant parameters. The demand curve (dark gray) shows the inventory demand for real money balances M/P, with M/P on the horizontal axis and the nominal interest rate on the vertical axis. Because the money demand function is only known approximately, it is shown as a thick line. In equilibrium, the *nominal* interest rate will average out to the equilibrium real interest rate (r^*) plus the inflation (π) that results from the central bank's money growth policy. Since neither r^* nor π is known with perfect certainty, their sum is depicted as a thick

FIGURE 1
THE QUANTITY THEORY OF MONEY

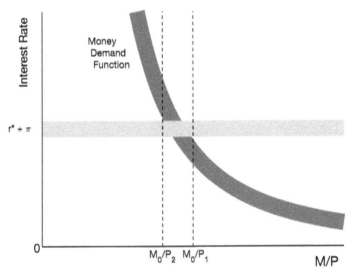

horizontal line (light gray). The intersection of the two curves determines real money balances and therefore the price level, but only imperfectly: given a nominal money stock M_0, the price level could be as high as P_2 or as low as P_1. So the price level is not determined precisely, but at least it's reasonably bounded.

Figure 2 illustrates the inventory demand for money (dark gray) as a function of its net opportunity cost, net of any interest paid on money or real return from deflation. As the opportunity cost approaches zero, this schedule coincides with the horizontal axis, for all practical purposes. The thick horizontal line (light gray) depicts the approximately zero opportunity cost under the Friedman Optiquan deflation rule. Because the neutral real rate r^* is uncertain and because the central bank cannot precisely control any deflation it engineers, this line again incorporates some uncertainty. Given a nominal money stock M_0, the price level is now indeterminate at any level between P_2 and P_1, and could be even lower than P_1.

In order for the value of a fiat money to be determinate, therefore, an appropriate monetary aggregate must have a clear and positive opportunity cost relative to nonmonetary assets. With all due respect to Friedman, his "optiquan model" is therefore just an interesting academic exercise that is in fact incompatible with the quantity

147

FIGURE 2
PRICE LEVEL UNCERTAINTY

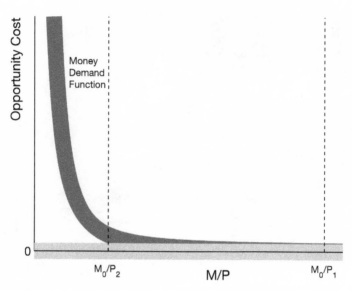

theory. Its reasoning does argue against high-inflation policies, and does make a case for reducing the opportunity cost of at least the deposit component of M1 through interest on checking accounts. However, in order for the quantity theory to function, there must be a substantial aggregate controlled by the central bank that pays zero or at least greatly reduced interest.

The Zero Lower Bound Issue

The extraordinary measures the Fed has taken since 2008 have tied in with the ZLB issue as it affects the Taylor rule.[3] This is an equation relating the FOMC's federal funds rate target i^* to a measure of anticipated inflation, $E\pi$, and, in its original formulation, the estimated percentage deviation of real output from its trend, $ygap$. The benchmark version of the equation, with coefficients as estimated by John Taylor (1993) on the basis of the Fed's behavior in the 1980s and early 1990s, is

(1) $i^* = 1.0 + 1.5\,E\pi + 0.5\,ygap.$

[3]The following three sections correct certain errors in McCulloch (2015). The present article therefore supplants the corresponding sections in that article.

There is widespread agreement among economists that weak (i.e., less than 100 percent) feedback from expected inflation to i^* was responsible for accelerating inflation prior to 1979, while strong (i.e., greater than 100 percent) feedback was responsible for bringing inflation down from double digits at the beginning of the 1980s to approximately 2 percent since 1990 (Clarida, Galí, and Gertler 2000). The actual coefficients depend on the Fed's inflation target, on its estimate of the equilibrium real interest rate, and on how aggressively it wants to fight inflation and/or the output gap. Furthermore, the coefficients the Fed is using appear to have varied over time (Clarida, Galí, and Gertler 2000; McCulloch 2007). I shall use the above benchmark coefficients for the sake of illustration, with the understanding that the Fed may in fact choose to modify these coefficients. The output gap variable is problematic, but by definition averages out to zero, so that the long-run inflation implications of the Taylor rule lie entirely in the first two terms.

If inflation has been running at the Fed's announced target of 2 percent and is expected to continue at this level, the above rule calls for a "normal" level of i^* of 4 percent. This will be neutral with respect to inflation if the equilibrium or "natural" short-term real interest rate r^* is 2 percent.[4] If inflation falls to 0 percent and is expected from the time-series evidence to stay there while the estimated output gap is 0, the benchmark rule calls for an i^* of 1 percent. This implies a real rate of 1 percent, which is less than its assumed equilibrium level of 2 percent, and hence would put upward pressure on inflation, driving it back toward the Fed's announced target of 2 percent.

But if inflation falls to 0 percent and at the same time the estimated output gap is -4 percent, the benchmark rule calls for an impossibly negative i^* of -1 percent, corresponding to a very stimulative real rate of -1 percent . Because of the ZLB on *nominal* interest rates, the lowest i^* can ordinarily go is 0 percent. This would imply a real rate of only 0 percent, which would not be as stimulative as desired. This supposed ZLB threat has been used as a rationale for deliberately targeting a positive inflation rate in order to give the Fed some additional space to reduce nominal rates before hitting the

---

[4]The equilibrium real interest rate is that determined in the absence of a monetary disequilibrium by the supply and demand for saving, as in the "loanable funds model" of Irving Fisher ([1930] 1974). This is equivalent to Knut Wicksell's "natural rate of interest," as discussed by Friedman (1968).

ZLB, in spite of the Fed's legislative mandate to stabilize prices. In 2012, the Fed in fact announced its intention to target 2 percent inflation, in part for this very reason.

We will see that this fear is unwarranted. But first, let us consider how the Taylor rule may be expected to operate when the ZLB is not binding.

The Taylor Rule When the ZLB Is Not Binding

Lowering the nominal interest rate $y(m_0)$ on loans of maturity m_0 by Δi, while holding forward rates beyond m_0 constant, reduces the cost of borrowing to any maturity beyond m_0 by $m_0\Delta i$.[5] Holding the public's inflationary expectations constant, this makes current consumption less expensive relative to consumption at any maturity beyond m_0, thereby creating a proportionate excess demand for current output, financed by an equal and opposite temporary excess supply of money created by the Fed and the banks (see McCulloch 2012). This excess demand for current output generates proportionate inflationary pressure over and above expectations. The opposite is true for an increase in interest rates.

The federal funds rate itself is overnight ($m_0 = 1/365$), and so in itself has only negligible effect on the cost of credit or inflationary pressure. However, the FOMC meets only eight times a year, so that the effective m_0 of the Fed's i^* is 1/8 year on average, or about six weeks.[6] The Fed typically (or at least prior to 2008) manipulates short-term rates through overnight loans to dealers via the repo market.[7] However, if dealers can count on a particular value of i^*

---

[5]If $y(m)$ is the continuously compounded nominal zero-coupon yield to maturity m, the discount factor $\delta(m) = \exp(-m\, y(m))$ is the current price of $1 payable at maturity m, and $f(m) = -d/dm \log \delta(m) = y(m) + m\, y'(m)$ is the instantaneous forward interest rate at maturity m. Changing $y(m_0)$ by Δi while holding $f(m)$ unchanged for all $m > m_0$ will change $\log \delta(m)$ by $-m_0\, \Delta i$ for all $m \geq m_0$.

[6]The FOMC has occasionally changed its fed funds target between regular meetings, via an emergency conference call meeting, but such meetings are rare enough to ignore for present purposes.

[7]A repurchase agreement, or repo for short, is in effect a short-term loan secured with Treasury securities. Legally, the effective borrower sells a security to the effective lender, and at the same time agrees to buy it back in the near future at a slightly higher price, reflecting the effective interest rate. In practice, "triparty" repos are often used, in which a custodial third party bank is the legal owner of the collateral securities throughout.

continuing for the next six weeks, they can make a virtually riskless arbitrage profit by buying six-week Treasury bills and using them as collateral for a series of overnight loans, until the six-week T-bill rate equals i^*. The Fed could achieve a very similar result without the intermediation of dealers by directly pegging the rate on T-bills maturing on or before the next FOMC meeting to i^*.[8] Since there is no reason for the credit premium on private loans to have changed, private loan rates will be similarly reduced, unless the Fed ends up holding a dominant fraction of all the maturing T-bills.

The direct effect of say a 100 basis point (1 percentage point) reduction in rates at even a 1/8 year maturity is still too subtle to create much inflationary pressure. However, if the market realizes this, it will recognize that conditions will most likely be similar to the present at the next FOMC meeting, and therefore that the FOMC will mostly likely choose a similar i^*. This will create speculative demand for longer-term Treasury securities, financed by further short-term borrowing from the Fed at i^*, until forward rates beyond 1/8 year on Treasury debt, and therefore private debt, reflect the probable trajectory of i^*, as adjusted for the empirical term premium (see McCulloch 1975).[9] This speculative demand for short-term loans from the Fed will magnify the direct and arbitrage demand, and can greatly increase the inflationary pressure of the low interest rate policy.

So long as the market is confident that the Fed will continue to fight high inflation (or below target inflation) with continuing tight (or easy) interest rate policy until inflation is back on target, there is therefore no need for the Fed to use "forward guidance" by announcing in advance a specific future interest rate target trajectory. Doing so is in fact counterproductive, because it may lead the Fed to feel bound to retain its promised interest rate trajectory despite conditions that in all likelihood will have changed somewhat, one way or

---

[8]Historically, maturing Treasury bills typically yield approximately 90 percent of the effective federal funds rate. This is presumably due to their exemption from state and local income taxes, in addition to their greater freedom from default risk. The fed might therefore in practice target a T-bill rate equal to about 90 percent of its fed funds target. In the text I have abstracted from this minor technicality.

[9]The present article abstracts from the term premium and assumes that the (log) expectations hypothesis is valid.

the other. It is sufficient for the market simply to expect the Fed to aggressively follow a policy that will stabilize inflation as well as may be expected under a Taylor-type rule, with hands untied by the past.

Unexpected changes in interest rates on the part of the Fed necessarily generate unexpected capital gains or losses on loans of all maturities. However, the FOMC does well ordinarily not to directly intervene in forward rates beyond the date of its next meeting, since otherwise the decisions at the next meeting may generate capital gains or losses in the opposite direction. Only in the case when the zero lower bound (or a self-imposed above-zero lower bound) is binding should it venture into maturities beyond its next meeting.

The Taylor rule approach to monetary policy has the advantage over a money growth rule motivated by the quantity theory of money because it does not rely on knowledge or stability of the demand for real money balances. Yet it has the disadvantage, even in the absence of the ZLB issue, that it relies instead on the knowledge and stability of the equilibrium real interest rate r^*. In practice, neither is fully known or stable, so that the monetary policymaker's choice is between the less imperfect of two options.[10]

The Taylor Rule When the ZLB Is Binding

Now suppose that the ZLB on i^* is binding. To take our earlier hypothetical example, suppose that experience with inflation and/or other variables would lead one to expect inflation to continue at 0 percent while $ygap$ is −4 percent, so that the benchmark Taylor rule calls for $i^* = -1$ percent, and the corresponding desired real rate of −1 percent is 3 percent below the natural real rate $r^* = 2$ percent. However, the most it can lower the real rate before hitting the ZLB is by 2 percent, which would be only 2/3 of the desired stimulus. Nevertheless, it can still achieve the equivalent of a 3 percent reduction out to a six-week maturity, simply by lowering nominal rates to 0 percent and, therefore, the real rate to 0 percent out to nine weeks (3/2 of the six-week meeting interval) instead.

Doing this with no direct disturbance to forward rates beyond nine weeks would require the Open Market Desk to peg the interest

---

[10]In an open economy with a fiat currency, a third option is to fix the exchange rate to a foreign fiat currency. However, this is superior only if the foreign country has solved the problem of stabilizing the value of its own currency.

rate on T-bills maturing within nine weeks of the current FOMC meeting to 0 percent, and to hold them there until the next FOMC meeting. At that time, the FOMC would then be free to continue the stimulus by moving the peg out another six weeks, or to alter the strength of the stimulus in either direction.

If the Fed, in our example, ends up holding a dominant share of all the outstanding T-bills maturing within nine weeks of the current meeting, it may have to supplement T-bill purchases with term repurchase agreements or term discount loans to insured commercial banks up to the same maturity date, in order to appropriately impact rates on private loans that compete with Treasuries.

If the Fed wished to avoid potential complications of 0 percent interest rates, it could alternatively achieve the same stimulus, in our example, by pegging rates at say 1 percent (a "unit lower bound," so to speak), so that the real rate is 1 percent below the natural rate of 2 percent rather than the desired 3 percent, out to 18 weeks (6 weeks × 3 percent / 1 percent) from the current meeting.

Thus, although the ZLB may require some adjustment of procedures, it does not in itself prevent the functioning of the Taylor Rule. In particular it does not justify the adoption of a positive inflation target in lieu of price stability. For example, if the Fed chose to target 0 percent inflation while retaining the 1.5 coefficient on expected inflation, the 0.5 coefficient on $ygap$, and the 2 percent assumption on r^*, it would have to raise the intercept in the Taylor rule to 2.0. Then if accidental deflation led the public to expect inflation to be -1 percent, while $ygap$ was -4 percent, the rule would call for $i^* = -3$ percent, or 4 percent below r^*. An equivalent stimulus could be achieved with a real rate of 1 percent (1 percent below r^*), at a maturity of 4 × 1/8 year, or 1/2 year. A "unit lower bound" as discussed in the preceding paragraph would not give the Fed much room to maneuver, but if it chose a 0.25 percent minimum Fed funds rate, which would correspond to a real rate of 1.25 percent with 1 percent expected deflation, or 0.75 percent below r^*, it could achieve the desired stimulus with $m_0 = 2/3$ year.

References

Baumol, W., and Tobin, J. (1989) "The Optimal Cash Balance Proposition: Maurice Allais's Priority." *Journal of Economic Literature* 27 (3): 1160–62.

Bernanke, B. S., and Kohn, D. (2016) "The Fed's Interest Payments to Banks." *Ben Bernanke's* blog, Brookings Institution (February 16).

Clarida, R.; Galí, J.; and Gertler, M. (2000) "Monetary Policy Rules and Macroeconomic Stability: Evidence and Some Theory." *Quarterly Journal of Economics* 115: 147–80.

Fisher, I. ([1930] 1974) *The Theory of Interest.* New York: Augustus M. Kelley.

Friedman, M. (1968) "The Role of Monetary Policy." *American Economic Review* 58: 1–17.

_____ (1969) "The Optimum Quantity of Money." In M. Friedman (ed.) *The Optimum Quantity of Money and Other Essays.* Chicago: University of Chicago Press.

Lipscomb, L.; Martin, A.; and Wiggins, H. (2017a) "Why Pay Interest on Required Reserve Balances?" *Liberty Street Economics* blog, Federal Reserve Bank of New York (September 25).

_____ (2017b) "Why Pay Interest on Excess Reserve Balances?" *Liberty Street Economics* blog, Federal Reserve Bank of New York (September 27).

McCulloch, J. H. (1975) "An Estimate of the Liquidity Premium." *Journal of Political Economy* 83: 95–119.

_____ (1981) "Misintermediation and Macroeconomic Fluctuations." *Journal of Monetary Economics* 8: 103–15.

_____ (2007) "Adaptive Least Squares Estimation of the Time-Varying Taylor Rule." Available at www.econ.ohio-state .edu/jhm/papers/TaylorALS.pdf.

_____ (2012). "The Theory of Money and Credit." NYU class notes (September). Available at https://newclasses.nyu.edu/ access/content/user/jhm406/MoneyAndCredit.pdf.

_____ (2015) "The Taylor Rule, the Zero Lower Bound, and the Term Structure of Interest Rates." In W. Barnett and F. Jawadi (eds.) *Monetary Policy in the Context of Financial Crisis: New Challenges and Lessons.* Bingley, U.K.: Emerald Press.

_____ (2017a) "The Rudderless Fed." *Alt-M* blog (September 8). Available at www.alt-m.org/2017/09/08/the-rudder-less-fed.

_____ (2017b) "Optiquandary: A Practical Problem with Friedman's 'Optimum Quantity of Money.'" *Alt-M* blog

(November 30). Available at www.alt-m.org/2017/11/30/optiquandary-practical-problem-with-friedmans-optimum-quantity-money.

Selgin, G. (2017) "Testimony before the U.S. House of Representatives Committee on Financial Services, Monetary Policy and Trade Subcommittee, Hearings on 'Monetary Policy versus Fiscal Policy: Risks to Price Stability and the Economy.'" (July 20). Available at https://financialservices.house.gov.

Taylor, J. B. (1993) "Discretion versus Policy Rules in Practice." *Carnegie-Rochester Conference Series on Public Policy* 39: 195–214.

9

NORMALIZING MONETARY POLICY
Martin Feldstein

The current focus of Federal Reserve policy is on "normalization" of monetary policy—that is, on increasing short-term interest rates and shrinking the size of the Fed's balance sheet. Short-term interest rates are exceptionally low, and the Fed's balance sheet has exploded from $800 billion in 2008 to $4.4 trillion now.

At the September 2017 meeting of the Federal Open Market Committee (FOMC), the Fed indicated its long-term goal for the federal funds rate and its near-term goal for shrinking the size of its balance sheet. In my judgment, the Fed's plan is too little, too late. I also believe the Fed's underlying goal is to increase inflation above its 2 percent target and that such a policy is wrong.

I think the Fed should have begun raising interest rates and reducing its balance sheet back in 2013 or 2014. I think the current goal of raising the federal funds rate from 1.4 percent now to 2.1 percent at the end of 2018 (when it would be a 0.1 percent real rate using the Fed's median inflation forecast) is just too slow and will continue to encourage a dangerous bidding up of asset prices.

In this article, I will begin by discussing the Fed's shift to the easy money policy. I will then turn to the adverse side effects of the quantitative easing (QE) policy, particularly the increases in asset prices that create a risk of financial instability. The next section considers the reasons that the FOMC members have continued to pursue the policy of excessively easy money. There is a brief concluding section.

Martin Feldstein is the George F. Baker Professor of Economics at Harvard University. This article is reprinted from the *Cato Journal*, Vol. 38, No. 2 (Spring/Summer 2018).

The Shift to Quantitative Easing

As we all know, Ben Bernanke introduced quantitative easing as a way to stimulate economic activity at a time when the unemployment rate was very high and the recovery was very slow. Conventional monetary policy had failed to stimulate the economy even after the federal funds interest rate was cut to zero in 2008. The fiscal stimulus legislation enacted in 2009 also failed to raise real GDP growth because it was so badly designed.

Bernanke explained that a Fed policy of buying long-term bonds and promising to keep the federal funds rate low for a long time would cause a significant decline in long-term interest rates. That would raise the price of equities and of homes. The resulting increase in household wealth would then lead to increased consumer spending and therefore to faster GDP growth.

Bernanke explained that this would be reinforced by what he called the "asset substitution effect" in which the reduced availability of bonds in which to invest would cause households to shift their portfolios to equities.

Not everyone was convinced by Bernanke's analysis. Why would investors buy equities that were made artificially high since they would know that those share prices would eventually decline? And how important could the asset substitution effect be when the household sector's holding of Treasury bonds was less than 10 percent of its investment in equities?

Moreover, the federal government deficits were pouring substantially more bonds into the market than the Fed was buying. The Fed's balance sheet grew by less than $2.5 trillion between the beginning of the large-scale asset purchase (LSAP) program and the end of 2011 while the government debt had grown nearly twice that amount.

The skeptics were initially correct. The value of equities owned by the household sector increased by less than 20 percent between 2009 and 2011. The unemployment rate continued to increase until October 2009 when it reached 10 percent and declined very little during the next two years to 8.8 percent in October 2011. Real GDP rose only 6 percent in the three years from the first quarter of 2009 to the first quarter of 2012.

But the volume of bond purchases then increased to $800 billion a year in 2013 and 2014 while the fiscal deficit fell to less than

$700 billion in 2013 and less than $500 billion in 2014. At last the Fed was buying more long-term assets than the Treasury was creating.

The shift in the Fed's net purchases and the strengthened commitment to keep short rates low caused equity prices to accelerate in 2012 and 2013. The value of equities owned by households rose 47 percent between 2011 and 2013. Overall household net worth increased nearly $10 trillion in 2013 alone.

Although Bernanke could feel vindicated by this increased value of net worth and the resulting 5.5 percent rise in real GDP between the beginning of 2013 and the beginning of 2015, he warned that the QE strategy could have adverse effects as well as the desired rise in aggregate demand. He identified those adverse effects of the extremely low interest rates as (1) excessive risk taking as investors and lenders reached for yield and (2) an unwanted acceleration of inflation.

The Adverse Effects of Quantitative Easing

The most obvious indicator of excessive risk taking is the rapid rise in share prices. The price–earnings ratio of the S&P 500 index rose from an average of 18.9 in the three years before the downturn to 25.6 now, an increase of 35 percent. The current price–earnings ratio is 63 percent higher than its historic average and higher than all but three years in the 20th century.

Robert Shiller's cyclically adjusted price–earnings ratio, which is based on average inflation-adjusted earnings from the previous 10 years, is now 31.5 and therefore 87 percent above it historic average and at a level exceeded in the past 100 years only during the period from 1998 through 2001.

While higher share prices no doubt make investors happy and contribute to aggregate consumer spending, there is obviously now an increased risk that share prices will decline. If the price–earnings ratio declines to the historic average, the implied fall of 39 percent would reduce the value of household equities held directly and through mutual funds by $9.5 trillion.[1] If every dollar of decline in

---

[1]The Flow of Funds data for the second quarter of 2017 put household sector ownership of equities at $24.9 trillion. The equity value of noncorporate businesses is estimated in the Flow of Funds data to be an additional $11.8 trillion.

wealth reduces spending by 4 cents, that would cut spending by $475 billion or more than 2 percent of GDP.

Bond prices are also out of line. With the consumer price index rising at about 2 percent and expected to continue at that pace, the yield on 10-year Treasury bonds would be expected to be about 4 percent or even a bit higher. In fact, it is now only about 2.25 percent. If the yield on a 10-year bond rises from 2.25 percent to 4 percent, the price of the bond would fall substantially. The lower price of bonds and other fixed income securities held by banks and insurance companies as well as by households could have a substantial destabilizing effect.

Commercial real estate prices have also risen in response to the lower cost of capital. Since these assets are often held in a significantly leveraged way, a decline in the asset prices would have a disproportionately large impact on the net value of the assets.

Banks and other lenders have also been responding to the very low level of interest rates by making riskier loans in order to get higher rates of return. Some of this reaching for yield involves lending to lower-quality borrowers. It also takes the form of lending with weaker conditions on the loans (i.e., covenant light loans). For both reasons, any weakness in the economy could be magnified by loan defaults that weaken the capital of the lending institutions.

Loans to consumers have also become more risky. The economic downturn that began in 2007 was increased by the widespread defaults on residential mortgages that happened as falling house prices caused loan-to-value ratios to rise well above 100 percent. After the downturn there was a general agreement that the loan-to-value ratio on new mortgages should be limited to 80 percent or less and that lenders should be required to keep a portion of the loans that they originate. Both of these conditions have been dropped in recent years as lenders seek ways to increase the yield on their portfolios.

In summary, the excessively easy monetary policy of the past decade has increased the fragility of the financial sector and therefore of the economy. Although the Fed has used its regulatory powers to strengthen the banks, it has not sought the power to limit the loan-to-value ratio on residential mortgages as other central banks have done.

More generally, Janet Yellen made it clear in a 2014 speech at the International Monetary Fund that the Federal Reserve does not believe that it should take into account the impact of its monetary policy on financial stability. She emphasized that the Fed has only two goals for monetary policy—price stability and maximum employment—and that macroprudential policies should be the responsibility of other agencies (Yellen 2014). Unfortunately it is not clear what those agencies are.

The excessively low interest rates that resulted from the Fed's monetary policy also increase the risk that the inflation rate will rise rapidly at some point in the future. Although the inflation rate has remained surprisingly low until now, the current unemployment rate of 4.1 percent is much lower than the Fed's own estimate of the sustainable level of unemployment. The September 2017 projections by the members of the Federal Reserve's Open Market Committee point to a range for the unemployment rate in the long run of between 4.4 percent and 5.0 percent with a median projected value of 4.6 percent. If inflation starts to rise rapidly at some point in the future, the Fed will be forced to increase the fed funds rate more rapidly, potentially causing a downturn of asset prices and economic activity.

Why Does the Fed Continue with Excessively Easy Monetary Policy?

The Federal Reserve justifies its continued low interest policies by noting that the core personal consumption expenditure measure of inflation is still below its target of 2 percent and that the excessively high asset prices are not a responsibility of the Fed even if they contribute to financial instability.

The Fed goes further and argues that the "equilibrium real interest rate" that is consistent with stable inflation and employment has been declining over the past years. According to the "Economic Projections" released after the September 2017 FOMC meeting, the "appropriate" projected long-run federal funds rate has declined to 2.8 percent even though the projected inflation is 2.0 percent, implying an equilibrium real rate of just 0.8 percent (Federal Reserve 2017).

My judgment is that the reasons given for a decline in the equilibrium real rate are too weak to support changing the Fed's target interest rate. I suspect that the claim of a declining equilibrium real rate is a reflection of the analysts' preferences rather than of hard evidence.

The primary reason given for a decline of the equilibrium real interest rate is the assertion of a rise in the saving rate, lowering the interest rate at which savings can be absorbed at full employment. It is hard to see evidence to support a rising saving rate. Between 1960 and 1980 the personal saving rate varied above 10 percent of disposable income, reaching a peak of 15 percent in the second quarter of 1975. After that it has been drifting lower and is now at 3.1 percent.

During the same years, the federal budget has moved from near balance to very large deficits that absorb household saving and reduce the national saving rate.

China's current account surplus adds to the funds available for investors worldwide. The current account surplus rose dramatically from 2000 to 2008, supporting Bernanke's comments about a savings glut. But in the decade since then, China's current account surplus has fallen sharply, from $420 billion in 2008 to $196 billion in 2016, back to its level in 2006. So the decline of China's surplus means that China has not been a source of downward pressure on global interest rates.

The other major source of current account surpluses has come from the oil-producing countries. But the price of oil has fallen from over $100 a barrel between 2011 and 2014 to about $60 a barrel now. Even a very low cost producer like Saudi Arabia has gone from significant current account surpluses before 2015 to current account deficits in recent years.

Putting all these pieces together implies that there is no increase in savings either in the United States or in the international economy to cause a fall in the equilibrium rate of interest.

A simpler explanation for the low global level of interest rates is that all of the major central banks have been keeping rates low by a combination of asset purchases and open market operations. This includes not only the Fed but also the European Central Bank and the Bank of Japan.

There are several reasons why the Federal Reserve has moved so slowly to raise interest rates. Different FOMC members no doubt have different reasons for their reluctance to raise rates, but the following three reasons probably capture all of the different opinions.

First, a more rapid increase in the federal funds rate could increase the risk of a sharp decline in asset prices. An asset price correction could of course happen even without a rise in the interest rate caused by the central bank, but the Fed would be severely criticized if it is seen as raising rates less cautiously.

Second, continuing the low interest rate environment helps to increase employment. Although the current 4.1 percent unemployment rate is very low, those who want easy money to stimulate employment point to the decline in the labor force participation rate and the large number of workers who are involuntarily working less than full time as indicating that a stronger expansion supported by low interest rates could increase employment further.

There are also those FOMC members who would welcome a rise of the inflation rate, not just to the 2 percent target level but to an even higher level. Some members would justify this goal by noting that the 2 percent target is not a ceiling but the midpoint of a desirable range. Since the actual inflation has been below 2 percent for an extended period, they would justify an inflation rate that is temporarily above 2 percent as a way of demonstrating that the 2 percent target is to be interpreted as the midpoint of an acceptable range.

Some FOMC members want a higher inflation rate for a different reason. They worry that the Fed lacks the ability to cut interest rates significantly when the next downturn occurs. A higher rate of inflation would allow the Fed to raise the nominal federal funds rate by a substantial amount without raising the real federal funds rate. That would put the Fed in a position to cut rates if necessary to deal with the next downturn.

My reaction to this clever argument is that little ability to deal with the next recession would be gained by an increase in the inflation rate to 3 percent and that the public's confidence in the Fed's attachment to a 2 percent inflation goal would be substantially weakened if the Fed allowed the inflation rate to rise to three percent and to remain at that level. If the Fed allowed the inflation rate to rise to 5 percent and then increased the federal funds rate to 6 percent, it would have acquired the ability to deal with the next downturn. But a 5 percent inflation rate would greatly undermine the Fed's credibility.

Conclusion

The Fed could reduce the risk of a financial correction by raising interest rates more quickly than it currently projects, reaching a federal funds rate of 4 percent by the end of 2019 or 2020 and aiming for a real federal funds rate of 2 percent. This could be achieved by increasing the pace of shrinking its balance sheet and by the way that it manages the overnight reverse repo policy.

References

Federal Reserve (2017) "Economic Projections" (September 20). Available at www.federalreserve.gov/monetarypolicy/files/fomc projtabl20170920.pdf.

Yellen, J. (2014) Remarks on "Monetary Policy: Many Targets, Many Instruments. Where Do We Stand?" International Monetary Fund Conference on "Rethinking Macro Policy II," Washington (April 16).

10

PRIORITIES ON THE PATH
TO NORMALIZATION
Kevin Warsh

I was honored to serve as a governor of the Federal Reserve System during the financial crisis. The times were tough, but the institution was strong—sustained by a Fed staff that was tired and tireless, hopeful and humble, brilliant without bravado. The internal battles among its leaders were consumed by big policy questions. We were sometimes divided in our assessments. And our proffered prescriptions.

We offered differing judgments in real time and in real candor. We had contrasting views on the origins of the turmoil, the wherewithal of the government-sponsored entities, the solvency of our banking system, the appropriate burden-sharing among actors in our government, the efficacy and limitations of quantitative easing (QE), the reliability of the Fed's dominant economic models, and the uncertainty around estimates for output and prices.

Our best days included our darkest hours. But complacency was set aside, owing to the exigencies of the circumstances. The search was for truth (as best we could measure it), not victory. And the quality and depth of debate were as large as the perils we faced.

Kevin Warsh is the Shepard Family Distinguished Visiting Fellow in Economics at the Hoover Institution, Stanford University. He is a former member of the Board of Governors of the Federal Reserve System. This article is reprinted from the *Cato Journal*, Vol. 38, No. 2 (Spring/Summer 2018).

Present Challenges

Today, the challenges to our central bank may be less urgent. But its task is no less large. So we should resist allowing the policy debate to be small or push aside ideas that depart from the prevailing consensus. The Fed's job is not easier today, and its conclusions are not obvious.

In recent, fiercely fought public debates, inflation hawks and doves are cast into ideological corners spoiling for a fight. The political class, especially in this season, emboldens factions to caricature the opposition and reduce policy prescriptions into simplistic, sloppy slogans. Those in the community of central banks should be wary of this affront. We should not respond in kind, but rather in the spirit of that which sets these institutions apart.

A robust debate between rules and discretion has marked the monetary policy literature for generations. It should not turn into an expedient means of back-solving for a preferred policy outcome.

In recent years, some commentators and academics seek to follow fixed monetary policy rules. The dominant view, however, purports to criticize adherence to preset policy rules. Most favor reliance on policymakers' discretion. I find it a bit puzzling, then, how to reconcile the widespread preference for policymaker discretion with the eagerness to follow a single, precise, unyielding inflation target as a key policy determinant.

The Knowledge Problem and Fed Policy

Our understanding of the macroeconomy, and the effects of extraordinary monetary policy, is decidedly imperfect. Modesty about what we know—and humility about what we do—have long shaped my views. I do not favor conducting monetary policy by fidelity to a fixed policy rule. Nor do I find a single, overly precise inflation measure to be the defining measure of price stability.

So, allow me to pose a question: Should the Fed's overriding policy objective be to lift the measure of the core personal consumption expenditure (PCE) inflation index, as calculated by the Bureau of Economic Analysis of the U.S. Department of Commerce, from 1.3 to 2.0 percent?

Inflation targeting frameworks represent an important advance in the consideration and conduct of monetary policy. If it were costless to move to a 2.0 percent target, and we were confident that the target was a well-measured and durable inflation indicator, then its achievement could be useful, not least because it would demonstrate the Fed delivering on its oft-repeated promise. But that should not preclude current practice from robust review.[1]

An inflation target of 2.0 percent is tantamount to price stability. But price stability does not always and everywhere require hitting a central bank–sanctioned, inflation target of 2.0 percent. There may be a sound argument for maintaining significant Fed accommodation, but the measured inflation shortfall is insufficient.

If, today, policymakers judge with perfect clarity and certainty the economy's post-2010 performance to be strong, cross-border trade and capital flows sustainable, financial assets prices in durable equilibrium, the future unwind of QE uneventful, the Fed well equipped to respond to the next shock, the financial regulatory system fixed, the too-big-to-fail problem solved, the macroprudential policy tool kit poised for prime time, and financial stability achieved, then I would suggest the Fed's fine-tuning around its inflation target is unobjectionable.

We would then have the luxury of debating the distance between current inflation readings and a professed, perfected inflation target. Absent that, I'd commend a more discerning discussion about Fed policy. And suggest that caricatured, confused commentary about hawks and doves be forgone.

We know far less than we purport about the price formation process; still less about the economy's resilience to economic and financial shocks; and less still about the current constellation of loose monetary policy, stagnant wages, and elevated financial asset prices. We should not allow an imperfect inflation measure to prevent consideration of other critical issues of inquiry. So, might the eagerness to lift core PCE to 2.0 percent be misplaced?

Reasons Why a Precise Inflation Target Is Misplaced

First, inflation is increasingly difficult to measure given mix changes in the economy, changing global trade flows, positive

---

[1]Chairman Bernanke (2017) recently proposed an alternative to existing practice.

supply shocks, and stale national accounts that make assigning price and quality changes difficult. Research by Marty Feldstein (2017) has ably demonstrated the imprecision of output and inflation estimates.

Second, measured inflation is taken by most as the dominant signal by which output is judged to approach its potential. When potential and actual output converge, it is presumed that the observed interest rate equals the natural rate, and the inflation gap is closed. Policymakers may take comfort in exploiting the theoretical relationship. But any tradeoff between prices and employment and ouput is, at best, temporary; yet the prevailing policy prescription appears permanent.

To mark the 50th anniversary of Milton Friedman's presidential address to the American Economic Association, Mankiw and Reis seek to reconcile the more recent contributions of monetarists and Keynesians. They remind us that "[a]s a scatterplot, [the Phillips curve] has shifted so often that no one takes it to be anything other than a transitory, reduced-form empirical relation" (Mankiw and Reis 2018: 92). More reliable, definitive models for predicting inflation, ouput, and interest rates are taking shape, and are worthy of considerable central bank attention. Until new models supplant those in practice, it's not obvious whether the Fed's new, permanently lower policy rate forecast is correct, coincident, or a contrivance with the Wicksellian natural rate.

Third, the natural rate needed to stabilize inflation and output is highly dependent on the conduct of both monetary and nonmonetary policy, here and abroad. If the current measured low inflation is a global phenomenon, is it the result of global supply or global demand shock? If it's a function of a positive supply shock with new impetus for labor and capital, is it temporary or permanent? If QE and forward guidance are powerful new tools for monetary policy, how "natural" is the rate being observed? And if domestic regulatory and tax policy changes are important determinants of potential output for the year or two ahead, might the natural rate reverse its recent fall with improved policies?

Fourth, the heated inflation rhetoric notwithstanding, the Fed sets the fed funds rates, not interest rates. If the Fed, belatedly, follows through on its promise to unwind QE—and that direction is matched by other large central banks—the Fed's influence on the medium and longer end of the treasury curve will be more limited in the next couple years. Policymakers have been price-making instead of price-taking for so long that they might be surprised by their own diminishing influence on prices.

Fifth, the inflation gap tells us little about financial stability. A separation principle works in theory—the Fed's interest policies are designed to satisfy the Fed's modal monetary mandate; micro- and macroprudential policy are said to suffice to deal with other risks. I am not at all persuaded that the separation principle works in practice.

Low growth, low rates, low inflation, and low market volatility have proven to be the ideal backdrop for large holders of wealth, explaining well the Fed's popularity among those on Wall Street. But we have little experience with the current policy mix. It may induce behavior that masks market signals, misallocates capital, and creates imbalances that ultimately undermine financial and price stability. If significant tail risks materialize, it is not obvious that markets will be ready, the central bank will be prepared, or the broader economy will be resilient.

The Role of the Fed in the Government

Central bankers themselves are more recognizable public figures than ever, which makes their profiles unrecognizable to their predecessors. The Fed rightfully played an outsized role in the crisis. The trend continues. The Fed is involved more directly in fiscal policy, credit allocation, and management of banking and finance than we would have expected or countenanced years ago.

If the Fed's imprint in the government, economy, and financial sector remains large and permanent, then it strikes me as imprudent to solve for a broader remit by subjecting policy to a single, precise, unyielding, inflation target.

Efforts to expand the Fed's powers and responsibilities in peace time have largely proven popular in the central bank community. Monetary and fiscal policies interact. So some believe that the central bank's modern Wilsonianism is necessary in light of the void left by warring legislators and government dysfunction. But we should be discomfited if important questions about the proper role of the Fed in our government and a balanced assessment of its objectives are reduced and caricatured into a fabled fight between hawks and doves—and somehow resolved by the achievement of a precise inflation target.

Conclusion

My hope is to reorient the discussion from a narrow target to the more difficult, important priorities on the Fed's path to normalization. With new leadership coming to the Fed, there is new opportunity to think more broadly about the challenges ahead. And I am hopeful that the Fed will do so.

Final judgments are likely to be quite different from the dominant narratives currently on offer. Remember that our understanding of the Great Depression did not crystalize until Milton Friedman and Anna Schwartz and Ben Bernanke, among others, wrote their definite accounts many decades later.

References

Bernanke, B. S. (2017) "Monetary Policy in a New Era." Paper prepared for "Rethinking Macroeconomic Policy," a conference sponsored by the Peterson Institute for International Economics, Washington, D.C. (October 12–13).

Feldstein, M. (2017) "Underestimating the Real Growth of GDP, Personal Income, and Productivity." *Journal of Economic Perspectives* 31 (2): 145–64.

Mankiw, N. G., and Reis, R. (2018) "Friedman's Presidential Address in the Evolution of Macroeconomic Thought." *Journal of Economic Perspectives* 32 (1): 81–96.

11

INTEREST ON EXCESS RESERVES: THE HOBIE CAT EFFECT
George Selgin

Forty years ago, in the spring of 1978, I had no intention of becoming an economist. Instead, I was studying marine biology at Duke University's Marine Lab at Pivers Island, on the beautiful North Carolina Coast. There, when the wind was up, my classmate Alan Kahana and I enjoyed going out on his Hobie 16, with Alan manning the tiller and myself hiked-out on the trapeze. We weren't, truth be told, especially prudent sailors. On the contrary: we were so inclined to push things to the limit that one day we took the Hobie out just as a gale was getting up, and ended up . . . well, that's a long, sad story. Suffice to say that it doesn't take much to capsize a Hobie, and that on that day we capsized Alan's boat once and for all.

What, you are no doubt wondering, has any of this to do with interest on excess reserves? I'm getting there. You see, although it doesn't take much to capsize a Hobie—a little over-trimming of the sail will suffice—once one capsizes, it's likely to start to turn turtle as its mast fills with water. And as that's happening, it may be all that two reasonably trim lads can do—by pulling for dear life on a righting line attached to the boat's mast, whilst leaning backwards on its uppermost hull—to lever the thing back upright. The more the mast fills, the harder it gets. And the same sort of thing goes for letting a central bank slip into, and then trying to wrest it out of, a floor system

---

George Selgin is Director of the Cato Institute's Center for Monetary and Financial Alternatives. This article is an expanded version of his *Alt-M* article (Selgin 2018a).

of monetary control: the more liquidity the banking system takes in while that system's in place, the more effort it takes to pull out of it.

Overturning the Fed's Traditional Monetary Control System

As faithful *Alt-M* readers know, I've long insisted that the modest interest rates the Fed began paying on excess reserves in October 2008 were enough to encourage bankers, who long made do with only the slimmest of excess reserve cushions, to hoard all the reserves they could lay their hands on. That modest little bit of Fed sail-trimming was enough to overturn the Fed's traditional monetary control system.[1] The Fed had long relied on a sort of asymmetrical "corridor" system, with a target fed funds rate set somewhere between zero and the Fed's discount rate, and the effective federal funds rate kept near that target by means of small-scale open market operations. Now it had flipped-over to a "floor" system, with changes in the Fed-administered IOER rate serving as its chief instrument of monetary control.

Some economists, to be sure, refuse to believe that the modest IOER rates the Fed paid in the early stages of the crisis could account for the switch in question, or for banks' subsequent tendency to hoard reserves. Paul Krugman (2014) even accused those who thought so of failing a "reality test" by overlooking how, in the United States in the 1930s and in Japan more recently, banks hoarded non-interest-bearing reserves. But Krugman himself might be said to have failed a "logic test," calling for an understanding of the difference between a necessary and a sufficient cause. Then there's the pesky fact that Ben Bernanke and other Fed officials secured permission to pay interest on bank reserves *for the express purpose of getting banks to hoard them.* Had they done so for no reason? Had Ben Bernanke himself forgotten about the 1930s?[2] The following passage from his *Macroeconomics* textbook is illuminating:

> In October 2008, the Federal Reserve began to pay interest on banks' reserve deposits at the Fed. The rationale is that paying interest on reserves would encourage banks to hold

---

[1]Selgin (2018b) offers a detailed history and critical appraisal of the Fed's floor system.

[2]Bernanke has long studied the Great Depression, which has shaped his policy ideas (see Ip 2005).

additional reserves, instead of trying to keep thei reserves as low as possible. . . . Not only did the move to paying interest on reserves lead banks to hold substantially more reserves, it also gave the Fed an additional tool to use to affect the money supply. By raising the interest rate on reserves, the Fed can encourage banks to hold additional reserves, thus reducing the money multiplier and the money supply [Abel, Bernanke, and Croushore 2014: 553].

But allowing that a modest above-zero return on bank reserves was indeed all it took to establish a floor system, and to get banks to stock-up on excess reserves, it doesn't follow that restoring the IOER rate to zero would have the opposite effects. The reason has to do with the immense growth in the total supply of reserve balances that has since taken place. That growth matters because, under a floor system, *the greater the nominal stock of bank reserves, the lower the IOER rate must be to reduce the quantity of excess reserves demanded to zero.* The accumulation of liquidity in a "floored" monetary control system thus acts like the accumulation of water in the mast of a capsized Hobie Cat, making it much harder to revert from a floor to a corridor system than it was to switch to the floor system in the first place. Call it the Hobie Cat effect.

The Hobie Cat Effect

The Hobie Cat effect can be illustrated formally using a diagram showing the supply of and demand for bank reserves or federal funds under a floor system (Figure 1). The supply schedule for federal funds is, as usual, a vertical line, the position of which varies with changes in the size of the Fed's balance sheet. The reserve demand schedule, on the other hand, slopes downward, but only until it reaches the going IOER rate, here initially assumed to be set at 25 basis points. At that point the demand schedule becomes horizontal, because banks would rather accumulate excess reserves that yield the IOER rate than lend reserves overnight for an even lower return.

For the initial stock of reserves R(1), starting at the equilibrium point "a," a slight reduction in the IOER rate would suffice to get the banking system back onto the sloped part of its reserve demand schedule, at point "b," where reserves are again scarce at the margin. But once the stock of reserves has increased to R(2), it takes a much more substantial reduction in the IOER rate—perhaps, as the move

FIGURE 1
THE HOBIE CAT EFFECT

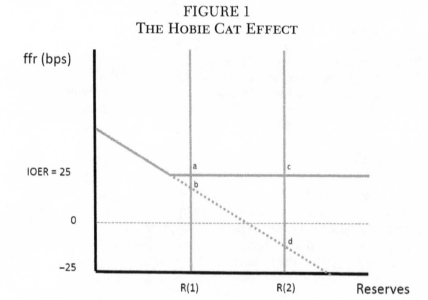

in the illustration from "c" to "d" suggests, even into negative territory—to make reserves scarce at the margin again, and to thereby make switching to a corridor system, by a modest further reduction in the IOER rate, possible without any need for central bank asset sales.[3]

Exiting the Floor System

Because the challenge of exiting from a corridor system becomes greater as central banks' operating such systems expand their balance sheets, its no surprise that the three central banks that expanded most during the crisis—the Fed, the Bank of England, and the ECB—are also the only ones that still rely on foor-style operating systems. In contrast, other central banks that entered the crisis with

---

[3]Because the move from "c" to "d," like that from "a" to "b," involves no change in the total stock of bank reserves, readers may be tempted to assume that it also involves no reduction in the quantity of *excess* reserves, and hence no change in banks' inclination to hoard such reserves. The temptation should be resisted: although banks hold the same total quantity of reserves at "d" as at "c," the former equilibrium involves a higher quantity of bank lending and deposit creation, hence a higher value of required reserves, with a correspondingly lower value of excess reserves.

corridor systems of some kind either (1) stuck to those systems all along (e.g. the Riksbank and the Reserve Bank of Australia); (2) switched to a floor system temporarily, and then reverted to a corridor (the Bank of Canada); or (3) switched first to floor systems and then to "tiered" or "quota" systems in which reserves can earn the policy rate only up to a certain limit, after which they earn lower, if not negative, rates (the Swiss National Bank, Bank of Japan, and Norges Bank). The only central banks that relied on floor systems before the crisis began—Norges Bank and the Reserve Bank of New Zealand—also switched to tiered systems afterwards.[4]

Does this mean that the Fed can never hope to escape from its current floor system unless it reduces its IOER rate substantially, and that it might even have to resort to a negative rate? It doesn't. And it's here that the Hobie Cat analogy fails, for while you can't drain the mast of a Hobie Cat that's turned turtle, the Fed *can* drain the banking system of any or all of the reserves it created after 2008. The obvious, and most prudent, way out of the floor system is, therefore, for the Fed to retrace the steps that got it into that system, by first shrinking its balance sheet far enough to return the stock of reserves to a point close to the kink in the federal funds demand schedule, and then reducing the IOER rate enough to make reserves scarce at the margin, thereby reviving interbank lending and establishing a corridor system.

Considering how many excess reserves banks are now holding, all of this is still a tall order. But it beats having an operating framework that leaves our monetary system sodden and adrift (see McCulloch 2017).

References

Abel, A. B.; Bernanke, B.; and Croushore, D. (2014) *Macroeconomics*, 8th ed. New York: Pearson.

Ip, G. (2005) "Long Study of Great Depression Has Shaped Bernanke's Views." *Wall Street Journal* (December 7).

---

[4]According to Norges Bank (2011), its switch from a floor to a quote system had two objectives. "One was to stop growth in central bank reserves. The other was to generate more interbank activity in the overnight market as rising quantities of reserves in the banking system entailed a risk that Norges Bank would assume some of the functions of the interbank market. The role of the central bank is to steer the total amount of reserves, while banks' should redistribute the reserves overnight in the interbank market." Concerning New Zealand's experience see Selgin (2018c).

Krugman, P. (2014) "Nobody Could Have Predicted, Monetary Edition." *New York Times* (March 19).

McCulloch, H. (2017) "The Rudderless Fed." *Alt-M* (September 8).

Norges Bank (2011) "Background for the System for Managing Bank Reserves in Norway." (June 20).

Selgin, G. (2018a) "Interest on Excess Reserves: The Hobie Cat Effect." *Alt-M* (April 4).

_____ (2018b) *Floored! How a Misguided Fed Policy Deepened and Prolonged the Great Recession*. Washington: Cato Institute (forthcoming).

_____ (2018c) "New Zealand's Floor System Experience." *Alt-M* (March 8).

Part 3

Monetary Rules

12

MONETARY POLICY IN AN UNCERTAIN WORLD: THE CASE FOR RULES

James A. Dorn

Since monetary policy operates in an uncertain world, discretionary policymaking relying on macroeconomic models of the economy is a weak reed upon which to base policy. The complexity of economic systems and constant changes in the underlying data mean errors may occur in a discretionary regime that can lead to monetary and financial instability.[1] The 2008 financial crisis is a case in point: central bankers and their expert staffs failed to anticipate the crisis, and may have worsened it by keeping policy rates too low for too long (Taylor 2012).

Moving to a rules-based regime would not eliminate radical uncertainty, but it could decrease institutional uncertainty—or what Robert Higgs (1997) has called "regime uncertainty"—and thus reduce the frequency of policy errors. Higgs focused on the uncertainty caused by fiscal and regulatory policies that attenuated private property rights by decreasing expected returns on capital.

James A. Dorn is Vice President for Monetary Studies and a Senior Fellow at the Cato Institute. This article is reprinted from the *Cato Journal*, Vol. 38, No. 1 (Winter 2018). He thanks Ari Blask, Kevin Dowd, Thomas M. Humphrey, Gerald P. O'Driscoll, Alex Schibuola, and George Selgin for comments on earlier versions of this article.

---

[1]Orphanides (2017: 1) holds that "the presence of uncertainty . . . cannot serve as a valid argument for defending discretionary policy. Indeed, uncertainty raises the potential costs of discretion as it makes it harder to understand how large a policy deviation may be from what would have been the desirable systematic response to a shock."

A discretionary monetary regime increases uncertainty about the future purchasing power of money and thereby undermines an important property right.

Radical uncertainty is a given, but institutional uncertainty can be reduced by adopting credible rules. As Karl Brunner (1980: 61) has pointed out:

> We suffer neither under total ignorance nor do we enjoy full knowledge. Our life moves in a grey zone of partial knowledge and partial ignorance. More particularly, the products emerging from our professional work reveal a wide range of diffuse uncertainty about the detailed response structure of the economy. . . . A nonactivist [rules-based] regime emerges under the circumstances . . . as the safest strategy. It does not assure us that economic fluctuations will be avoided. But it will assure us that monetary policymaking does not impose additional uncertainties . . . on the market place.

In a similar vein, Allan Meltzer (1983: 95), a long-time collaborator with Brunner, has noted:

> The flexibility that permits government to change policy has a cost: Anticipations about the future conduct of policy are altered. The effect of uncertainty is an important, but often neglected, characteristic that affects the cost of following alternative rules in a world subject to unpredictable changes.

Some congressional leaders think it's time to create a rules-based monetary regime. The Financial CHOICE Act of 2017 (H.R 10), which recently passed the House, would make the Fed responsible for specifying a monetary rule and justifying to Congress any Fed deviations from it.[2]

Whether the CHOICE Act passes or not, it is important to consider alternative monetary rules and to be prepared to make the case for rules over discretion when the opportunity for reform arises.

This article begins with a discussion of the case for rules over discretion in the conduct of monetary policy and draws upon the theory of monetary disequilibrium to support that case. In particular, a

---

[2]See Financial CHOICE Act of 2017 (H.R. 10): https://financialservices.house-.gov/uploadedfiles/hr_10_the_financial_choice_act.pdf.

credible monetary rule can eliminate what Clark Warburton (1949) called "erratic money," which he viewed as the chief cause of business fluctuations.[3]

Various monetary rules will be examined, so will the difficulty of implementing them under the current environment in which unconventional Fed policy has plugged up the monetary transmission mechanism. Particular attention will be paid to rules designed to stabilize the path of nominal spending. The article ends with a call to establish a Centennial Monetary Commission to evaluate the Federal Reserve's performance over its 100-plus years and to consider the effectiveness of alternative rules to reduce regime uncertainty.

The Case for Rules over Discretion

It is sometimes argued that discretionary monetary policy is superior to a rules-based monetary regime because discretion includes the option to adopt a rule. That argument, however, begs the question. The real issue is whether a robust, credible monetary rule that constrains policymakers to a long-run objective, and is strategic in nature, is superior to a discretionary regime that focuses on period-by-period optimization using various tactics without committing to any rule.

Those who favor discretion over rules also argue that no rule is permanent and thus judgment is needed to choose among rules. But choosing among rules is different from having no rule to guide policymakers, which is what is generally understood by a discretionary monetary regime. Under the Taylor rule, for example, one has to define the goal variables—the inflation gap and GDP gap—and use discretion in assigning numerical values to the coefficients on the goal variables. Nevertheless, it is still a rules-based monetary regime with a definite strategy as opposed to a regime that gives monetary authorities wide discretion ("the rule of experts").

At the 2013 American Economic Association meeting, Lawrence H. Summers debated John Taylor on the issue of rules versus discretion. Summers used a medical analogy to make the case

---

[3]The analysis of alternative monetary rules in this article focuses on rules that are potentially stabilizing and omits rules such as the real bills doctrine that could be destabilizing. For an in-depth discussion of the real bills doctrine, see Humphrey and Timberlake (2017).

for discretion, arguing that he wants his doctor "to be responsive to the medical condition" rather than "to be consistently predictable." Taylor responded by arguing that "relying on an all-knowing expert" who practices medicine without "a set of guidelines" is risky—"checklists are invaluable for preventing mistakes" just as a rules-based monetary strategy is. This argument in favor of rules is not to say that doctors don't need to exercise good judgment in designing checklists. They do. But that kind of discretion needs to be distinguished from "a checklist-free medicine."[4] One could also argue that underlying Summers's preference for "a doctor who most of the time didn't tell me to take some stuff" is a fundamental rule: "Do no harm."

Taylor (2015: 10) recognizes that "some rules are better than others, and it makes perfect sense for researchers and policymakers to be looking for new and better rules." The focus should be on long-run strategy, not short-run tactics. The Fed did implicitly follow a Taylor rule during the Great Moderation, from the mid-1980s to 2007, and Taylor thinks that rule "does a good job at keeping nominal GDP on a steady growing trend."

Taylor (2015: 4) does not recommend following "a rule mechanically"—"judgment is required to implement the rule." He is thinking primarily of rules within the context of a government fiat money system. The question then becomes what is to bind policymakers to the rule. Although the Fed appears to have followed the Taylor rule in setting its policy rate during the Great Moderation, that adherence began to erode around 2003–05, when the fed funds rate was pushed significantly below the rate prescribed by the Taylor rule (ibid., p. 5).

The Fed has not returned to any rules-based monetary policy even though Fed chairman Ben Bernanke argued in 2015 that the central bank was following a rule of "constrained discretion." Yet, as Taylor observes, what Bernanke viewed as a rule— namely, setting goals (e.g., targeting inflation and employment)—differs substantially from adopting a rules-based monetary *strategy*. According to Taylor (2015: 12), "Simply having a specific numerical goal or objective function is not a rule for the instruments of policy; it is not a strategy; in my view, it ends up being all tactics."

In order to better understand the case for rules over discretion, it is essential to recognize the knowledge problem confronting

---

[4]For a summary of the debate, see Taylor (2015: 11).

policymakers, the value of having time-consistent rules to reduce uncertainty, and the need to reduce the risk that monetary policy may become politicized as public choice theory describes.[5]

The Knowledge Problem

In his classic essay "The Use of Knowledge in Society," F. A. Hayek (1945: 519–20) defined the "economic problem of society" as "a problem of the utilization of knowledge which is not given to anyone in its totality." That problem implies monetary policymakers are not omniscient: they cannot know the structure of a complex economic system; their models will have serious flaws and forecast errors; there are long and variable lags in the effects of monetary policy, as noted by Milton Friedman (1968); and constant changes in economic data make it difficult to distinguish between permanent and transitory changes.

A discussion of the Hayekian knowledge problem, as it relates to monetary policy, is presented in O'Driscoll (2016). He argues that "unavoidable errors are an essential feature of discretionary policy" (p. 343), and that a rules-based monetary regime could help reduce uncertainty—an idea that both Hayek and Milton Friedman accepted. According to O'Driscoll (p. 350), "Hayek and Friedman agreed that we know too little to design an optimal monetary policy. . . . A monetary rule facilitates the emergence of a monetary order."

Glenn Hubbard, former chairman of the Council of Economic Advisers under President George W. Bush, echoed those problems when he recently remarked, "Ignorance of economic conditions or doctrinaire attention to false models may blow Fed policy off course" (Hubbard 2017).

Nevertheless, Fed Vice Chairman Stanley Fischer, speaking at a Hoover Institution conference on May 5, 2017, argued that committees of experts rather than rigid rules are the best approach to sound monetary policymaking.[6] According to Fischer, experts must "be continuously on the lookout for structural changes in the economy and for disturbances to the economy that come from hitherto unexpected sources." However, the knowledge problem precludes such

---

[5]A useful overview of the case for rules over discretion is provided in Salter (2017: 444–48). See also Taylor (2017).

[6]For a critique of Fischer's "rule-by-experts" approach to monetary policymaking, see White (2017).

changes and disturbances from being known beforehand; hence, Fed action is often destabilizing.

A discretionary monetary regime suffers most from these flaws and can be improved upon by moving to a rules-based regime (Friedman 1968). Monetary rules that are operational, credible, and enforceable could help reduce uncertainty.

Rules that are market based, don't rely on experts, and can evolve as learning occurs would be in line with Hayek's warning against the "pretense of knowledge." In his Nobel Memorial Lecture, Hayek ([1974] 1989: 7) stated: "To act on the belief that we possess the knowledge and the power which enable us to shape the processes of society entirely to our liking, knowledge which in fact we do not possess, is likely to make us do much harm." In monetary policy, relying on the Phillips curve and aggregate demand management to obtain full employment is an evident example of hubris.

The Fed's recent *Monetary Policy Report* (July 7, 2017) reflects the thinking of many Fed officials on the adoption of a money rule: "The U.S. economy is highly complex, and these rules, by their very nature, do not capture that complexity" (Board of Governors 2017: 36–37). In fact, it is the complexity of the economy that makes rules beneficial and more likely to bring about monetary and financial stability than pure Fed discretion.

Absence of Credible Commitment under a Discretionary Regime

Even if monetary authorities could centralize all the relevant information, a discretionary regime would not escape the problem of "time inconsistency" that Kydland and Prescott (1977) have pointed out.[7] Under discretion, there is no guarantee that future policy will be consistent with current policy: monetary policymakers will be tempted, for example, to deviate from a commitment to maintain price stability in order to stimulate full employment by exploiting the short-run Phillips curve. Adherence to a monetary rule can improve policy outcomes if the rule amounts to a credible commitment.

---

[7]See White (1999: chap. 10) for an overview of the time-inconsistency case for rules, as first presented by Kydland and Prescott (1977) and elaborated on by Barro and Gordon (1983).

In his classic book *Interest and Prices*, Michael Woodford (2003) criticizes optimal control theory as applied to monetary policy while supporting the case for credible rules to reduce regime uncertainty and achieve long-run price stability. He opposes period-by-period policymaking, which he sees as destabilizing, compared to a rules-based regime:

> It is not enough that a central bank have sound objectives . . . , that it make policy in a systematic way, using a correct model of the economy and a staff that is well-trained in numerical optimization, and that all this be explained thoroughly to the public. A bank that approaches its problem as one of optimization under *discretion*—deciding afresh on the best action in each decision cycle, with no commitment regarding future actions except that they will be the ones that seem best in whatever circumstances may arise—may obtain a substantially worse outcome, from the point of view of its own objectives, than one that commits itself to follow a properly chosen *rule* [Woodford 2003: 18–19].

Bennett McCallum, a member of the Shadow Open Market Committee, offers a similar criticism of discretionary policy:

> The absence of rule-based policymaking means the absence of any systematic process that the public can understand and use as the basis for its expectations about future policy. The Fed apparently sees communication as a device for affecting expectations, but rational private agents form expectations on the basis of their understanding of the process by which the central bank actually conducts policy. If the central bank fails to adopt a process involving rule-based policymaking—that is, a commitment to some clearly stated objectives—its attempts to influence expectations are unlikely to be productive [McCallum 2004: 370].

A monetary rule is a constraint on the monetary authority in line with the rule of law. In addition to reducing regime uncertainty and increasing predictability of money and prices, a credible rule reduces the concentration of power over monetary matters and expands economic freedom. As Milton Friedman notes, in reference to the Fed's failure to maintain monetary stability during the Great Depression when the money supply contracted by nearly 30 percent, "much harm can be done by mistakes on the part of a few men when they wield vast power over the monetary system of a country" (Friedman 1962: 50).

When policymakers have to follow known rules that recognize the limits of monetary policy and the social value of maintaining sound money, markets will be better able to perform their incentive, information, and allocation functions. There will be less risk of government intervention (e.g., price controls, credit allocation, and the politicization of investment) under a rules-based monetary regime than a discretionary regime. Government power grows, and economic freedom declines, when money and markets are in disorder, as we learned from the Great Depression, the high inflation and ensuing price controls of the 1970s, and the Great Recession, which greatly increased the Fed's monetary and regulatory powers.

The Case for a Monetary Constitution

Monetary authorities have an incentive to increase their discretionary powers, especially during a crisis. When the Federal Reserve started operating in 1914, its powers were narrowly limited. Today, the Fed's balance sheet has reached $4.5 trillion and it engages in massive credit allocation and financial regulation. The 2008 financial crisis greatly expanded the Fed's powers, and there is little incentive for Federal Reserve Board members to relinquish those powers.

Public choice theory describes how incentives operate within the public sector and how the administrative state feeds on itself. Constitutional political economy makes the case for limited government and the rule of law. To stem the incentives for monetary bureaucrats to expand their fiefdoms, their powers need to be limited by a strict monetary rule or constitution.

To be credible, a rule must be enforceable. In this regard, Selgin (2016b) distinguishes between "real and pseudo monetary rules." In contrast to a pseudo monetary rule, which merely acts as a policy guide and is subject to change, a real monetary rule "must be rigorously enforced so that the public is convinced there will be no deviations from the rule." It must also be "robust," meaning "the rule must be capable of perpetuating itself, by not giving politicians or the public reason to regret its strict enforcement and to call either for its revision or its abandonment in favor of discretion" (p. 282).

The network of private contracts that characterized the classical gold standard, for example, were strictly enforced and allowed markets to determine the quantity of money without interference from central banks. People had confidence in the long-run value of their money, which enabled them to borrow at reasonable interest rates for long periods of time. Commerce and investment were energized as a result.

While some economists (e.g., Buchanan 1962, 1989) favor a monetary constitution that retains a central bank but limits its powers, others (e.g., Hayek 1978) prefer a free-market monetary system. Between those two extremes there are many other sorts of monetary rules, many of which retain some degree of discretion for policymakers. For example, under inflation targeting, the monetary authority can arbitrarily change the target. Likewise, under the Taylor rule, more emphasis can be placed on reducing unemployment or closing the output gap rather than on achieving long-run price stability.

In making the case for rules over discretion, one should recognize that, under discretion, "the money-using public, uncertain about what the central bank experts will decide to do will hedge more and invest less in capital formation than they would with a credibly committed regime" (White 2017: 3). In contrast, "a commodity standard— especially without a central bank to undermine the redemption commitments of currency and deposit issuers—more completely removes policy uncertainty and with it overall uncertainty." Consequently, there is a strong case for "a market-guided monetary system" rather than "expert-guided monetary policy" (ibid.).

The Theory of Monetary Disequilibrium

The case for a rules-based monetary regime can be better appreciated by an understanding of the theory of monetary disequilibrium—and thus the importance of limiting the power of central banks to manipulate money and interest rates.

Discrepancies between the quantity of money demanded and supplied at some prevailing price level set into motion an adjustment process during which real variables are influenced as the economy works its way toward a new equilibrium price level. Sticky prices and wages, as well as other institutional rigidities and the fact that money has no market of its own, mean not only that monetary disturbances are possible but also that they can have pervasive effects on real economic activity during the transition process.

According to Warburton (1949: 107), "The duration and amplitude of a business depression resulting from monetary disequilibrium depends not only on the degree of that disequilibrium, but also on the tenaciousness of rigidities in the cost-price structure." Thus, the theory of monetary disequilibrium may properly be called "a theory of the effect of price rigidities under an erratic supply of money."[8] Moreover, liquidity effects and other shorter-run real interest rate effects of monetary policy occur precisely because the price level doesn't instantly adjust to disturbances in the demand and supply of money.

The fact monetary disequilibrium can persist for a significant time means that monetary policy can distort relative prices, especially intertemporal prices (i.e., interest rates) and misallocate capital. As Claudio Borio, head of the Monetary and Economic Department at the Bank for International Settlements, notes, "Monetary policy can fuel financial booms and their subsequent bust," and in the process lead to long-lasting misallocation of resources, lower productivity, and a permanent loss of output (Borio 2016: 219–20).

Borio also addresses the idea that monetary disequilibrium can affect asset prices by driving a wedge between the market rate of interest and the equilibrium or natural rate that brings voluntary saving in line with private investment. According to Borio (2016: 214–19), in thinking about the Wicksellian natural rate of interest, it is not sufficient to consider only potential output and expected inflation; one must also consider financial stability. One cannot say that market rates are at equilibrium if there is financial instability. The natural rate of interest is unobservable; it is misleading to assume that the absence of inflation and the attainment of full employment signal that market rates are at their equilibrium levels—one must also check for a "build-up of financial imbalances."

In Borio's view, monetary policy

> has failed to lean against unsustainable financial booms. The booms and, in particular, subsequent busts have caused long-term economic damage. Policy has responded very aggressively and, above all, persistently to the bust, sowing the seeds of the next problem. Over time, this has imparted a downward bias to interest rates and an upward one to debt [Borio 2016: 226].

[8]For a detailed discussion of the theory of monetary disequilibrium, see Warburton (1966, especially his list of postulates underlying that theory, pp. 28–29). Also see Yeager (1986, 1997) and Dorn (1987).

Central banks find it hard to increase interest rates because of fear that higher rates will deflate asset bubbles created by previous policy decisions to reduce interest rates. Moreover, politicians favor lower rates to keep the cost of deficit financing at bay. In such an environment, rates are likely to stay too low for too long, thus increasing the ultimate cost of adjustment.

It is also misleading, argues Borio (2016: 222–25), to view all episodes of deflation as bad. In particular, a gently falling price level during times of high real economic growth should be distinguished from sharply falling prices due to a prior monetary collapse, as happened from 1929–33, when the money supply fall by one-third during the Great Contraction (Friedman and Schwartz 1963). What should be avoided is demand-driven deflation, not productivity-induced deflation (Selgin 1997).

Finally, the idea that monetary policy can directly affect asset prices and distort investment decisions—even when official measures of inflation (such as the CPI or PCE) remain stable—is evident in the impact of recent, unconventional monetary policy on the prices of stocks, bonds, and real estate, with little impact on conventional measures of inflation.

Monetary disequilibrium theory holds that financial stability is best achieved by minimizing monetary instability, which means controlling the growth of money and credit to achieve stable growth of nominal GDP and long-run price stability. Under the classical gold standard, long-run price stability was ensured as the supply of money responded to changes in the demand for money. As Lawrence H. White (2017: 2) notes,

> The actual track record of the classical gold standard *is superior* in major respects to that of the modern fiat-money alternative. Compared to fiat standards, classical gold standards kept inflation lower (indeed near zero), made the price level more predictable (deepening financial markets), involved *lower* gold-extraction costs . . . , and provided stronger fiscal discipline. The classical gold standard regime in the US (1879–1914), despite a weak banking system, *did no worse* on cyclical stability, unemployment, or real growth.

Central banks tried to improve on that regime but have ended up with a pure fiat money system not subject to any clearly defined monetary rule to reduce uncertainty about the future path of money and prices—and business fluctuations in the United States have not lessened (Selgin, Lastrapes, and White 2012).

Alternative Monetary Rules

Monetary rules can be classified either as (1) limits placed on a discretionary central bank issuing government fiat money or (2) the replacement of a central bank with a market-based monetary system.[9] Rules applicable to the first category include inflation targeting, a price-level rule, a Taylor rule, and demand rules aimed at achieving a stable growth path of nominal income. The second category of "rules" is greater in scope, but could, for example, consist of defining the dollar in terms of gold and allowing private banks to issue currencies convertible into gold.

Broad "meta-rules," such as Peter Bernholz's (2017: 100) call for "a concrete plan for a monetary constitution"—the key provision of which is "a constitutional safeguard that prevents governments and central bankers from influencing the stock of money"—are in line with Hayek's call for "a constitution of liberty."[10] True meta-rules, such as the gold standard unconstrained by central banks, would be virtually devoid of discretionary elements. There would be no need to worry about defining and measuring policy objectives or estimating coefficients in equations representing the rule. Free markets, rather than policymakers, would operate to bring about monetary equilibrium.

Under Article 1, Section 8, of the U.S. Constitution, Congress has the authority "to coin Money [and] regulate the Value thereof." Those enumerated powers have been delegated to the Federal Reserve, but with little oversight and wide discretion. As James Buchanan (1988: 33) has noted:

> The dollar has absolutely no basis in any commodity base, no convertibility. What we have now is a monetary authority [the Fed] that essentially has a monopoly on the issue of fiat money, with no guidelines that amount to anything; an

---

[9]For an in-depth discussion of alternative monetary rules, see White (1999), Dorn (2017), and Salter (2017).

[10]For a discussion of meta-monetary rules, see Boettke, Salter, and Smith (2016). On the idea of a "monetary constitution," see Yeager (1962) and White, Vanberg, and Köhler (2015).

authority that never would have been legislatively approved, that never would have been constitutionally approved, on any kind of rational calculus.

Indeed, today's pure fiat money system, and the lack of any monetary rule to limit discretion, is not something the Framers would have sanctioned. James Madison, the chief architect of the Constitution recognized that

> the only adequate guarantee for the uniform and stable value of a paper currency is its convertibility into specie—the least fluctuating and the only universal currency. I am sensible that a value equal to that of specie may be given to paper or any other medium, by making a limited amount necessary for necessary purposes; but what is to ensure the inflexible adherence of the Legislative Ensurers to their own principles and purposes? [Madison 1831].

The courts and culture have eroded the Framers' monetary constitution (Timberlake 2013, Vieira 2017). Any link of the dollar to gold was officially ended in August 1971, when President Nixon closed the gold window. However, long before that event the Fed abandoned what Clark Warburton called "the convertibility theory of monetary control," and never explicitly adopted the "responsibility theory of monetary control" to manage a fiat money regime. Under the convertibility theory, which was incorporated into the original Federal Reserve Act of 1913 but discarded by the monetary legislation of the early 1930s, the decisions of households and firms determine the quantity of money. The government's role is to ensure convertibility of notes and deposits into base (commodity) money. Under the responsibility theory, the decisions of central bankers determine the quantity of fiat money and maintain its value (Warburton 1966: 291–92).

The fact that present monetary law in the United States incorporates neither the *convertibility theory* nor the *responsibility theory* means monetary law remains in the same unsettled condition Warburton found it in 1946: "Monetary law in the United States is ambiguous and chaotic, does not contain a suitable principle for the exercise of the monetary power held by the Federal Reserve System, and has caused confusion in the development of Federal Reserve policy" (Warburton 1966: 316).

The Federal Reserve Reform Act of 1977 amended the Federal Reserve Act and implicitly adopted a monetary rule to limit growth in the monetary aggregates to long-run economic growth in order to achieve price stability. However, there was no operational rule and other objectives were added—namely, "maximum employment" and "moderate long-run interest rates."[11] Moreover, there was no enforcement mechanism to hold the Fed responsible. Section 2A stated: "Nothing in this Act shall be interpreted to require that such ranges of growth or diminution [in the monetary aggregates] be achieved if the Board of Governors and the Federal Open Market Committee determine that they cannot or should not be achieved because of changing conditions."

Today Section 2A simply reads:

> The Board of Governors of the Federal Reserve System and the Federal Open Market Committee shall maintain long run growth of the monetary and credit aggregates commensurate with the economy's long run potential to increase production, so as to promote effectively the goals of maximum employment, stable prices, and moderate long-term interest rates.

Yet the Fed pays little attention to monetary aggregates, has engaged in credit allocation to satisfy special interest groups, pays interest on excess reserves (IOER), and fails to recognize the limits of monetary policy in promoting long-run economic growth.

The Fed has rejected arguments for rules over discretion, showing that the Reform Act of 1977 did not succeed in truly implementing a monetary rule. Still, Congress can have the final say. Indeed, Congress is currently considering moving toward a rules-based regime and establishing a Centennial Monetary Commission to examine the Fed's performance since its creation in 1913 and to consider various reforms.

The Financial CHOICE Act of 2017 makes the Fed responsible for specifying a monetary rule, while Congress would be required to use the Taylor rule as a benchmark or default rule. That rule specifies how the fed funds rate is to be adjusted based on the output gap (i.e., deviations of actual from potential output) and desired inflation, or more precisely, deviations of actual inflation from the chosen

[11]See Pub. L. 95–188, 91 Stat. 1387, enacted November 16, 1977.

192

target (Taylor 1993). The Taylor rule rests on guesstimates of potential output and the Wicksellian natural rate of interest. The uncertainty regarding the value of those elements makes implementing the Taylor rule problematic, especially during times of financial turmoil. Furthermore, the rule formulates current policy based on past information as output and inflation measures are made available with lags.[12]

Simpler rules include: (1) Milton Friedman's (1960) k percent rule, which calls for money growth to be constant; (2) a price-level rule designed to achieve long-run price stability by controlling the monetary base; (3) inflation targeting; and (4) nominal income targeting. Friedman's k percent rule assumes that the demand for money (or its velocity) is stable. However, after the velocity of money became less stable, Friedman (1987) advocated freezing the monetary base and allowing the issuance of private bank notes.[13]

A price-level rule is plagued by long and variable lags in the relationship between money and prices,[14] while an inflation-target rule may be destabilizing in the sense that a negative supply shock could temporarily increase inflation, leading to a tightening of monetary policy that would worsen the fall in output. For those reasons, there has been a resurgence of interest in demand rules aimed at stabilizing nominal GDP (NGDP).[15]

Scott Sumner, director of the Program on Monetary Policy at George Mason University's Mercatus Center, is a well-known proponent of NGDP targeting, which he thinks superior to alternative

---

[12]For these and other reasons, Beckworth and Hendrickson (2016) argue that the basic Taylor rule is inferior to a nominal GDP rule. Also see Selgin, Beckworth, and Bahadir (2015) on the case for a nominal GDP rule.

[13]One could argue that Friedman's k percent rule was never really tried and that if it had been, monetary velocity may have been more stable (see White 1999: 223).

[14]Haraf (1986: 361) has argued that, under a properly specified price-level rule, there would be increased certainty about future price levels that would improve the environment for nominal contracting. That improvement would reduce the lag between changes in the monetary base and the speed at which the observed price level approaches the target level. If so, a major objection to price-level targeting is removed. For further support of a price-level rule, see McCulloch (1991) and Dittman, Gavin, and Kydland (1999).

[15]Early proponents of nominal income targeting include Robert Hall (1981) and Robert Gordon (1985). George Selgin's "productivity norm" is also a type of demand rule, in which the price level would be allowed to vary inversely with real output while maintaining a stable path of aggregate spending (Selgin 1997).

monetary rules (Sumner 2014). One benefit of NGDP targeting is that it bypasses the issue of assigning weights under the Fed's dual mandate to achieve price-level stability and maximum employment. All that needs to be done is to set a target path for the growth of NGDP (i.e., the sum of real GDP growth and inflation). So, if the NGDP growth target is set at 5 percent, market forces will determine real growth and the Fed will supply the monetary base sufficient to hit the designated NGDP target. This strategy avoids having to fine tune monetary policy and would help circumvent the knowledge problem (see Beckworth 2017).

William Niskanen (1992: 284) has made a strong case for a demand rule targeting nominal domestic final sales. He argues that "a demand rule is superior to a price rule because it does not lead to adverse monetary policy in response to unexpected . . . changes in supply conditions. Similarly, a demand rule is superior to a money rule because it accommodates unexpected changes in the demand for money," meaning unanticipated changes in the velocity of money. Niskanen sees base money as the best *instrument* to achieve a stable path for nominal income—and thus superior to using the fed funds rate.[16]

Bennett T. McCallum (1989: chap. 16) also calls for using the monetary base as an instrument. However, he prefers a feedback rule that, like Sumner's, "would aim at a zero inflation rate on average and would not attempt to be highly ambitious with regard to its effect on cyclical variation of real variables." Accepting Warburton's (1949) argument against erratic money, McCallum seeks to avoid "abrupt changes in conditions due to monetary policy itself" (p. 338). He would allow the monetary base to grow in line with long-run real output growth adjusted for the growth in velocity averaged over the past four years. Nominal income would then tend to grow at a stable, non-inflationary rate reflecting the trend growth in real output.[17]

---

[16]Interest rates are not a good indicator of the stance of monetary policy: if the Fed increases money growth, and money incomes and inflation expectations rise, nominal interest rates will follow. Changes in base money are a better indicator, but only if base velocity is stable so there is a predictable relationship between base money, monetary aggregates, and nominal income. The best indicator is the behavior of spending itself.

[17]See White (1999: 223–24) for the simple analytics of the McCallum rule. Christensen (2011) provides "a market monetarist version of the McCallum rule."

A Club of Financial Stability

Karl Brunner (1987: 49–51) once called for an international "club of financial stability" in which member states would agree to bind themselves to a monetary rule and thereby help reduce the uncertainty inherent in a discretionary government fiat money regime.[18] Allan Meltzer (1989: 83) has argued that internal and external stability could be achieved if major countries each set "the rate of growth of the monetary base equal to the difference between the moving average of past real output growth and past growth in base velocity." Doing so would anchor future expected prices and, with anticipated inflation stable, reduce the "variability of exchange rates arising from differences in expected rates of inflation" (ibid.).[19]

Meltzer's rule is mildly activist but nondiscretionary; characteristics also present in McCallum's (1984) rule. Choosing to stabilize the *anticipated* price level, rather than the actual price level, eliminates the need "to reverse all changes in the price level" (Meltzer 1989: 79). Instead, under Meltzer's rule, the actual price level is allowed "to adjust as part of the process by which the economy adjusts real values to unanticipated supply shocks" (ibid.). In other words, Meltzer's monetary rule "adjusts fully to permanent changes in growth rates of output and intermediation (or other changes in the growth rate of velocity) within the term chosen for the moving averages," but ignores "short-term, transitory changes" (p. 81). Unlike a strict NGDP rule, Meltzer's rule would accommodate persistent output changes with correspondingly more or less rapid money growth to achieve a mean-reverting long-run price level, much like that seen under the classical gold standard.

---

[18]On the importance of rules for obtaining monetary order and reducing the uncertainty present in a discretionary government fiat system, see Brunner (1985).

[19]Meltzer's rule to stabilize the *anticipated* domestic price level of those countries who adopt his rule would still allow nominal exchange rates to vary with real exchange rates. In particular, "anticipated and actual exchange rates would be subject to change with changes in relative productivity growth, rates of growth of intermediation, differences in rates of saving, in expected returns to capital, in labor-leisure choice or other real changes" (Meltzer 1989: 80–81).

Unconventional Monetary Policy and the Plugged-Up Monetary Transmission Mechanism

In the current environment, with the Fed paying interest on excess reserves at a rate above what banks can get on highly liquid assets, the absence of a fully functioning fed funds market, and complex macroprudential regulations that discourage bank lending,[20] Meltzer's monetary rule (as well as other rules relying on the traditional links between base money, broader monetary aggregates, spending, and prices) would be difficult, if not impossible, to implement. In particular, by paying interest on excess reserves above the opportunity cost of those reserves, the Fed has increased the demand for holding excess reserves (rather than lending them out and creating a multiple expansion of deposits).[21] Consequently, there has been a significant reduction in the size of the money multiplier, meaning there is a much weaker link between base growth and money growth than in the precrisis era (see Selgin 2017a, 2017b, 2017d).

Before serious consideration can be given to implementing any rule-based monetary regime, the Fed needs to normalize monetary policy by ending interest on excess reserves and shrinking its balance sheet to restore a precrisis fed funds market. Once changes in base money can be effectively transmitted to changes in the money supply and nominal income, the adoption of a monetary rule would reduce uncertainty and spur investment and growth.

Under the Fed's unconventional monetary policies, the growth rate of base money has far exceeded the growth of monetary aggregates and has not led to substantial, let alone rapid, growth of nominal income. Conventional price inflation has been tame.

---

[20]On the impact of unconventional monetary policy on bank lending, especially the effect of overly zealous maroprudential regulation, see Calomiris (2017).

[21]There is no doubt that payment of interest on excess reserves (beginning in October 2008) at a rate exceeding interest on highly liquid assets (such as short-term Treasuries), has sterilized much of the newly created base money from the Fed's large-scale asset purchases. Humphrey (2014: 7) argues that paying IOER increases the "demand for idle reserves" and prevents them from being "lent out into active circulation in the form of bank deposit money." He notes that the Fed's attempt to expand the broad money supply to counter the financial crisis was hampered by paying IOER, which defeated the Fed's lender-of-last-resort function. According to Humphrey (in personal correspondence with the author), instead of paying a positive interest rate on excess reserves, the Fed should have charged a negative (penalty rate) to spur bank lending and deposit creation.

The large-scale purchases of longer-term Treasury securities and mortgage-backed securities have swelled the Fed's balance sheet to $4.5 trillion from less than $1 trillion before the crisis. However, banks have not lent out most of the new base money, and private investment has remained sluggish. Meanwhile, the Fed has used administrative measures to set a range for the fed funds rate—interest on excess reserves to set the upper limit and reverse repos to set the lower limit (see Selgin 2017a and Jordan 2016, 2017). The Fed has also engaged in credit allocation, used forward guidance to influence market perceptions of future rates, encouraged risk by underpricing it, penalized savers with ultra-low interest rates, and encouraged debt.

The problem is that, with massive amounts of excess reserves, there is no viable market for fed funds—more precisely, the only trading is arbitrage between GSEs that are not eligible for IOER and banks that are. Ending unconventional monetary policy by shrinking the Fed's balance sheet, while eliminating interest on excess reserves and the use of reverse repos, would help normalize monetary policy and restore the money multiplier to its precrisis values. The implementation of a demand rule would then be feasible.[22]

Although the Fed has begun to increase the target range for the fed funds rate and has announced plans to shrink its balance sheet, the expectation is that the Fed will move very slowly and reverse course if asset prices tumble, disinflation occurs, or recession sets in.

Toward a Forecast-Free Monetary Regime

Leland Yeager (1992: 71) has proposed eliminating monetary disequilibrium by decentralizing and privatizing money, defining the unit of account "by a comprehensive bundle of goods and services," and letting competition among private issuers "keep meaningful the denomination of their bank notes and deposits (and checks) in the stable, independently defined unit."[23] He argues that those steps would take us much closer to a forecast-free monetary regime than our current government fiat money system under a highly

---

[22]Belongia and Ireland (2015) have argued that the Fed could use Divisia monetary aggregates to make long-run targeting of NGDP feasible.

[23]For a more detailed discussion, see Greenfield and Yeager (1983), and Yeager and Greenfield (1989).

discretionary central bank. Moreover, he is skeptical of "ideally managed government fiat money," because that approach to monetary reform "precludes decentralizing and privatizing the issue of money" (ibid.). Absent a fundamental reform, he would favor a price-level rule over a demand rule.[24]

Monetary Freedom and Monetary Order

A rules-based monetary system would increase economic freedom and lead to a more harmonious monetary order. The choice of what rule to follow will depend on whether one has more confidence in the convertibility theory of monetary control or the responsibility theory. There is no perfect monetary system, so tradeoffs must be made among competing rules. Furthermore, as digital currencies evolve, there may be completely novel ways to achieve monetary and financial stability.

Some critics of government fiat money believe that a gold standard could supply a desirable rule. Others would combine the properties of a gold standard with free banking or digital currencies. Still others would prefer binding the Fed by a monetary rule that is aimed at stabilizing NGDP, the price level, or inflation.

Lawrence H. White (2012) favors restoring "a gold definition of the U.S. dollar," removing legal restrictions that prevent the emergence of a "parallel gold standard," and allowing the issuance of private gold-backed currencies that could be used as legal tender. He provides a roadmap for making the transition to a new gold standard, but recognizes the difficulty of doing so without a broad public consensus. If that consensus does develop, however, financial innovation could help facilitate the transition.

Much of the criticism of monetary freedom has rested on the argument that free-market currencies are inherently unstable and inferior to a government-directed monetary system. Kevin Dowd (2017) constructs a hypothetical model of a laissez-faire monetary regime—asking how a free market in currencies would emerge

---

[24]Bradley and Jansen (1989: 40) contend that changes in the assumptions about the labor market can make a price-level rule theoretically superior to a demand rule. Also, they argue that "ignorance of the correct equations, parameter values and lag structure that characterize the U.S. economy reduces the appeal of nominal GNP targeting."

absent any central bank—and finds that its operating properties are consistent with stability and optimality, not chaos and inefficiency. The harmony that emerges under a market-based monetary system, argues Dowd, stems from the freedom to choose alternative currencies and the rule of law that binds the system together. White and Selgin discuss some historical examples of that stability.[25]

Conclusion

Congress is currently considering moving toward a rules-based regime and establishing a Centennial Monetary Commission to examine the Fed's performance since its creation in 1913, and to consider various reforms. In doing so, it should not neglect the importance of restoring constitutional money and understanding how alternative monetary regimes affect uncertainty.

Normalizing monetary policy requires restoring the fed funds market and reducing the size of the Fed's balance sheet, which means eliminating interest on excess reserves and ending reverse repos so that selling longer-term Treasuries and mortgage-backed securities is accompanied by an equal reduction in excess reserves.

As Tatom (2017: 51) notes:

> The Fed could repair its balance sheet and boost bank credit simply by reversing past actions. Since the last recession began, the Fed has accumulated about $3.5 trillion of securities; 77 percent of bank receipts from these Fed purchases were added to excess reserves. Simply ending the subsidized interest on excess reserves would allow the Fed to sell the $2.7 trillion of its securities held at the peak of excess reserves in August 2014 and incur a matching decline in banks' excess reserves. Such an operation would have no effect on the effective monetary base, monetary aggregates or total credit created in the money creation process. Fed credit and excess reserves would contract by $2.7 trillion, but commercial bank credit would rise by an equal amount. This is precisely where risky assets should be held if banks are to promote growth and if the Fed is to get out of the credit allocation business.[26]

---

[25]See, e.g., White (1989), Selgin (2017c), Selgin and White (1987, 1994).
[26]Selgin (2016a) provides a similar analysis.

The problem is that any reduction or even announcement of such a reduction in Fed assets could trigger a sharp fall in asset prices (especially in bond markets where duration risk is high) and shake market confidence—as seen in the 2013 Bernanke "taper tantrum" when he announced that the Fed would exit its large-scale asset purchase program. Financial markets have relied on the Fed "put" for a long time, and that expectation has made it difficult to change policy.

Also, unplugging the monetary transmission mechanism by ending interest on excess reserves, while desirable, would force the Fed to confront the problem of how to stop existing excess reserves from leaking out into the financial system and thereby creating inflation. The Fed may then face a period of stagflation and decide to revert back to unconventional monetary policy to "stimulate" the economy. Thus, the Fed is essentially in a trap that will be difficult to exit.[27] That is why it is essential to have a national debate over the direction of monetary policy and how best to reform the Fed.

References

Barro, R. J., and Gordon, D. B. (1983) "A Positive Theory of Monetary Policy in a Natural Rate Model. *Journal of Political Economy* 91 (August): 589–610.

Beckworth, D. (2017) "The Knowledge Problem in Monetary Policy: The Case for Nominal GDP Targeting." Mercatus on Policy Series (July 18). Mercatus Center, George Mason University.

Beckworth, D., and Hendrickson, J. R. (2016) "Nominal GDP Targeting and the Taylor Rule on an Even Playing Field." Mercatus Working Paper, George Mason University (October).

Belongia, M. T., and Ireland, P. N. (2015) "A 'Working' Solution to the Question of Nominal GDP Targeting." *Macroeconomic Dynamics* 19 (3): 508–35.

Bernanke, B. S. (2015) "Objections to Federal Reserve Accountability Bill." Remarks presented at the conference on "The Fed in the 21st Century: Independence, Governance, and Accountability," Brookings Institution, March 2. Available at www.youtube.com/watch?v=KJmA5JDNpKg.

---

[27]On the unsustainability of unconventional monetary policies and the exit problem, see Dowd and Hutchinson (2017: 313–17).

Bernholz, P. (2017) "The Implementation and Maintenance of a Monetary Constitution." In J. A. Dorn (ed.) *Monetary Alternatives: Rethinking Government Fiat Money*, chap. 8. Washington: Cato Institute.

Board of Governors, Federal Reserve System (2017) *Report on Monetary Policy* (July 7). Available at www.federalreserve .gov/monetarypolicy/files/20170707_mprfullreport.pdf.

Boettke, P. J.; Salter, A. W.; and Smith, D. J. (2016) "Money as Meta-Rule: Buchanan's Constitutional Economics as a Foundation for Monetary Stability." George Mason University Working Paper in Economics, No. 16–49.

Borio, C. (2016) "Revisiting Three Intellectual Pillars of Monetary Policy." *Cato Journal* 36 (2): 213–38.

Bradley, M. D., and Jansen, D. W. (1989) "Understanding Nominal GNP Targeting." Federal Reserve Bank of St. Louis *Review* 71 (6): 31–40.

Brunner, K. (1980) "The Control of Monetary Aggregates." In *Controlling Monetary Aggregates III*, 1–65. Boston: Federal Reserve Bank of Boston.

_____ (1985) "Monetary Policy and Monetary Order." In *Monetary Policy and Monetary Regimes*, 4–21. Center Symposia Series No. CS-17. Rochester, N.Y.: Center for Research in Government Policy and Business, Graduate School of Management, University of Rochester.

_____ (1987) "Policy Coordination and the Dollar." Shadow Open Market Committee: Policy Statement and Position Papers (PPS 87-01). Center for Research in Government Policy & Business, University of Rochester.

Buchanan, J. M. (1962) "Predictability: The Criterion of Monetary Constitutions." In L. B. Yeager (ed.) *In Search of a Monetary Constitution*, 155–83. Cambridge, Mass.: Harvard University Press.

_____ (1988) "Comment by Dr. Buchanan." In *Prospects for a Monetary Constitution*, 32–35; special issue of *Economic Education Bulletin* 28 (6).

_____ (1989) "Reductionist Reflections on the Monetary Constitution." *Cato Journal* 9 (2): 295–99.

Calomiris, C. W. (2017) "The Microeconomic Perils of Monetary Policy Experiments." *Cato Journal* 37 (1): 1–15.

Christensen, L. (2011) "A Market Monetarist Version of the McCallum Rule." *The Market Monetarist*: https://marketmonetarist.com/2011/10/09/a-market-monetarist-version-of-the-mccallum-rule.

Dittman, R.; Gavin, W. T.; and Kydland, F. E. (1999) "Price-Level Uncertainty and Inflation Targeting." Federal Reserve Bank of St. Louis *Review* (July/August): 23–33.

Dorn, J. A. (1987) "The Search for Stable Money: A Historical Perspective." In J. A. Dorn and A. J. Schwartz (eds.) *The Search for Stable Money: Essays on Monetary Reform*, 1–28. Chicago: University of Chicago Press.

_____, ed. (2017) *Monetary Alternatives: Rethinking Government Fiat Money*. Washington: Cato Institute.

Dowd, K. (2017) "Monetary Freedom and Monetary Stability." In J. A. Dorn (ed.) *Monetary Alternatives: Rethinking Government Fiat Money*, chap. 18. Washington: Cato Institute.

Dowd, K., and Hutchinson (2017) "From Excess Stimulus to Monetary Mayhem." *Cato Journal* 37 (2): 303–28.

Fischer, S. (2017) "Committee Decisions and Monetary Policy Rules." Speech presented at "The Structural Foundations of Monetary Policy," a Hoover Institution Monetary Policy Conference, Stanford University (May 5).

Friedman, M. (1960) *A Program for Monetary Stablity*. New York: Fordham University Press.

_____ (1962) *Capitalism and Freedom*. Chicago: University of Chicago Press.

_____ (1968) "The Role of Monetary Policy." *American Economic Review* 58 (1): 1–17.

_____ (1987) "Monetary Policy: Tactics versus Strategy." In J. A. Dorn and A. J. Schwartz (eds.) *The Search for Stable Money*, 361–82. Chicago: University of Chicago Press.

Friedman, M., and Schwartz, A. J. (1963) *A Monetary History of the United States, 1867–1960*. Princeton, N. J.: Princeton University Press.

Gordon, R. J. (1985) "The Conduct of Domestic Monetary Policy." In A. Ando et al. (eds.) *Monetary Policy in Our Times*. Cambridge, Mass.: MIT Press.

Greenfield, R. L., and Yeager, L. B. (1983) "A Laissez-Faire Approach to Monetary Stability." *Journal of Money, Credit, and Banking* 15 (August): 302–15.

Hall, R. (1981) "Lowering Inflation and Stimulating Economic Growth." In *Politics and the Oval Office: Toward Presidential Governance*, 207–27. San Francisco: Institute for Contemporary Studies.

Haraf, W. S. (1986) "Monetary Velocity and Monetary Rules." *Cato Journal* 6 (2): 641–62.

Hayek, F. A. (1945) "The Use of Knowledge in Society." *American Economic Review* 35 (4): 519–30.

_____ ([1974] 1989) "The Pretense of Knowledge: Nobel Memorial Lecture of December 4, 1974." *American Economic Review* 79 (6): 3–7.

_____ (1978) *The Denationalisation of Money*. 2nd ed. London: Institute of Economic Affairs.

Higgs, R. (1997) "Regime Uncertainty: Why the Great Depression Lasted So Long and Why Prosperity Resumed after the War." *The Independent Review* 1 (4): 561–90.

Hubbard, G. (2017) "How to Keep the Fed from Following Its Models Off a Cliff." *Wall Street Journal* (June 15).

Humphrey, T. M. (2014) "Averting Financial Crises: Advice from Classical Economists." Federal Reserve Bank of Richmond *Economic Focus* 18 (4): 4–7.

Humphrey, T. M., and Timberlake, R. H. (2017) "The Real Bills Doctrine, the Gold Standard, and the Great Depression." Unpublished manuscript.

Jordan, J. (2016) "Tools of Monetary Policy." *Sound Money Project* (December 13): http://soundmoneyproject.org/2016/12/tools-of -monetary-policy. A project of the Atlas Network.

_____ (2017) "Rethinking the Monetary Transmission Mechanism." *Cato Journal* 37 (2): 361–84.

Kydland, F. E., and Prescott, E. C. (1977) "Rules Rather than Discretion: The Inconsistency of Optimal Plans." *Journal of Political Economy* 85 (June): 473–91.

Madison, J. (1831) "[Letter] to Mr. Teachle" (Montpelier, March 15). In S. K. Padover (ed.), *The Complete Madison: His Basic Writings*, 292. New York: Harper and Bros. (1953).

McCallum, B. T. (1984) "Monetary Rules in the Light of Recent Experience." *American Economic Review* 74 (May): 388–96.

_____ (1989) *Monetary Economics: Theory and Policy*. New York: Macmillan.

_____ (2004) "Misconceptions Regarding Rules vs. Discretion for Monetary Policy." *Cato Journal* 23 (3): 365–72.

McCulloch, J. H. (1991) "An Error-Correction Mechanism for Long-Run Price Stability. *Journal of Money, Credit, and Banking* 23 (August, Part 2): 619–24.

Meltzer, A. H. (1983) "Monetary Reform in an Uncertain Environment." *Cato Journal* 3 (1): 93–112. Reprinted in J. A. Dorn and A. J. Schwartz (eds.) *The Search for Stable Money: Essays on Monetary Reform*, 201–20. Chicago: University of Chicago Press, 1987.

_____ (1989) "On Monetary Stability and Monetary Reform." In J. A. Dorn and W. A. Niskanen (eds.) *Dollars, Deficits, and Trade*, 63–85. Boston: Kluwer. This paper was originally presented at the Third International Conference of the Institute for Monetary and Economic Studies at the Bank of Japan, June 3, 1987.

Niskanen, W. A. (1992) "Political Guidance on Monetary Policy." *Cato Journal* 12 (1): 281–86.

O'Driscoll, G. P. Jr. (2016) "Monetary Policy and the Knowledge Problem." *Cato Journal* 36 (2): 337–52.

Orphanides, A. (2017) "The Case Against the Case Against Monetary Rules." Paper presented at the Shadow Open Market Committee meeting, Princeton Club, New York City (May 5).

Salter, A. W. (2017) "Some Political Economy of Monetary Rules." *The Independent Review* 21 (3): 443–64.

Selgin, G. (1997) *Less than Zero: The Case for a Falling Price Level in a Growing Economy*. Hobart Paper No. 132. London: Institute of Economic Affairs.

_____ (2016a) "Interest on Excess Reserves, Part 2." *Alt-M* (January 5): www.alt-m.org/2016/01/05/interest-reserves-part-ii.

_____ (2016b) "Real and Pseudo Monetary Rules." *Cato Journal* 36 (2): 279–96.

_____ (2017a) "On Shrinking the Fed's Balance Sheet." *Alt-M* (February 23): www.alt-m.org/2017/02/23/shrinking-the-feds-balance-sheet.

_____ (2017b) "A Monetary Policy Primer, Part 10: Discretion or a Rule?" *Alt-M* (May 11): www.alt-m.org/2017/05/11/a-monetary-policy-primer-part-10-discretion-or-a-rule.

_____ (2017c) *Money: Free and Unfree*. Washington: Cato Institute.

_____ (2017d) "Monetary Policy v. Fiscal Policy: Risks to Price Stability and the Economy." Testimony before the U.S. House of Representatives Committee on Financial Services (July 21). Available at www.cato.org/publications/testimony/monetary-policy-v-fiscal-policy-risks-price-stability-economy.

Selgin, G.; Beckworth, D.; and Bahadir, B. (2015) "The Productivity Gap: Monetary Policy, the Subprime Boom, and the Post-2001 Productivity Surge." *Journal of Policy Modeling* 37 (2): 189–207.

Selgin, G.; Lastrapes, W. D.; and White, L. H. (2012) "Has the Fed Been a Failure?" *Journal of Macroeconomics* 34 (3): 569–96.

Selgin, G., and White, L. H. (1987) "The Evolution of a Free Banking System." *Economic Inquiry* 25 (July): 439–57.

_____ (1994) "How Would the Invisible Hand Handle Money?" *Journal of Economic Literature* 32 (December): 1718–49.

Sumner, S. B. (2014) "Nominal GDP Targeting: A Simple Rule to Improve Fed Performance." *Cato Journal* 34 (2): 315–37.

Tatom, J. A. (2017) "How to Fix the Fed: The Ineffectiveness of the U.S. Central Bank's Credit Policy." *The International Economy* (Winter): 48–51.

Taylor, J. B. (1993) "Discretion versus Policy Rules in Practice." *Carnegie-Rochester Conference Series on Public Policy* 39: 195–214.

_____ (2012) "Monetary Policy Rules Work and Discretion Doesn't: A Tale of Two Eras." *Journal of Money, Credit, and Banking* 44 (6): 1017–32.

_____ (2015) "Getting Back to a Rules-Based Monetary Strategy." Written version of keynote address given at the Shadow Open Market Committee's Conference on "Getting Monetary Policy Back on Track," Princeton Club, New York City, March 20.

_____ (2017) "Rules versus Discretion: Assessing the Debate over the Conduct of Monetary Policy." Paper presented at the Federal Reserve Bank of Boston Conference on "Are Rules Made to Be Broken? Discretion and Monetary Policy" (October 13).

Timberlake, R. T. (2013) *Constitutional Money: A Review of the Supreme Court's Monetary Decisions*. New York: Cambridge University Press.

Vieira, E. Jr. (2017) "Gold and Silver as Constitutional Alternative Currencies." In J. A. Dorn (ed.) *Monetary Alternatives: Rethinking Government Fiat Money*. Washington: Cato Institute.

Warburton, C. (1949) "Erratic Money: An Outline of the Theory of Monetary Disequilibrium." Box 16, Warburton Collection, Special Collections, George Mason University Library, Fairfax, Va. (Unpublished book-length manuscript.)

_____ (1966) *Depression, Inflation, and Monetary Policy: Selected Papers, 1945–1953*. Baltimore: The Johns Hopkins University Press.

White, L. H. (1989) *Competition and Currency: Essays on Free Banking and Money*. New York: New York University Press.

_____ (1999) *The Theory of Monetary Institutions*. Oxford: Basil Blackwell.

_____ (2012) "Making the Transition to a New Gold Standard." *Cato Journal* 32 (2): 411–21.

_____ (2017) "Experts and the Gold Standard." *Alt-M* (June 13). Available at www.alt-m.org/2017/06/13/experts-gold-standard.

White, L. H.; Vanberg, V. J.; and Köhler, E. A., eds. (2015) *Renewing the Search for a Monetary Constitution*. Washington: Cato Institute.

Woodford, M. (2003) *Interest and Prices: Foundations of a Theory of Monetary Policy*. Princeton, N.J.: Princeton University Press.

Yeager, L. B., ed. (1962) *In Search of a Monetary Constitution*. Cambridge, Mass.: Harvard University Press.

_____ (1986) "The Significance of Monetary Equilibrium." *Cato Journal* 6 (2): 369–99.

_____ (1992) "Toward Forecast-Free Monetary Institutions." *Cato Journal* 12 (1) 53–73.

_____ (1997) *The Fluttering Veil: Essays on Monetary Disequilibrium*. Edited by G. Selgin. Indianapolis: Liberty Fund.

Yeager, L. B., and Greenfield, R. L. (1989) "Can Monetary Disequilibrium Be Eliminated?" *Cato Journal* 9 (2): 405–21.

13
REFORMING THE RULES THAT GOVERN THE FED
Charles W. Calomiris

As historians of the Fed such as Allan Meltzer (2003, 2009a, 2009b, 2014) frequently note, the Fed has failed to achieve its central objectives—price stability and financial stability—during about three-quarters of its first 100 years of operation. Although the Fed was founded primarily to stabilize the panic-plagued U.S. banking system, since the Fed's founding the United States has continued to suffer an unusually high frequency of severe banking crises, including during the 1920s, the 1930s, the 1980s, and the 2000s. Unfortunately, research shows that the Fed has played an active role in producing most of those crises, and its failure to maintain financial stability has often been related to its failure to maintain price stability. The Fed-engineered deflation of the 1930s was the primary cause of the banking crises of that era.

Charles W. Calomiris is Henry Kaufman Professor of Financial Institutions at Columbia University, Director of the Program on Financial Studies at Columbia Business School, Research Associate of the National Bureau of Economic Research, Member of the Shadow Open Market Committee, Member of the Financial Economists Roundtable, Co-Director of the Hoover Institution Initiative on Regulation and the Rule of Law, and a Fellow at the Manhattan Institute. This article is reprinted from the *Cato Journal*, Vol. 38, No. 1 (Winter 2018). An earlier version of this article was presented as testimony on April 4, 2017, before the U.S. House of Representatives Subcommittee on Monetary Policy and Trade of the Committee on Financial Services. This article draws upon prior work, including a coauthored 2015 Shadow Open Market Committee (SOMC) presentation to congressional staff written by Charles Calomiris, Greg Hess, and Athanasios Orphanides. Allan Meltzer, Mickey Levy, John Taylor, Athanasios Orphanides, and Deborah Lucas provided helpful comments.

The Fed's lax monetary policy produced the Great Inflation of the 1960s and 1970s, which was at the heart of the interest rate spikes and losses in real estate, agricultural, and energy loans during the 1980s, which produced the banking crisis of that period. A combination of accommodative monetary policy from 2002 to 2005, alongside Fed complicity with the debasement of mortgage underwriting standards during the mortgage boom of the 2000s, and Fed failures to enforce adequate prudential regulatory standards, produced the crisis of 2007–09 (Calomiris and Haber 2014: chs. 6–8).

It is worth emphasizing that the U.S. experience with financial crises is not the global norm; according to the IMF's database on severe banking crises, the two major U.S. banking crises since 1980 place our country within the top quintile of risky banking systems in the world—a distinction it shares with countries such as Argentina, Chad, and the Democratic Republic of Congo (Laeven and Valencia 2013, Calomiris and Haber 2014).

In his review of Fed history, Allan Meltzer (2003, 2009a, 2009b, 2014) points to two types of deficiencies that have been primarily responsible for the Fed's falling short of its objectives: (1) adherence to bad ideas (especially its susceptibility to intellectual fads); and (2) politicization, which has led it to purposely stray from proper objectives. Failures to achieve price stability and financial stability reflected a combination of those two deficiencies.

Unfortunately, the failures of the Fed are not merely a matter of history. Since the crisis of 2007–09, a feckless Fed has displayed an opaque and discretionary approach to monetary policy in which its stated objectives are redefined without reference to any systematic framework that could explain those changes, has utilized untested and questionable policy tools with uncertain effect, has been willing to pursue protracted fiscal (as distinct from monetary) policy actions, has grown and maintains an unprecedentedly large balance sheet that now includes a substantial fraction of the U.S. mortgage market, has been making highly inaccurate near-term economic growth forecasts for many years, and has become more subject to political influence than it has been at any time since the 1970s. The same problems that Meltzer pointed to—bad ideas and politicization—now, as before, are driving Fed policy errors. I am very concerned that these Fed errors may result, once again, in departures from price stability and financial stability (Calomiris 2017a, 2017b, 2017c).

In this article, I show that the continuing susceptibility of the Fed to bad thinking and politicization reflects deeper structural problems that need to be addressed. Reforms are needed in the Fed's internal governance, in its process for formulating and communicating its policies, and in delineating the range of activities in which it is involved. I will focus on three types of reforms that address those problems: (1) internal governance reforms that focus on the structure and operation of the Fed (which would decentralize power within the Fed and promote diversity of thinking); (2) policy process reforms that narrow the Fed's *primary* mandate to price stability and that require the Fed to adopt and to disclose a systematic approach to monetary policy (which would promote transparency and accountability of the Fed, thereby making its actions wiser, clearer, and more independent); and (3) other reforms that would constrain Fed asset holdings and activities to avoid Fed involvement in actions that conflict with its monetary policy mission (which would improve monetary policy and preserve Fed independence).

Together these three sets of reforms would address the two most important recurring threats to monetary policy—short-term political pressures and susceptibility to bad ideas—and thereby improve the Fed's ability to achieve its ultimate long-run goals of price stability and financial stability, which are crucial to promoting full employment and economic growth. Table 1 summarizes the reforms proposed here, and Figure 1 outlines the primary channels through which reforms would improve monetary policy.

The Need for Internal Governance Reforms

The Fed needs broad and fundamental changes to its internal governance. Internal governance reform should make the Fed more institutionally democratic and more diverse in its thinking. Those improvements, in turn, would make the Fed less susceptible to political pressure—because centralization of power *in* the chair invites more political pressures *on* the chair. They also would make the Fed less likely to adhere to bad ideas, because of a reduced likelihood of "group think." My proposed changes are unlikely to have strong internal advocates within the Fed system (at the very least inside the beltway, at the Board of Governors), and therefore will require legislation. Ironically, although the Fed has been a

TABLE 1
SUMMARY OF PROPOSED REFORMS

Internal Governance Reforms to Fed Structure and Operation

1. Require at least two of seven Fed governors to be people with significant financial markets experience.
2. Governors should each have at least two staff members under their direct control.
3. Require governors to resign other positions as a condition for appointment.
4. Require governors to pledge that they expect to stay for at least half of their appointed terms.
5. Increase salaries for governors to ensure that the Fed remains able to attract talented people.
6. Enhance retirement benefits for governors, contingent on a sufficient number of years of service.
7. Federal Reserve Bank presidents should be selected by their Board of Directors, not subject to the approval of the Board of Governors. At the very least, adopt a sunshine law that requires the Board of Governors to provide summary information to Congress regarding any candidates the Federal Reserve Board rejects, as well as information about candidates that the Board suggests for consideration, or asks to be dropped from consideration prior to being formally proposed by the Banks.
8. All Reserve Bank presidents should vote at every FOMC meeting.
9. Budgetary authority should rest in a committee comprising representatives of all the Federal Reserve Banks and the Board of Governors, and perhaps even some outsiders, to determine the budgets of each Bank and each governor's staff.
10. Prohibit Reserve Bank presidents from being promoted from within their own Bank.

Policy Process Reforms

11. Replace the "dual mandate" with a single price-stability primary objective.
12. Require the Fed to maintain and state a systematic approach to monetary policy. The policy framework would be controlled by the Fed, and subject to change as the Fed sees fit.

(Continued)

TABLE 1 *(Continued)*
SUMMARY OF PROPOSED REFORMS

Avoiding Inappropriate Policies or Conflicts of Interest

13. Prohibit the Fed from holding securities other than U.S. Treasury securities in its portfolio (except during emergencies, in the context of assistance approved under its emergency lending powers).
14. Interest on reserves should be set at 10 basis points below the federal funds rate.
15. Prohibit the Fed from engaging in its current reverse repos as a substitute for open market operations.
16. Remove the Fed from writing and enforcing regulations. The Fed would still participate in examinations and have full access to all information necessary to fulfill its role as a lender of last resort. At the very least, the Fed should be removed from merger decisions and oversight of highly politically sensitive matters, such as CRA examinations.

U.S. Budgetary Reform

17. The Fed's surplus revenues should not be used as an off-budget means of funding the Consumer Financial Protection Bureau (CFPB), other regulatory actions, highway expenditures (including those undertaken by the Fed), or other programs.

champion of governance reform for banks as a means of improving their performance, it is much less receptive to recognizing its own governance problems.

In recent years, there has been an unhealthy increase in the centralization of power within the Fed, which has two parts: (1) the power of the Fed chair over the Federal Reserve Board; and (2) the concentration of power within the Federal Reserve System at the Board of Governors.

Daniel Thornton and David Wheelock (2014), both economists who have served for many years at the Federal Reserve Bank of St. Louis, provide some heuristic evidence on the need to reduce the power of the Fed chair over the Board of Governors. Thornton

FIGURE 1
HOW PROPOSED GOVERNANCE REFORMS WOULD
IMPROVE MONETARY POLICY

Internal governance reforms to Fed structure and operation
Policy process reforms (price stability mandate, systematic policy)
Avoid inappropriate policies or conflicts of interest

↓

More diversity of thinking within the Fed
Democratization of power within the Fed
Fewer political entanglements for the Fed
Less seat-of-the-pants bias in monetary policy
Greater Fed accountability
Greater Fed independence

↓

Less adherence to bad ideas and intellectual fads
Less myopic politicization of monetary policy
More effective and predictable monetary policy

and Wheelock report that Federal Reserve Board governors have dissented from the chair only two times from 1995 to 2014. This compares to 65 dissents during the same period of time by Federal Reserve Bank presidents. Interestingly, presidents and governors had a similar pattern of dissents from 1957–95, about eight dissents per year for each group.

Surely, a well-informed and diligent group of six independent (nonchair) governors would find reason to disagree from time to time with the chair. Federal Reserve Bank presidents dissent frequently, and Supreme Court justices dissent with aplomb. Dissents remain common at the Bank of England. But somehow, Fed governors in recent years have become restrained from expressing their dissenting views.

This lack of dissent would seem strange to architects of the current Fed structure. When then-Fed chair Marriner Eccles testified before the Senate Banking Committee on March 4, 1935, regarding the proposed structure of the Federal Open Market Committee (FOMC), he complained that including only three Federal Reserve Board governors ran the risk that "a minority of the Board [of Governors] could adopt a policy that would be opposed to one favored by the majority [of the seven board members]." That argument convinced Congress to structure the FOMC to include all seven governors. Clearly, Eccles envisioned a healthy degree of potential dissent within the Board of Governors about monetary policy. That is no longer the case.

Three possible explanations emerge for this unhealthy trend toward uniformity at the Board of Governors, each of which indicates a need for reform. One possibility is that governors are selected based on their willingness to compromise and "to go along, to get along." The chair has substantial discretionary power that can be wielded against uncooperative governors. This possibility, if true, is indicative of an unhealthy internal governance system that quashes independent thinking.

A second possibility is that many of the governors have become, de facto, short-timers who may not have a permanent stake in the system's long-run management or performance. Why bother to dissent if you are leaving soon after arriving? If this explanation has merit, it indicates that Fed governors are not playing the role intended by the Federal Reserve Act, which entrusted them with significant authority, gave them long-term (14-year) appointments, and envisioned them as important contributors to shaping the policies of the Fed.

Finally, a third possibility is that governors may not have the information or background needed to support the formation of independent decisions. This is quite possible given that (nonchair) governors do not have *any* staff to support their own lines of research and inquiry, and historically their access to the Board's staff has been limited. To the extent that limits are sometimes relaxed by the chair, this is a discretionary decision that can be reversed (and perhaps *would* be reversed if governors made use of staff to support positions that opposed the chair). Fed governors have complained publicly about the lack of independent staff to advise them, or the inability to speak to staff without permission. Former vice chairman Alan Blinder frequently complained about the limitations placed on his ability to communicate with Fed staff, and also complained about the "real reluctance to advance alternative points of view" at the Fed. Former governor Laurence Meyer said that he was "frustrated by the disproportionate power the chairman wielded over the FOMC," and said that dissents were viewed as disruptive to the process of monetary policymaking (Calomiris 2014).

Not only is there a disturbing power imbalance within the Board of Governors, but also there has been a shift in power within the System toward Washington. Throughout the founding and operation of the Fed, it has always been recognized that the Board of Governors is more attuned to political pressures than the Fed presidents. The presidents, therefore, play a crucial role in deterring political influences that tend to make monetary policy myopic. The shift of power toward the Board has made it harder for Federal Reserve Bank presidents to challenge the point of view coming from the chair, and serves to politicize the Fed (e.g., through pressures applied by the administration to the chair).

One symptom of the shift of power toward Washington has been an increasingly aggressive "approval" process by the Board of Governors for nominees to be presidents of Federal Reserve Banks. The Fed Board of Governors has approval authority over the appointment of presidents, but recently they have been taking a more aggressive role in suggesting nominees and refusing to approve others. Although the discussion of this issue has been limited to those within the system—as well as journalists—recent presidential searches have purportedly resulted in the nonapproval of multiple finalist candidates put before the Federal Reserve Board by Boards of Directors of the Federal Reserve Banks.

In addition to the problems of excessive centralization of power in Washington and in the Fed chair, there has been a cultural shift at the Fed that has reduced the diversity of thinking and made the Fed more susceptible to academic fads. As recently as the 1970s, Fed governors and presidents typically were not academics steeped in the latest modeling fads of macroeconomics. But in recent years, it has become rare for governors or presidents to be people coming from backgrounds other than academia. This likely reflects several influences, including the increasing centralization of power within the system noted above, and changes in the structure of the banking industry; but it also probably reflects the increasing technical complexity of macroeconomic modeling, which many non-PhD economists find challenging to comprehend.[1]

The models the Fed has employed for policy purposes, however, have not proven to be of much value. The fashionable "dynamic stochastic general equilibrium" (DSGE) model, which was all the rage in Fed and academic thinking during the years leading up to the crisis, conceived of the economy as divorced from the banking sector (a sector that was not important enough to be included in the DSGE model). Needless to say, the banking crisis proved that this was an important omission. Since the 2007–09 crisis, DSGE models have been modified to try to incorporate the financial sector. Nevertheless, the consistent failure of the Fed to forecast economic growth over the past decade gives little reason for confidence in current Fed modeling.

In the past, many of the most successful Fed leaders did not put much stock in the latest fads of macroeconomic modeling. It is widely believed that Paul Volcker was the most successful Fed chair of the past several decades. In one Fed cartoon prepared for high school students, Paul Volcker is lovingly portrayed as a superhero wearing a red cape. Few would object to that characterization. Mr. Volcker's combination of integrity, judgment, and courage stand alone:

- Integrity because—prior to his appointment—he leveled with President Carter about his intention to attack inflation aggressively.
- Judgment because he rejected the model-driven advice of some top Fed economists who adhered to "Phillips curve"–based projections; Volcker recognized that only a draconian policy change would be sufficient to establish Fed credibility in lowering inflation.

---

[1] The rise of nationwide branch banking in the 1990s caused important local and regional banks to largely disappear, which has changed the profiles of Federal Reserve Banks' boards. The increasing rigor of Fed modeling at FOMC meetings (despite the inaccuracy of that modeling, especially in the years leading up to the subprime crisis) has fostered a culture that makes it quite difficult for nonacademics to challenge the assumptions of the chair's preferred econometric model, however misspecified it may be. Even someone like Alan Greenspan, a trained economist who worked outside of academia and who resisted placing too much weight on forecasts from the Fed's macroeconomic models, is missing in the ranks of Fed leadership today.

- Courage because he stayed the course despite sustained high unemployment and vilification from many academics who derided his policies—because they contradicted the received academic wisdom of the day.

If the Fed were to face a similar challenge again—and the risks associated with its balance sheet's size and structure make that a real possibility—would someone emerge with the same combination of virtues? Sadly, the answer is perhaps not. People like Volcker—who took macroeconomic modeling with the appropriately large grain of salt, whose spine was stiffened by years in the trenches of global banking, and who deeply understood the psychology of financial markets—are unlikely to end up as leaders of today's Fed.

That fact would not have pleased the Fed's founders. The structure of the System, as originally conceived, and as reformed in 1935, was designed to ensure a healthy diversity of experience among its leaders. Fed leadership was supposed to combine those with experience in banking with political appointees with different life experience. Academics were absent from leadership positions, as they were not selected as political appointees until much later— Arthur Burns was the first academic to serve as chair. A system of 12 Federal Reserve Banks was intended to ensure that Fed leaders would be guided by diverse regional *banking* perspectives. Even at the Board, banking professionals sometimes dominated (e.g., Marriner Eccles was a Utah banker, and Paul Volcker worked at Chase when he wasn't at the Treasury or the Fed).

Some Fed leaders I have spoken with tell me that nonacademics often lack understanding of key economic issues. That may be true, but every governor or president doesn't have to understand statistics deeply to be able to contribute to the collective wisdom of the Fed. Sometimes the most important contribution one can make in a meeting is to question things that economists as a group accept too easily. It is worth emphasizing that group think about models has been a perennial problem at the Fed. In the 1920s–60s, it was the Riefler-Burgess "net free reserves" model; later it was the Phillips Curve; and more recently, the New Keynesian DSGE model.

Don't get me wrong: technical modeling is necessary, but it is not helpful to fill the FOMC with people who use the same model. We need multiple models, and we need people who bring other facts and thinking to bear on economic questions. There is no better antidote to Fed group think than having FOMC members who are willing to scoff at economists' certainties, especially if their own experiences provide credible alternative perspectives about how markets and people behave.

Promoting Democratization of Power and Diversity of Thinking within the Fed System

It is possible to construct new rules for Fed leadership that will reduce the centralization of power, enhance diversity, and reduce group-think risk.

Congress could require, for example, that at least two of the seven Fed governors be people with significant financial markets experience. Having at least two people on the Board with backgrounds in the financial industry—like Peter Fisher and Kevin Warsh—would create a critical mass of market-savvy opinion.

To further build diverse thinking at the Board, the power of the chair should be limited. For starters, to ensure that governors have access to necessary information and can act independently in their voting, governors should each have at least two staff members under their direct control, which would enable them to develop independent views.

Perhaps that reform would help to solve another problem: the short tenure of most governors. Governors' terms are 14 years, but most leave after only two years. Before governors become fully educated to the intricacies and challenges of monetary policy, they are on their way back to the universities whence they came (to avoid losing their chaired professorships). Congress should require governors to resign their other positions, including university professorships, as a condition for appointment, and also ask them to pledge that they expect to stay on as governors for at least half of their appointed terms. Salaries for governors should also be increased to ensure that the Fed remains able to attract talented people. Part of the reason that governors return to academia so quickly is that for most of them their salaries as governors are much less than what they earn at universities. Furthermore, after two years on the FOMC, lucrative consulting and private board of directors appointments beckon. Retirement benefits for governors could also be enhanced, and made contingent on a sufficient number of years of service.

In addition to reforming the Board of Governors, Congress should increase the role of Federal Reserve Banks within the FOMC and increase their independence within the Fed System. Federal Reserve Bank presidents should be selected based on the independent decisions of their Board of Directors, and should not be subject to the approval of the Board of Governors. At the very least, if the Board of Governors is to retain its approval power, let's adopt a sunshine law that requires it to provide summary information to Congress (which maintains all candidates' privacy) regarding any candidates the Federal Reserve Board rejects, as well as information about candidates that the Board suggests for consideration, or asks to be dropped from consideration prior to being formally proposed by the Banks.

Congress also should change FOMC voting rules so that all Reserve Bank presidents vote at every meeting. That would promote diversity by giving more power and voice to the research staffs of the Reserve Banks. Current FOMC rules of rotation are designed to give greater weight to the Board, which effectively means the huge research staff controlled by the Fed chair.

Perhaps most important, the 12 Federal Reserve Banks should also be freed from the budgetary control of the Fed Board and its chair, who can use budgetary power (e.g., to limit the size and scope of their research activities) as a threat to gain cooperation on policy matters. For example, the Federal Reserve System could establish a committee comprising representatives of all the Federal Reserve Banks and the Board of Governors, and perhaps even some outsiders, to consider the budgets of each Bank and each governor's staff.

It would further promote diversity of thinking if Federal Reserve Banks were prohibited from appointing Reserve Bank presidents from within their own Bank. When Federal Reserve Banks' Boards were composed of regional banking and business leaders, Boards had a direct stake in Fed decisionmaking and presidents were selected from a broad pool of outsiders. Now, almost all Fed presidents are former Bank research economists (usually research directors). Although formal searches are always undertaken, it is hard to attract qualified outsiders to participate in that process when they know that the internal candidate has the inside track, based on his or her relationship with the Board, and even if they do participate, risk-averse Boards often prefer the devil they know to the one they don't. The result is unhealthy inbreeding.

Policy Process Reforms: A Primary Price-Stability Mandate and Systematic Policy

The internal governance reforms outlined above must be supplemented with policy process reforms that ensure the right kind of accountability for the Fed by improving policy transparency, constraining unaccountable discretion, and discouraging politicization of monetary policy. Fed history shows that some of the Fed's worst errors were the result of the wrong kind of accountability. As Allan Meltzer's (2003, 2009a, 2009b, 2014) work shows, including his three volume *History of the Federal Reserve*, Fed failures often have reflected political pressures on the Fed to accommodate deficits, or an excessive focus on short-term unemployment goals (with an eye to upcoming elections) at the expense of long-term inflation and unemployment goals. An important safeguard against monetary policy errors, therefore, is to promote greater independence of the Fed.

Paradoxically, unlimited Fed discretion does not result in greater independence of action because unlimited discretion invites political interference. Fed independence is best achieved by imposing discipline on the process of monetary policy in a way that sets clear objectives for policy and enhances accountability with respect to achieving those objectives.

The most obvious policy process improvement would be to repeal the "dual mandate" imposed on the Fed in the 1970s and replace it with a single primary price-stability mandate, as Paul Volcker and Alan Greenspan, among many others, have publicly championed.[2] The sole primary objective of price stability is embodied in many other central banks' charters, including those of the European Central Bank and the Bank of England. There are three arguments for adopting this policy in the United States.

First, price stability is an achievable long-run objective, and thus the Fed can be held accountable for achieving it. Indeed, long-run inflation is *completely* under its control. The Fed has a monopoly over the supply of currency. Inflation is the (inverse of the) value

---

[2]With respect to the financial stability mandate, focusing monetary policy on price stability would also tend to avoid financial instability. Of course, aside from monetary policy, there are other important regulatory policy tools that should be used to promote financial stability (see Calomiris 2017a).

of money; if you control its supply, you control its value. Unpredictable short-term changes in demand and measurement problems make this hard to do on a short-term basis, but over sufficient time the Fed can control inflation. In contrast, the Fed cannot be held accountable for achieving a given unemployment target in the long run; indeed, economists agree that the long-run rate of unemployment is the result of factors outside of the control of the Fed.

Second, inflation matters for growth. High levels of inflation, or volatile inflation, result in lower output and higher unemployment in the long run. As Milton Friedman and many others correctly argued for many years, the reason to target price stability is not that we care about price stability per se (no one should), but rather because we care about employment and output; by making price stability the primary long-run objective of the Fed we ensure that *the average levels of output and employment will be maximized in the long run.* Paradoxically, the point of narrowing the Fed's long-term mandate to inflation is to boost average employment.

Third, narrowing the Fed's primary mandate protects it from myopic political pressures that are inherent in any democracy. Elections can lead politicians to pressure the monetary authority to make the wrong tradeoffs, such as boosting output today (in the interest of current voters) at the expense of higher inflation and lower output tomorrow (at the expense of future voters). Giving the Fed a narrow price stability primary objective provides cover for the Fed in defending itself against opportunistic attacks. Complicating monetary policy by introducing multiple goals (unemployment alongside price stability) makes it hard to hold the Fed accountable for its actions in the long run, while encouraging political pressures on the Fed to achieve an amorphous employment objective. I believe that the Fed's risky QE3 program of purchasing mortgage-backed securities (MBS) and long-term Treasury bonds in an effort to demonstrate its commitment to reducing unemployment (which had very little effect in boosting employment) is an example, among many, of how such myopic political pressures can distort monetary policy.

The call for a single price-stability mandate is often misunderstood as reflecting a callous lack of interest in unemployment, but the opposite is the case. Economic studies have shown that in the long run there is no tradeoff between price stability and maximum employment; it follows that a single primary long-run commitment to price stability in no way requires a tradeoff of lower employment. Holding the Fed primarily to account for price stability does not preclude it from supporting the economy during slumps with countercyclical policy over the short or medium terms, as a *secondary* objective. Indeed, the Taylor Rule is an example of a policy that is consistent with both meeting a long-run inflation target and providing countercyclical influence. There is no doubt that a Fed with a single inflation mandate would continue to execute countercyclical policy aggressively. However, making price stability its sole primary objective ensures maximum *sustainable* growth and employment over the long run, while defending the independence of the Fed from short-term political pressures.

In addition to narrowing the Fed's primary mandate to price stability, it would also enhance accountability and independence to require the Fed to maintain a *systematic approach* to monetary policy. This is crucial for two reasons: First, systematic policy defends against the dangers of discretionary, seat-of-the-pants policymaking that is susceptible to biases and socio-political pressures. One of the most important seat-of-the-pants biases is "dynamic inconsistency." As academics and Fed researchers have long recognized, a non-rule-based monetary policy will tend to err both with respect to hitting its inflation target and with respect to optimally stabilizing the economy over the business cycle. These twin seat-of-the-pants biases are sometimes referred to as "inflation bias" and "stabilization bias" (see, for example, Faust and Henderson 2004), and are part of a long tradition in monetary policy research emphasizing the social welfare improvements that come from adherence to long-term commitments by the monetary policy authority (e.g., Friedman 1948, 1959, 1968; Phelps 1968, 1972; Kydland and Prescott 1977; Orphanides 2003a, 2003b). Systematic rule-based policy is key to avoiding undue focus on the short term at a long-term cost to society.

Second, because businesses and households take decisions that depend on expectations about the future, including future policy decisions and their economic consequences, a systematic policy framework that makes monetary policy more predictable facilitates better private-sector decisions over time and enhances social welfare.

What constitutes systematic monetary policy? Clearly, not the status quo, which delegates monetary policy to Fed policymakers with broad mandates and allows these policymakers to employ unconstrained judgment in meeting those mandates.

Over its first century of operation, however, the Fed sometimes acted relatively systematically. Variation in the quality of Fed policy-making over time reflects, in part, variation in the degree to which policy was systematic and oriented toward clear long-term objectives. One reason for this diversity in outcomes over different periods is the immense discretionary power that the Federal Reserve has exercised over time in interpreting its mandate and in deciding monetary policy, as well as the lack of any effective oversight of the monetary policy process. Recognizing that appointed policymakers are humans and are susceptible to all the pressures and biases that humans face, reform legislation can play a crucial role in giving monetary policy a clear long-term focus and forcing it to implement a systematic policy process. Policy so conceived would be more predictable and less susceptible to fads, to short-term seat-of-the-pants biases, and to myopic political influences.

Does a systematic approach to monetary policy imply adherence to a rigid, static rule? If economists had a perfect understanding of the economy and the ability to observe and properly interpret shocks, and if the structure of the economy were unchanging, then monetary policy could be guided by a fixed policy rule that would specify how the Fed would react to observed shocks to maintain price stability and smooth the business cycle. But that is not a realistic vision of what systematic monetary policy would mean in the real world of changing economic structure and imperfect economic understanding.

Economists always have an incomplete understanding of the economy and face limitations in observing and interpreting shocks hitting the economy in real time, when policy decisions counteracting potential adverse effects of various shocks have to be made. As a result, there are divergent views and considerable uncertainty regarding precisely what the best monetary policy response to macroeconomic conditions may be. Furthermore, as the structure of the economy evolves over time, any algebraic rule characterizing the appropriate policy response to macroeconomic factors will have to adapt to changing circumstances. In addition, policymakers learn over time, and their understanding of appropriate policy responses, therefore, is also subject to change even if the structure of the economy is not changing.

The limitations introduced by these sources of uncertainty have been used by some to justify relying on policymakers' "best judgment" with unlimited discretion. That is a fatuous argument. So long as the systematic formulation of monetary policy is flexible and able to adapt to changes in the economy's structure and our understanding, uncertainty cannot justify the resistance to making policy systematic.

This point bears emphasis: the adoption of a simple, but flexible, monetary policy rule is clearly desirable because it can tackle uncertainty about the economy while avoiding the adverse consequences of unlimited discretion.

Let me be clear: a policy rule must be a specific algebraic formula that can be used to determine how monetary policy should respond to changes in macroeconomic conditions, as summarized by specific observable variables such as the current inflation and unemployment rates. By its very nature, such a policy rule ensures that policy is systematic, transparent, and accountable. If well designed (based on existing empirical evidence), the policy rule will also deliver good economic performance. Research with estimated models of the U.S. economy over the past few decades suggests that simple policy rules can be designed that would deliver good economic performance. Of course, there is reasonable disagreement about what the best rule would be, and care is required both in the evaluation of alternative policy rules and in their implementation. Sifting through this evidence and reaching appropriate judgments about which rule to apply, and adapting the rule over time as needed, should be the central functions of any monetary policy authority.

Taylor (2016) discusses recent progress in the evaluation of macroeconomic models, like those that would form the basis for the evolving Fed policy rule. Two important characteristics of the model evaluation process are noteworthy. First, models must be developed in what Taylor calls the "rules space" rather than the "path space." Models in path space conceive of policy as the execution of isolated, hypothetical one-time policy actions. Models in rules space evaluate alternative policy rules in a framework in which policy actions occur within the context of the rules that produce them. Not only are rules-space models the only coherent approach to model the effects of policy on the economy (because, for example, they take account of expectations that are influenced by the existence of the rule), they are also ideally suited to inform an FOMC that is charged with developing and constantly improving its explicit monetary rule. Second, the model evaluation process must identify common performance criteria that would be used to evaluate the relative validity of a diverse range of models. Volker Wieland's pioneering efforts to develop "The Macroeconomic Model Data Base" (see www.macro-modelbase.com) shows that this is possible (see Wieland et al. 2016). Wieland's website invites all comers to propose models, and provides a platform in which they can be compared, debated, and verified empirically. An FOMC charged to follow and disclose its systematic approach to monetary policy could benefit from making use of just such a website. And a Fed structured to encourage diverse thinking would make effective use of it.

One might ask whether a flexible policy rule could be an effective constraint on unbridled discretion. After all, the FOMC would be free to change its rule at every meeting. Yes, it would, but it would have to do so as a committee, reaching agreement on the changes needed, and embodying those beliefs in observable parameter changes that outsiders could challenge. Outside opinions about the quality of FOMC deliberations and decisions about its rule would be a source of accountability, including at Congressional hearings, and the FOMC would have reason to care about its reputation as a crafter of empirically defensible rules.

To help fix ideas about how FOMC discussions would be likely to proceed, consider an example policy rule for the federal funds rate, f, based on the well-known Taylor (1993) rule:

$$(1) \qquad f = r^* + \pi + a\,(\pi - 2) - b\,(u - u^*)$$

This rule suggests that when the inflation rate equals the 2 percent target and the unemployment rate equals the natural rate of unemployment, u^*, monetary policy should be neutral, that is, the federal funds rate should be equal to the sum of the real natural rate of interest, r^*, and the inflation target. If inflation is above the target, then policy should be tighter, with the degree of the policy response depending on the parameter a (in Taylor's original formulation this was equal to 0.5). If the unemployment rate is above the natural rate of unemployment, as is typically observed in recessions, monetary policy should be eased, with the response governed by the parameter b. Considering different values for the parameters a and b is a simple way to see that care is required to ensure that a policy rule, if followed, will contribute to good economic outcomes over time. If b is set to zero, this rule does not respond at all to employment conditions and may lead to undesirable volatility in unemployment. If b is set to a very high value, say 10, this rule becomes very activist and may result in undesirable instability in both inflation and unemployment. Choosing parameters that would deliver the best macroeconomic performance depends on one's beliefs about the economy. Alternative estimated models typically suggest somewhat different values for the parameters that work best.

The Taylor-type rule above also highlights an important issue relating to the natural rate of unemployment and the natural rate of interest. These concepts are unobservable and are typically estimated. However, estimates are uncertain and may vary considerably both over time and due to differences in estimation methodologies. Using a Taylor-type rule with the wrong estimates of the natural rates introduces a bias that results in deviations from price stability. As an example, the original formulation of the Taylor rule was based on the assumption that the natural rate of interest is 2 percent. Some analysts, including Federal Reserve officials, presently suggest that their preferred current estimates of the natural rate of interest are zero or even negative. The same policy rule with these two alternative assumptions would give policy prescriptions from the Taylor rule that would differ by 200 basis points or more.

I emphasize, however, that such disagreements about hard-to-measure concepts like the natural rate of interest are not insurmountable obstacles to agreeing on a rule. Indeed, alternative policy rules could be specified that do not depend on estimates of the natural rates to set policy and are therefore not subject to related uncertainty. For example, a rule might employ the values of the federal funds rate and the unemployment rate in the previous quarter, f_{-1} and u_{-1}.

$$(2) \qquad f = f_{-1} + a\,(\pi - 2) - b\,(u - u_{-1})$$

Compared to the Taylor rule, this rule suggests that the federal funds rate should be raised (relative to its value a quarter earlier) if inflation is above the target and should be reduced if the unemployment rate is higher than it was in the previous quarter.

Simple rules, based on the examples above, can also make use of forecasts of economic activity and inflation. Indeed, there are many reasonable candidates for a simple policy rule. A critical issue in determining which rule the monetary authority should adopt among the many alternatives is how robust the rule is to the various sources of uncertainty and potential error. In a committee setting, such as the FOMC, there may be differences of opinion about what is the appropriate way to think about the U.S. economy that may not be possible to distinguish on the basis of available empirical evidence.

A reasonable criterion for designing a simple rule for the Federal Reserve would be the robustness of the rule to reasonable alternative models. This is how policy ought to be designed to defend against major inference errors in an environment of uncertainty.

Requiring the Fed to identify and adopt a policy rule along the lines highlighted above would replace meeting-by-meeting discretion and thus ensure that the harmful consequences of seat-of-the-pants policy are avoided. But as I have noted, given the complexity and continuous change of the economy, it would not be expected that any simple algebraic formula could be the basis for robust policymaking forever.

The goal in making monetary policy systematic is not to replace discretionary policy with an immutable rule, but rather to replace it with a systematic framework for selecting a simple and robust rule that foresees periodic reviews and adaptation. Nor would this process of discussing and disclosing come as an unprecedented innovation within the Fed. Publication of the simple rule that the FOMC would follow has a precedent in the Fed's current publication of principles regarding its longer-run goals, which the FOMC has been publishing every January since 2012. As the FOMC adapts its rule over time, to ensure that best practices prevail in the evaluation process, it would be important that a high degree of transparency accompany the process of evaluation of alternative rules and any adaptations under consideration.

Crucially, the selected rule should be specified with sufficient detail to hold the FOMC accountable and eliminate meeting-by-meeting discretion. An outside observer should be able to determine the meeting-by-meeting setting of policy *using only public information*. If the rule's implementation requires use of unobserved concepts that may vary from quarter to quarter, such as the natural rate of interest, then the methodology for tracking those changes over time should be made explicit so that it could be replicated with public information. Similarly, if the rule employs short-term projections of inflation, these projections should be in line with those available to the public. In other words, unaccountable discretion should not be introduced through the back door, for example by using a simple rule that responds to inflation projections based on policymakers' "judgment" that cannot be independently reproduced and evaluated.

Because no simple rule can encompass satisfactorily crisis situations that might require a rapid policy response, an escape clause should be included that allows policy to deviate from the simple rule. In the past few decades, a few instances could be identified, perhaps once every decade or two, when a deviation from a simple rule could be necessary. To cover such contingencies, a comply-or-explain approach should be adopted, with the understanding that deviations are rare and related explicitly to crisis circumstances.

Providing the Fed with a single primary mandate of price stability and requiring it to maintain a systematic, flexible approach to policy are reforms that are long overdue. Several senior Fed policymakers recently mischaracterized the current legislative proposal (U.S. House of Representatives 2016) to require monetary policy to be systematic as dictating an immutable rule, such as the Taylor Rule, to the Fed. This is disingenuous. My understanding of the current proposed legislation is that it conforms to the proposal I lay out here: the Fed would determine its own policy rule, which would be subject to its decisions to alter the rule over time, and in emergency circumstances the Fed would not be rigidly bound to adhere to its stated framework.

The methodology and expertise necessary for the Federal Reserve to adopt a simple and robust policy rule that can preserve price stability and deliver good stabilization performance are available. Requiring a systematic approach will have a constructive effect on the substance of FOMC deliberations and their information content for outside observers, by encouraging much of the debate to focus on whether to revise the existing framework, and how to do so. This will make monetary policy more predictable, more understandable to the market, more accountable to Congress, and more independent of myopic political pressure. Given the undisputed benefits of avoiding seat-of-the-pants policymaking, preserving the Fed's unlimited discretionary approach cannot be reasonably defended.

Limits on Fed Activities and Holdings

There are major problems that arise from combining monetary policy with other functions and powers. Most obviously, a systematic rule for monetary policy may mean little if it is only one of many things that the monetary policy authority is doing. Unaccountable discretion could arrive through the back door of other policies and undermine the commitment to systematic policy. And those other policies, because they would not be subject to the discipline of systematic thinking and accountability, would invite myopic political influence. Furthermore, other mandates on the Fed related to regulatory policy, or its own financial interests, may conflict with its role as a monetary policy authority.

These are not hypothetical problems. The Fed's current fiscal and regulatory policy actions give it many policy levers other than those related to traditional monetary policy. Without reforms that limit Fed actions and holdings, even if the internal governance and policy process reforms suggested above were implemented, the Fed would continue to suffer from conflicts of interest and politicization risk that could encourage it to choose inferior monetary policy rules, or to undermine the effects of its systematic monetary policy rule with other actions. Additional reforms, therefore, are needed to avoid the conflicts and politicization that result from the current multiple roles, powers, and instruments of the Fed.

The Fed's powers and toolkit have grown since the crisis of 2007–09. One of the most remarkable aspects of Dodd-Frank was the confidence it evinced in the Fed. The Office of Thrift Supervision was abolished after the 2007–08 crisis in response to its perceived incompetence. But Dodd-Frank enhanced the supervisory and regulatory powers of the Fed (which was a primary regulator of several of the most deeply troubled banks, including Citi and Wachovia).

That enhancement of Fed power was all the more remarkable when one considers that in March 2008, the U.S. Treasury circulated a "blueprint" explaining why it would be desirable to redesign the U.S. financial regulatory structure along functional lines. That change also would have reduced the conflicts of interest inherent in exercising of monetary policy and regulatory authority by removing many supervisory and regulatory powers from the Fed (Calomiris 2006, 2013). Under the "blueprint," the Fed would continue playing a key role in examinations, with full access to information that might be useful to it in its capacity as lender of last resort, but it would not play a central role in the rule setting or supervision of banks. The "blueprint" was put aside after the crisis, which largely reflected the skill of Fed advocates (especially Chairman Bernanke) in convincing Congress that the Fed was the most able and trustworthy party in which to vest many of the new regulatory powers created by Dodd-Frank.

Since the crisis, as the Fed's powers have grown, so have its conflicts of interest. In particular, monetary policy experimentation has involved the Fed as a direct participant in financial markets in unprecedented ways. As of February 22, 2017, the Fed holds $1.8 trillion dollars in MBS on its balance sheet (which amounts to roughly one-sixth of the U.S. mortgage market), reflecting the Fed's new role in spurring the economy by subsidizing mortgage finance costs. It is noteworthy that this new fiscal policy role of the Fed was not primarily the result of crisis support, but rather of Fed purchases of mortgage-backed securities as part of its "quantitative easing" experiments.

Many critics regard this as an inappropriate incursion into fiscal policy by the Fed. It also creates numerous conflicts of interest with respect to the Fed's role as a regulator of banks. As a holder of MBS, the Fed has an incentive to avoid actions that might increase mortgage interest rates, even if that would be desirable as a matter of monetary policy. This is true for two reasons. First, any accounting losses on its MBS portfolio would increase the Fed's contribution to the measured deficit, with obvious adverse political ramifications.[3] Second, housing finance is a magnet for political interests, which implies severe continuing pressures on the Fed not to sell its mortgage portfolio, even if failing to do so serves to prop up a destabilizing housing bubble.

The Fed also sets interest rates banks earn on reserves. The Fed apparently intends to use this tool to potentially offer very high interest rates, if necessary, to dissuade banks from lending, as an alternative to selling its portfolio (and recognizing politically unappealing capital losses when doing so). Although Title II, Sec. 201, of the Financial Services Regulatory Relief Act of 2006, which authorized the payment of interest on reserves, clearly limited Fed discretion in setting interest payments by specifying that "balances maintained at a Federal Reserve Bank . . . may receive earnings . . . at a rate or rates not to exceed the general level of short-term interest rates," the Fed appears to intend to side-step this legislative limit by creating a

---

[3]According to the Fed's accounting rules, the Fed does not mark its portfolio to the market; it incurs losses on securities only if those securities are sold. The Fed's capital losses affect the measured deficit, but on a consolidated basis they have no economic effect on the government's deficit. Nevertheless, they matter politically, as critics of the Fed are likely to make use of its measured contribution to the deficit. Because that threat is real, the Fed will seek to avoid sales of assets that cause its measured contribution to the deficit to rise.

"range" of targeted values, with the interest on reserves expected to lie at the top of the specified range, and by reserving its right to "adjust the interest on excess reserves rate . . . as necessary for appropriate monetary control, based on policymakers' assessments of the efficacy and costs of their tools."[4] Some politicians have already challenged the Fed to explain why it is appropriate for it to pay above-market rates on bank reserves. Clearly, this is a fiscal expenditure, just as paying zero interest is the commonly understood "reserve tax." It is inappropriate for the Fed to make fiscal decisions about the taxes or subsidies transferred from the government to banks, and it is doubly inappropriate, given the Fed's role as a bank regulator.

Not only do the Fed's holdings of MBS and its setting of interest on reserves entail new fiscal actions and politicization risks, but also the Fed now acts as a repo counterparty, and will do so increasingly over time. This new activity (like setting interest on reserves) appeals to the Fed because it provides the Fed a means for avoiding the politically embarrassing recognition of capital losses that it would otherwise incur if it sold long-duration securities into the market as interest rates rise. Rather than sell securities from its portfolio to contract its balance sheet, the Fed engages in reverse repos, repeatedly lending those securities into the market until they mature, and thus avoiding sale while effectively reducing its balance sheet size.

Over the past several decades, repo has been an important alternative source of funding for lending in the U.S. economy, by both regulated banks and nonbank lenders. The massive expansion of the Fed's balance sheet over the past decade has withdrawn a large amount of low-risk collateral from the market, thereby making repo funding of loans and other financial transactions harder to arrange.

Furthermore, the Fed's imposition of the Supplementary Leverage Ratio (SLR) requirement has also reduced the supply of repo funding. This policy was announced in late 2012 and became effective in 2013. It includes the quantity of repos (and other items) in the regulatory measure of leverage. In effect, including repo in the SLR means that repo funding is more costly to banks that use it as a source of funding. Allahrakha, Cetina, and Munyan (2016) find that this new requirement significantly increased the cost of repo finance for regulated U.S. institutions.

---

[4]See the September 2014 FOMC statement, available at www.federalreserve .gov/monetarypolicy/policy-normalization.htm.

The Fed's dual role as regulator and repo counterparty raises important and disturbing questions about a new conflict of interest. As a repo counterparty, the Fed benefits financially from imposing the Supplementary Leverage Ratio, which reduces competitors' abilities to transact in repo. Might the Fed have taken into account its own financial benefits from being able to engage in reverse repo on more favorable terms when setting regulations for its competitors?

When the Fed began contemplating its reverse repo tool (as a means to avoid sales of securities), it was already cognizant that it might want to engage in a large number of such transactions to avoid the political consequences of suffering losses on securities sales and thereby being perceived as contributing to government deficits. I do not claim to know whether the Fed's new SLR rule was motivated in part by a desire to improve its own competitive position in the repo market, but the coincidence in timing between the SLR rule and the Fed's entry into the repo market is disturbing, and there is no question that the Fed suffers a conflict of interest from being both a repo counterparty and a repo regulator.

These conflicts of interest are nothing new. The Fed's regulatory power has long been a lightning rod for politicization, which has often placed the Fed at the center of highly contentious power struggles, often with disastrous consequences for both the economy and the Fed's independence. There are many examples, but the most obvious one has been the Federal Reserve Board's role as the arbiter of bank mergers in the last three decades. The Fed was given that role precisely because it could be counted upon to go along with an ill-conceived government policy, which designed the merger approval process to be a source of rent creation for merging mega banks in the 1990s, and ensured that those rents would be shared between merging banks and urban activist groups, which were given power to influence the merger approval process.

According to Fed officials with whom I have spoken, fears of possible congressional or administrative reprisals against the Fed that might have threatened its monetary policy actions were a major part of the explanation for the Fed's willing participation in this farce. As Stephen Haber and I show in our book, *Fragile by Design: The Political Origins of Banking Crises and Scarce Credit*, Fed bank merger hearings focused on the testimony of activist groups about whether the merging banks were "good citizens," a trait that was measured by the amount of loans and grants the merging banks had contractually promised to give the activists as the quid pro quo for their testimony. Those contractual promises exceeded $850 billion from 1992 to 2006. The Fed's role in overseeing these unseemly political bargains not only lessened the Fed as an institution, but also helped to precipitate the risky mortgage lending that was at the heart of the recent subprime crisis.

The destabilizing debasement of mortgage standards and prudential bank regulatory standards—which were part and parcel of the political deal the Fed oversaw through its merger powers—profoundly contributed to the financial crisis of 2007–09. If the Fed had not been given the authority to approve mergers and set prudential capital standards, and if merger approval and prudential standards had been based on clear rules enforced by an independent regulatory body, then the subprime crisis might have been avoided, or at least substantially mitigated.

Removing the Fed from its regulatory role would not in any way prevent the Fed from examining banks and pursuing all the related supervisory functions that are necessary to a central bank's lending function. Examination powers and some continued shared supervisory authority should be preserved. But there is no reason for the central bank to determine merger policy, whether banks should be permitted to act as real estate brokers, or other matters unrelated to central banking. And allocating that decisionmaking to the Fed does positive harm by putting the Fed in the line of fire with respect to highly charged political battles, which often results in inferior regulatory decisions and jeopardizes independent monetary policy.

Four reforms would avoid most of the problems that stem from combining the Fed's monetary policy authority with its other authorities and powers. First, the Fed should not hold securities other than U.S. Treasury securities in its portfolio (except briefly in the context of assistance approved under its emergency lending powers).[5] Second, rather than permit the Fed to set the interest rate paid on reserves, interest on reserves should be fixed at 10 basis points below the federal funds rate. Third, the Fed should be prohibited from competing with other intermediaries in the repo market. Fourth, the 2008 Treasury "blueprint" provided a thoughtful vision of how to

---

[5]See also Plosser (2017). For a discussion of how to make Fed lender-of-last-resort lending more credibly rule-based, see Calomiris et al. (2017).

reorganize the administration of financial regulation. Avoiding duplication of effort by consolidating regulatory functions (not only in banking, but also by creating a federal charter for insurance companies) is long overdue. This approach also would remove the Fed from the job of writing and enforcing regulations, which would free monetary policy from the conflicts that arise when it is combined with those tasks. The Fed would still participate in examinations and have full access to all information necessary to fulfill its role as a lender of last resort, as envisioned under the Treasury blueprint. At the very least, the Fed should be removed from merger decisions and oversight of highly politically sensitive matters, such as Community Reinvestment Act examinations.

Conclusion

Table 1 summarizes the three sets of reforms proposed in this testimony: internal governance reforms, policy process reforms, and limits on Fed asset holdings and activities. Together these proposed reforms would provide a new approach to governing monetary policy, which would result in better monetary policy decisionmaking than we have witnessed in the troubled first century of the Fed's history (through the channels of influence summarized in Figure 1). A central bank that operates as a more democratic institution, is able to benefit from more diverse thinking, is required to follow transparent and systematic policy actions in pursuit of achievable objectives, is held accountable for its actions, and is freed from myopic political pressures and less conflicted by nonmonetary policy mandates and tools would be much more likely to achieve the proper objectives of monetary policy.

There are practical political considerations that make 2018 an ideal time to push forward on needed reforms. A majority of Republicans have long favored many of the reforms listed here, but they have not been able to gain sufficient support from enough Democrats to enact policy reforms. Over the next two years, all seven Fed governors may be appointed by President Trump and confirmed by a Republican-majority Senate. It seems likely that many Democrats who have opposed Fed reforms in the past now may find it appealing to support measures that would make Fed policymaking more systematic, more receptive to diverse viewpoints, and more immune to political influences.

There is another reform relating to the Fed that should also be implemented, which does not fit into any of the categories discussed above. The Fed's surplus revenues should not be used as an off-budget means of funding the Consumer Financial Protection Bureau, other regulatory activities (including those undertaken by the Fed itself), highway expenditures, or other programs. Those practices undermine honest government budgetary accounting and discipline. If the U.S. government wants to be taken seriously as an instrument of monetary reform, it must also be willing to subject itself to honest accounting.

References

Allahrakha, M.; Cetina, J.; and Munyan, B. (2016) "Supplementary Leverage Ratio and Repo Supply." Working Paper, Office of Financial Research, U.S. Treasury.

Calomiris, C. W. (2006) "Alan Greenspan's Legacy: An Early Look: The Regulatory Record of the Greenspan Fed." *American Economic Association Papers and Proceedings* 96 (2): 170–73.

_____ (2013) "How to Promote Fed Independence: Perspectives from Political Economy and History." Working paper, Columbia University (March).

_____ (2014) "Diversity Now." *The International Economy* (Winter): 46–49, 83.

_____ (2017a) *Reforming Financial Regulation.* Manhattan Institute.

_____ (2017b) "Taming the Two 800 Pound Gorillas in the Room." In R. Bliss and D. Evanoff (eds.) *Public Policy and Financial Economics,* forthcoming.

_____ (2017c) "The Microeconomic Perils of Monetary Policy Experiments." *Cato Journal* 37 (1): 1–15.

Calomiris, C. W., and Haber, S. H. (2014) *Fragile By Design: The Political Origins of Banking Crises and Scarce Credit.* Princeton, N. J.: Princeton University Press.

Calomiris, C. W.; Holtz-Eakin, D.; Hubbard, R. G.; Meltzer, A. H.; and Scott, H. (2017) "Establishing Credible Rules for Fed Emergency Lending." *Journal of Financial Economic Policy* 9 (3): 260–67.

Eccles, M. (1935) "Testimony of Governor Marriner Eccles of the Federal Reserve Board on Banking." *Hearings before the Senate*

Committee on Banking and Currency, 74th Congress, 1st Session (March 4): 179 ff.

Faust, J., and Henderson, D. W. (2004) "Is Inflation Targeting Best-Practice Monetary Policy?" International Finance Discussion Paper No. 807 (May). Federal Reserve Board.

Friedman, M. (1948) "A Monetary and Fiscal Program for Economic Stability." *American Economic Review* 38 (3): 245–64.

_____ (1959) *A Program for Monetary Stability*. New York: Fordham University Press.

_____ (1968) "The Role of Monetary Policy." *American Economic Review* 58 (1): 1–17.

Kydland, F., and Prescott, E. (1977) "Rules Rather Than Discretion: The Inconsistency of Optimal Plans." *Journal of Political Economy* 85 (3): 473–91.

Laeven, L., and Valencia, F. (2013) "Systemic Banking Crises Database." *IMF Economic Review* 61 (2): 225–70.

Meltzer, A. H. (2003) *A History of the Federal Reserve, Volume 1*. Chicago: University of Chicago Press.

_____ (2009a) *A History of the Federal Reserve, Volume 2, Book 1*. Chicago: University of Chicago Press.

_____ (2009b) *A History of the Federal Reserve, Volume 2, Book 2*. Chicago: University of Chicago Press.

_____ (2014) "Current Lessons from the Past: How the Fed Repeats Its History." *Cato Journal* 34 (3): 519–39.

Orphanides, A. (2003a) "Monetary Policy Evaluation with Noisy Information." *Journal of Monetary Economics* 50 (3): 605–31.

_____ (2003b) "The Quest for Prosperity without Inflation." *Journal of Monetary Economics* 50 (3): 633–63.

Phelps, E. S. (1968) "Money-Wage Dynamics and Labor-Market Equilibrium." *Journal of Political Economy* 76 (4): 678–711.

_____ (1972) *Inflation Policy and Unemployment Theory*. London: Macmillan.

Plosser, C. I. (2017) "Why the Fed Should Own Only Treasuries." *Defining Ideas* (June 10). Available at www.hoover.org/research-/why-fed-should-only-own-treasuries.

Taylor, J. B. (1993) "Discretion versus Policy Rules in Practice." *Carnegie-Rochester Series on Public Policy* 39: 195–214.

_____ (2016) "Central Bank Models: Lessons from the Past and Ideas for the Future." Keynote presentation at the workshop,

"Central Bank Models: The Next Generation," Bank of Canada (November 17).

Thornton, D. L., and Wheelock, D. C. (2014) "Making Sense of Dissents: A History of FOMC Dissents." Federal Reserve Bank of St. Louis *Review* 96 (3): 213–27. Available at research.stlouis-fed.org/publications/review/2014/q3/thornton.pdf.

U.S. Department of the Treasury (2008) "The Department of the Treasury Blueprint for a Modernized Financial Regulatory Structure" (March). Available at www.treasury.gov/press-center/press-releases/Documents/Blueprint.pdf.

U.S. House of Representatives Committee on Financial Services (2016) "The Financial CHOICE Act: Creating Hope and Opportunity for Investors, Consumers, and Entrepreneurs: A Republican Proposal to Reform the Financial Regulatory System" (June 23). Available at financialservices.house.gov/uploadedfiles-/financial_choice_act_comprehensive_outline.pdf.

Wieland, V.; Afanasyeva, E.; Kuete, M.; and Yoom, J. (2016) "New Methods for Macro-Financial Model Comparison and Policy Analysis." In J. B. Taylor and H. Uhlig (eds.) *Handbook of Macroeconomics, Volume 2*. Amsterdam: Elsevier.

14

IMPROVING MONETARY POLICY BY ADOPTING A SIMPLE RULE

Athanasios Orphanides

Monetary theory as well as monetary practice over the past few decades suggest that economic outcomes in our economy are better when monetary policy is systematic and respects the importance of maintaining price stability.[1] Despite broad agreement of the benefits of systematic policy, the Fed continues to set policy on a meeting-by-meeting discretionary basis. This article examines how policy can be improved by replacing discretion with a transparent process of selecting and periodically adapting a simple policy rule.

The Case for a Simple Rule

The Fed's decision to adopt a precise quantitative definition of price stability in January 2012 was an important step in the right direction. With the adoption of an inflation target—2 percent, measured by the PCE index—in its *Statement on Longer-Run Goals and Monetary Policy Strategy* (Federal Reserve Board 2012), the Fed can facilitate well-anchored inflation expectations in line with price stability and can be held accountable over time more easily.

Athanasios Orphanides is Professor of the Practice of Global Economics and Management at the MIT Sloan School of Management and a member of the Shadow Open Market Committee (SOMC). This article is reprinted from the *Cato Journal*, Vol. 38, No. 1 (Winter 2018). It is a revised version of the author's presentation at the May 5, 2017 meeting of the SOMC (Orphanides 2017).

[1] See Taylor and Williams (2011) for a comprehensive review of the literature on policy rules.

However additional progress is required. The Fed's current policy framework places too much emphasis on meeting-by-meeting discretion and is not sufficiently systematic to be in line with best policy practice. This is particularly problematic because of the Fed's so-called dual mandate—to achieve simultaneously maximum employment and price stability.

It is well known that the mandate of the Federal Reserve can create difficulties for the institution when tightening policy is required to keep inflation at bay. The combination of meeting-by-meeting discretion and multiple conflicting goals makes the Fed vulnerable to all the pitfalls that monetary theory and history teach us are associated with the absence of systematic policy. This can be corrected if the Fed adopts and communicates a simple policy rule that it can then use as a guide for setting monetary policy. Adopting an appropriate simple rule would allow the Fed to respond in a countercyclical fashion to economic developments while protecting price stability over time.[2]

Countering Key Arguments against Rules

Unfortunately, the Fed has not shown the willingness to move in that direction and continues to prefer to operate with meeting-by-meeting discretion. In recent speeches, Fed Chair Yellen and Vice Chair Fischer have presented a case *against* monetary rules (Fischer 2017a, 2017b; Yellen 2017). It is instructive to examine the key arguments presented against rules and provide counterarguments to make progress in this policy debate.

Perhaps the most common argument against monetary rules is that discretion allows greater flexibility to take into account uncertainty. It is certainly important to acknowledge uncertainty. Policymakers face numerous dimensions of uncertainty. Our understanding of how the macro economy works is incomplete. Estimated macroeconomic models are imperfect, and often competing models with quite different policy implications may be equally plausible. Key concepts that would have been very useful for policy, if they could be measured accurately in real-time (e.g., the natural rate of interest), are in fact unknown.

---

[2] See Orphanides (2015) for a more detailed exposition.

The presence of uncertainty, however, cannot serve as a valid argument for defending discretionary policy. Indeed, uncertainty raises the potential costs of discretion as it makes it harder to understand how large a policy deviation may be from what would have been the desirable systematic response to a shock.

The reasons why systematic policy is preferable to discretion are no less important under uncertainty. Consider dynamic inconsistency, one of the major policy problems associated with discretionary policy that the adoption of a rule solves. When policy does not follow a rule, households and businesses cannot trust that the policymaker will follow through with any policy that was communicated in the past, even if nothing has changed in the economy. Under discretion, the policymaker has the incentive to deviate from earlier plans and households and businesses must adapt their behavior to protect against these future discretionary decisions. Dynamic inconsistency makes everyone worse off when policy is set under discretion. Dynamic inconsistency is as much a feature of the macroeconomic policy problem under uncertainty about the structure of the economy as it is when, for simplicity, we assume this uncertainty away.

Consider the issues associated with the formation of expectations, most importantly about inflation. A major advantage of monetary rules over discretion is that when the Fed is systematic and follows policy based on a rule, financial market participants, households, and businesses can better understand what the Fed is doing and take that into account in forming expectations. Again, this is the case regardless of whether we assume perfect knowledge about the structure of the economy or acknowledge imperfect knowledge. Systematic policy is even more important when the economy is buffeted by uncertain and potentially destabilizing shocks: when policy follows a well-designed rule, inflation expectations can remain well-anchored, which in turn helps maintain stability both in prices and in the real economy.

Uncertainty is also invoked in another way that is important to address and often used as an excuse to promote discretionary policy. It is *correctly* noted by advocates of discretionary policy that since our knowledge about the structure of the economy is incomplete and our understanding of this structure evolves over time, no simple fixed and immutable monetary rule can possibly be best at all times. Hence, it is argued, it is best for policy to remain discretionary.

The Taylor rule can be used as an example. Some versions of the Taylor rule state that policy should be set with the implicit assumption that the natural rate of interest is constant. The classic Taylor rule, for example, has embedded in it the assumption that the natural rate of interest equals 2 percent. If policy is set in accordance with this version of the Taylor rule and the wrong assessment of the natural rate of interest, policy would be systematically too easy or too tight, leading to inferior economic outcomes. Thus, it is argued, discretion is better.

This argument, however, is not right. What it suggests is that care is needed in selecting a policy rule that properly accounts for uncertainty, including about the natural rate of interest. Furthermore, it suggests that a simple policy rule should not always be seen as fixed and immutable. Fixed and immutable rules can indeed be problematic if they cannot be adapted as our understanding of the economy evolves.[3]

As our knowledge improves, we must reevaluate the simple rules-of-thumb embedded in our models and embrace modifications suggested by new analysis. This ought to be the case both for those who argue in favor of formulating policy in a systematic manner and for those who prefer meeting-by-meeting discretion.

For this reason, it is important to describe more precisely a process for selecting a rule that ensures that policy is systematic. To account for our evolving understanding of the economy, the Fed could adopt a framework that relies on a simple policy rule that is subject to periodic reviews and adaptation.

Selecting a Robust Rule

The Fed could select a rule following a rigorous evaluation process that ensures robustness, taking into account all the dimensions of

---

[3]Adaptation is required of virtually any rule to avoid systematic errors. This includes interest rate rules and rules regulating the growth rate of the money supply. For example, k-percent money-growth rules require estimates of trend velocity and potential output growth to deliver a 2 percent inflation goal. With no drift in velocity a k-percent rule would suggest 4 percent money growth if potential output growth is believed to be 2 percent but only 3 percent money growth if potential output growth is believed to be 1 percent.

uncertainty that can be incorporated into macroeconometric policy evaluation. The evaluation process should include uncertainty about natural rates, about the structure of the economy, about expectations formation, and so forth.

The Fed could communicate its selected rule, as part of an expanded and more detailed *Statement on Longer-Run Goals and Monetary Policy Strategy*. Adding the Fed's monetary rule to this statement would complete it by actually providing the Fed's policy strategy, which is absent from the current meeting-by-meeting discretionary framework.

It is important to acknowledge that setting policy following a monetary rule is a living process that requires periodic review and adaptation. This would allow the Fed the flexibility to account for and adapt to the evolving understanding of the economy.

The Fed could publish an evaluation of its rule on an annual basis and adapt its rule, if needed. Updates to the Fed's rule could be presented with the annual revision of the *Statement on Longer-Run Goals and Monetary Policy Strategy* that the Fed has published each January since 2012.

Replacing the meeting-by-meeting discretion with a transparent process of selecting and periodically adapting a simple and robust policy rule would ensure that monetary policy is systematic and contributes to social welfare over time while also retaining the flexibility to account for the evolution of the economic environment and of our knowledge. To ensure transparency and accountability, the Fed should communicate its preferred rule with sufficient detail so that an outside observer could track policy using incoming information and data without additional input from the Fed. The detail required would depend on the selected rule. For example, if the rule's implementation required use of unobserved concepts that evolve over time, such as the natural rate of interest, the methodology for arriving at the pertinent estimates should also be specified in advance to make the rule meaningful and avoid discretion.

The framework just described outlines how the Fed could adopt a monetary rule and maintain systematic policy in a manner that addresses the key concerns advanced when a case against monetary rules is argued. It may be noted that congressional legislation could guide the Fed in this direction. For example, the Federal Oversight Reform and Modernization (FORM) Act that was introduced in

Congress and passed by the House in 2015, includes a provision for a Directive Policy Rule which is developed by the FOMC to provide the basis for the Open Market Operations Directive.

Indeed, as the FORM Act implies, the Fed is best placed to select the simple rule that should guide its systematic monetary policy. However, legislation is not necessary for the Fed to adopt a simple rule. The Fed could embrace this improvement on its own, within its current mandate. No change in the Federal Reserve Act is needed for the Fed to include a simple policy rule in its annual *Statement on Longer-Run Goals and Monetary Policy Strategy*. The improvement could be seen as an added step, building on the improvement that started with the adoption of an explicit inflation target in 2012, which did not require a change in the Federal Reserve Act.

Conclusion

I will close by recounting a recent exchange I had with Vice Chair Fischer on this matter. Professor Stanley Fischer, who was one of my teachers at MIT, has been an active participant in the rules versus discretion debate for many decades. In the early 1970s, together with Phillip Cooper, he was among the first to do econometric policy evaluation of monetary rules in competing models such as the FRB-MIT-Penn Model and the St Louis Monetarist model, which were used at the time for policy analysis.[4] In 1990, he published an influential review of the literature, presenting the rules versus discretion debate that was then "at least 150 years old" (Fischer 1990: 1181). At that time, the research appeared inconclusive and Fischer suggested that a new generation of models needed to be developed. However, in reflecting about what could guide monetary policy in the meantime, he also suggested that "it might

---

[4]These contributions include Cooper and Fischer (1972a, 1972b, 1974) and Fischer and Cooper (1973). The research program in these papers involved comparative evaluations of active countercyclical monetary rules that were more elaborate than many of the simple Taylor-type rules that have been advocated more recently.

be possible to find simple feedback rules that perform well in a variety of models, and to recommend them as a basis for monetary policy" (p. 1169).

Last February, Vice Chair Fischer delivered a speech arguing in favor of discretion over monetary rules (Fischer 2017a). For the title, he used part of a famous quote by Paul Samuelson highlighting the value of judgement and models for policy analysis. Samuelson said, "I'd rather have Bob Solow than an econometric model, but I'd rather have Bob Solow with an econometric model than without one." While I fully subscribe both to the use of models and to the value of judgment, I thought that the case presented against rules was incomplete. I wrote an email to the vice chair with the subject line: "I'd rather have Bob Solow with a model and a rule (following a careful evaluation process)" and went on to describe how the Fed could go about selecting a policy rule, relying on the superb research of Fed system staff.

The vice chair responded with a subsequent speech in March (Fischer 2017b). While acknowledging how a careful evaluation process could proceed, he appeared to remain unconvinced and noted, "However, I tend to agree with John Taylor and my Fed colleague John Williams when they write that 'the search for better and more robust policy rules is never done.'"[5]

Once again, I find myself in agreement with the quote but not with the suggested conclusion. It is indeed true that the search for better rules is never done. It is also true that our knowledge will always remain imperfect. But is this sufficient to justify the Fed's emphasis on meeting-by-meeting discretion? Perhaps we should acknowledge our imperfect knowledge and promote systematic policy with a robust rule that reflects our current state of knowledge. We could also accommodate potential amendments by embracing a transparent process of periodically adapting the simple and robust policy rule selected to guide monetary policy.[6]

---

[5]The quote is from the conclusion of Taylor and Williams (2011).
[6]Indeed, such a process would heed the advice: "Prudence . . . suggests that the rule include procedures for its own amendment" (Fischer 1990: 1169).

References

Cooper, P. J., and Fischer, S. (1972a) "Simulations of Monetary Rules in the FRB-MIT-Penn Model." *Journal of Money, Credit, and Banking* 4 (2): 384–96.

_____ (1972b) "Stochastic Simulation of Monetary Rules in Two Macroeconomic Models." *Journal of the American Statistical Association* 67 (340): 750–60.

_____ (1974) "Monetary and Fiscal Policy in the Fully Stochastic St. Louis Econometric Model." *Journal of Money, Credit, and Banking* 6 (1): 1–22.

Federal Reserve Board (2012) "Federal Reserve Issues FOMC Statement of Longer-Run Goals and Policy Strategy." Press Release (January 25).

Fischer, S. (1990) "Rules versus Discretion in Monetary Policy." In B. M. Friedman and F. Hahn (eds.) *Handbook of Monetary Economics*, Vol. 2, 1155–84. Amsterdam: North-Holland.

_____ (2017a) " I'd Rather Have Bob Solow Than an Econometric Model, But . . . ." Remarks at the Warwick Economics Summit, Coventry, U.K. (February 11).

_____ (2017b) "Monetary Policy: By Rule, By Committee, or By Both?" Remarks at the 2017 U.S. Monetary Policy Forum, New York (March 3).

Fischer, S., and Cooper, P. J. (1973) "Stabilization Policy and Lags." *Journal of Political Economy* 81 (4): 847–77.

Orphanides, A. (2015) "Fear of Liftoff: Uncertainty, Rules, and Discretion in Monetary Policy Normalization." Federal Reserve Bank of St Louis *Review* 97 (3): 173–96.

_____ (2017) "The Case Against the Case Against Monetary Rules." Position paper for the May 7, 2017 meeting of the Shadow Open Market Committee.

Taylor, J. B., and Williams, J. C. (2011) "Simple and Robust Rules for Monetary Policy." In B. M. Friedman and M. Woodford (eds.) *Handbook of Monetary Economics*, Vol. 3B, 829–60. Amsterdam: North-Holland.

Yellen, J. (2017) "The Economic Outlook and the Conduct of Monetary Policy." Remarks at the Stanford Institute for Economic Policy Research, Stanford (January 19).

15

NUDGING THE FED TOWARD A RULES-BASED POLICY REGIME
Scott Sumner

There is a great deal of academic research suggesting that monetary policy should use a rules-based approach (e.g., Kydland and Prescott 1977, McCallum 1985, Plosser 2014). However, Fed officials have generally been opposed to any sort of rigid policy rule.

There are two types of policy rules, both of which the Fed finds problematic. One involves a commitment to target a macroeconomic variable such as inflation, or nominal GDP, at a specified rate of growth. Today many central banks aim for approximately 2 percent inflation, although such rules are generally regarded as being flexible—with some weight also being given to output and/or employment stability. Even the European Central Bank, which has a simple inflation mandate, must also ensure that the eurozone monetary regime remains stable and viable.

The Fed has a dual mandate for stable prices and high employment, which it interprets as 2 percent inflation and unemployment close to the natural rate. However, there is no clear indication of the weights assigned to each variable, and hence current policy cannot be viewed as a fully rules-based monetary regime. If both inflation and unemployment are above target, the Fed has discretion as to which problem deserves more attention.

Scott Sumner is the Ralph G. Hawtrey Chair of Monetary Policy at the Mercatus Center at George Mason University. He is also a Professor of Economics at Bentley University and Research Fellow at the Independent Institute. This article is reprinted from the *Cato Journal*, Vol. 36, No. 2 (Spring/Summer 2016).

In other cases, the term "policy rule" refers to an instrument rule, such as the famous Taylor rule, which would require that the Fed target the nominal fed funds rate (see Taylor 1993). Key Fed officials also oppose instrument rules, which they suggest do not provide adequate flexibility. They worry that if the natural rate of interest and/or the natural rate of unemployment change, then the Taylor rule could lead to a suboptimal policy. In principle, the rule can adapt to changes in these parameters, but it may be very difficult to estimate the natural rate of either unemployment or the real interest rate.

Elsewhere, I have argued that the Fed's discretionary approach did very poorly during the Great Recession and that the Fed should adopt level targeting of nominal GDP (Sumner 2012). I have also suggested that policymakers should target the market forecast of future nominal GDP, or at least the Fed's internal forecast, if a market forecast is not available (Sumner 2015).[1] In this article, I will simply assume that a nominal GDP-level target is the best option; however, all of the arguments presented here could equally be applied to a different policy target, such as one for 2 percent inflation.

Given the Fed's opposition to a rigid policy rule, it's worth asking whether the Fed can be "nudged" in the direction of a policy rule, through some more modest and less controversial policy reforms. Here I'll suggest three such reforms: first, asking the Fed to more clearly define the stance of monetary policy; second, asking the Fed to more clearly evaluate past policy decisions; and third, asking the Fed to define the outer limits of acceptable deviation in aggregate demand from the target path. I will also argue that if the Fed starts down this road, it will likely lead to the eventual adoption of nominal GDP-level targeting.

What Do We Mean by the "Stance" of Monetary Policy, and Why Does It Matter?

Economists frequently refer to monetary policy using terms such as "expansionary" or "contractionary," "easy" or "tight," and "accommodative" or "restrictive." Those terms are said to refer to the

---

[1]Svensson (2003) discusses targeting the Fed's internal forecast—that is, setting the policy instrument at a level expected to lead to on-target outcomes, according to the central bank's internal model.

"stance" of monetary policy. Given their frequent use, one might assume that they have a clear meaning, at least to professional economists. Unfortunately, that is not the case. References to the stance of monetary policy are often vague and misleading, and frequently hinder clear thinking about the role of monetary policy in the business cycle. Given that the Fed discusses its policy stance while communicating with the public, it is essential that policymakers clearly define what these terms mean. We need some metric for evaluating the stance of monetary policy.

I am not the first economist to express frustration with the way pundits characterize real-world monetary policy stances. Milton Friedman made a similar complaint in 1997:

> Low interest rates are generally a sign that money has been tight, as in Japan; high interest rates, that money has been easy. . . . After the U.S. experience during the Great Depression, and after inflation and rising interest rates in the 1970s and disinflation and falling interest rates in the 1980s, I thought the fallacy of identifying tight money with high interest rates and easy money with low interest rates was dead. Apparently, old fallacies never die [Friedman 1997].

Friedman thought monetary policy in Japan was quite contractionary during the 1990s, despite near-zero interest rates and quantitative easing (QE). Of course, in 1963, Friedman and Schwartz famously argued that contractionary monetary policy had caused the Great Depression. And, as with Japan, this occurred despite near-zero interest rates and rapid growth in the monetary base.[2]

This raises an interesting question: If Friedman were alive today, would he have regarded Fed policy during 2008 and 2009 as expansionary or contractionary? Indeed, is it possible that the recession of 2008 was caused by tight money? I won't definitively answer that question here. Rather, I will show that this hypothesis should not be summarily rejected merely because most economists saw monetary policy during 2008 and 2009 as being "obviously" highly expansionary.

---

[2]In the United States, the monetary base expanded from $6,978 million in December 1929 to $23,738 million in December 1941.

The Problem of Identifying the Stance of Monetary Policy

Joan Robinson (1938) argued that easy money could not have caused the German hyperinflation, because interest rates were not low. Modern economists might be inclined to smile at this example of "old Keynesian" thinking, perhaps recalling the more than billion-fold increase in the German monetary base between 1920 and 1923, when currency was being printed at a furious pace. On the other hand, modern economists are not supposed to rely on changes in the monetary base as an indicator of the stance of monetary policy. So is that really a good reason to dismiss Robinson's claim (which applied to the first part of the hyperinflation)?

For instance, in the United States, the monetary base had been growing at about 5 percent a year in the period leading up to August 2007. Then, over the next nine months, growth in the base came to a sudden halt. And yet you would be hard pressed to find many economists who regarded this sudden change in the growth rate of the monetary base as a contractionary move by the Fed. The reason is obvious: interest rates were cut repeatedly during this nine-month stretch, from 5.25 percent all the way down to 2 percent. Contemporaneous discussion of monetary policy during 2007–08 almost invariably referred to the Fed's actions as expansionary or "easy money." This characterization implicitly rejected the monetary base as a useful indicator, and (presumably) relied instead upon changes in interest rates.

A more sophisticated argument against Joan Robinson's claim would be that nominal interest rates don't matter, and that real interest rates are the proper measure of the stance of monetary policy. Certainly, real interest rates would be a superior policy indicator during a period of hyperinflation. But once again it seems highly unlikely that this is the variable that economists actually focus on—or *should* focus on. Between early July and early December 2008, the real interest rate on five-year inflation indexed Treasury bonds rose from less than 0.6 percent to more than 4 percent, one of the sharpest increases ever recorded in such a short period of time. If economists regarded real interest rates as the proper indicator of the stance of monetary policy, then one might have expected almost universal outrage about the Fed's "highly contractionary" policy shift during a period of financial turmoil and deepening recession. Yet it is difficult to find any criticism of this sort during the second half of 2008.

On the contrary, most commentators claimed that monetary policy was expansionary.[3]

We have already seen that nominal interest rates might be highly misleading due to the effects of inflation. But, in fact, the same sort of criticism can be lodged against real interest rates, which reflect other macroeconomic variables, such as expected real GDP growth. A real interest rate of 2 percent during a period of rapid economic growth certainly represents a different monetary policy stance from a 2 percent real interest rate during a deep depression. So it is not at all clear that real interest rates are actually a good indicator of policy.

Milton Friedman is not the only economist to criticize the way members of his profession describe the stance of monetary policy. Other highly regarded economists, in many cases those closer to the (new Keynesian) mainstream, have expressed similar concerns. Take Frederic Mishkin, who served on the Federal Reserve Board, and wrote the number one monetary economics textbook in the United States (Mishkin 2007). Toward the end of the book he listed several important points about monetary policy. Here are the first three as they appeared back in 2008:

1. It is dangerous always to associate the easing or the tightening of monetary policy with a fall or a rise in short-term nominal interest rates.
2. Other asset prices besides those on short-term debt instruments contain important information about the stance of monetary policy because they are important elements in various monetary policy transmission mechanisms.
3. Monetary policy can be highly effective in reviving a weak economy even if short-term rates are already near zero [Mishkin 2007: 606–7].

One of the most striking features of these three key lessons for monetary policy is how incompatible they seem with the consensus view of events circa 2008 and 2009. Policy was almost universally viewed as being expansionary precisely because the Fed cut interest rates sharply to near-zero levels. Yet almost all other asset markets were signaling a highly contractionary monetary policy. For instance, between July and December 2008, commodity prices fell roughly by

---

[3]Robert Hetzel (2009, 2012) is one of the few Fed officials to consider the possibility that excessively tight money might have contributed to the Great Recession.

half, stock prices crashed, the dollar appreciated 15 percent in trade-weighted terms, the decline in real estate prices spread from the subprime states to areas of the country that had not experienced a bubble, and inflation expectations in the Treasury Inflation-Protected Securities (TIPS) markets fell into negative territory. And as we've already seen, real interest rates rose sharply. Virtually every asset market was signaling extremely tight monetary policy; yet the pundits ignored those asset markets and focused on the only thing that suggested easy money—falling *nominal* interest rates. That's the very same indicator that led Joan Robinson to insist that money couldn't have been easy during the German hyperinflation.

It is also interesting to note that, in 2008 and 2009, most economists seem to have thought monetary policy was not particularly effective when short-term interest rates are near zero. After all, few blamed the Fed for allowing a sharp drop in aggregate demand. This view conflicts with Mishkin's third key point, and it raises the question of whether the profession is in sync with the material taught in the most popular monetary economics textbooks.

Ben Bernanke is, of course, another highly respected mainstream economist, and he was head of the Federal Reserve Board in 2008 and 2009. It is therefore interesting to examine how he thinks about the stance of monetary policy. The following comes from a speech given by Bernanke at a dinner honoring Milton Friedman on his 90th birthday:

> The only aspect of Friedman's 1970 framework that does not fit entirely with the current conventional wisdom is the monetarists' use of money growth as the primary indicator or measure of the stance of monetary policy. . . .
>
> The imperfect reliability of money growth as an indicator of monetary policy is unfortunate, because we don't really have anything satisfactory to replace it. As emphasized by Friedman (in his eleventh proposition) and by Allan Meltzer, nominal interest rates are not good indicators of the stance of policy, as a high nominal interest rate can indicate either monetary tightness or ease, depending on the state of inflation expectations. Indeed, confusing low nominal interest rates with monetary ease was the source of major problems in the 1930s, and it has perhaps been a problem in Japan in recent years as well. The real short-term interest rate,

another candidate measure of policy stance, is also imperfect, because it mixes monetary and real influences, such as the rate of productivity growth. . . .

Ultimately, it appears, one can check to see if an economy has a stable monetary background only by looking at macroeconomic indicators such as nominal GDP growth and inflation [Bernanke 2003].

There's a great deal to be said for using nominal GDP growth and inflation as indicators of the stance of monetary policy. However, this leads to the same puzzle that we've discovered with other possible indicators: it doesn't seem to match the way real world economists think about monetary policy. In the five years after mid-2008, nominal GDP growth was slower than during any comparable period since the early 1930s. Indeed, even an average of nominal GDP growth and inflation was the slowest since the early 1930s. And yet you'd be hard pressed to find many economists who thought monetary policy was at its tightest since the Herbert Hoover administration. Rather, most economists (including Ben Bernanke) regarded policy as being quite easy.

We've seen that Friedman, Mishkin, and Bernanke were all somewhat critical of the orthodox view that low interest rates mean easy money. Interestingly, however, these three distinguished economists did not seem to agree on which alternative was better. Friedman tended to favor broad monetary aggregates such as M2. Mishkin cited asset prices, while Bernanke pointed to nominal GDP growth and inflation. None favored using the monetary base. In the quotation above, Bernanke alludes to the fact that, in the early 1980s, most economists became skeptical of the reliability of monetary aggregates, at least in part because the velocity of money was shown to be unstable. In my view, the options mentioned by Mishkin and Bernanke both have appeal. But before giving them further consideration, let's dig a little deeper into *why* interest rates and the monetary base make for such unreliable indicators of the stance of monetary policy.

Why Interest Rates and the Monetary Base Are Particularly Unreliable

Recall Milton Friedman's words, as cited earlier in this article: "[L]ow interest rates are generally a sign that money *has been* tight" (emphasis added). Friedman is not just claiming that interest rates are unreliable; he is saying they are a perverse indicator—sending precisely the wrong signal. And yet, quite clearly, that cannot always be the case; economists would surely not have come to the conclusion that low interest rates represent easy money without at least some empirical justification.

So what is the short- and long-run impact of monetary policy on nominal interest rates? A one-time increase in the monetary base tends to reduce nominal interest rates in the short run (the liquidity effect), and then bring interest rates back to the original level in the long run (income and price-level effects.) Indeed, an increase in the growth rate of the money supply may well leave nominal interest rates higher in the long run as people expect inflation—something economists refer to as the Fisher effect. This is, presumably, what Friedman had in mind when he suggested that low rates are a sign that money *has been* tight.

Of course, economists are aware of these short- and long-run effects. The mistake comes in mistakenly equating short run with "right now" and long run with "sometime in the future." But that is not what short and long run mean at all. In fact, at any given moment in time, the condition of the economy reflects the long-run effects of policies adopted earlier—that may be obvious when you think about it, but it is easy to overlook when evaluating current events.

As a result, while we can expect money market interest rates—especially short-term ones—to immediately fall when the Fed injects money into the economy, it does not follow that the Fed *must have* injected money simply because interest rates were seen to fall. For example, let's suppose that the Fed were to adopt a highly expansionary monetary policy, which reduced interest rates in the short run but led to higher inflation and economic growth over the medium to long term. In that case, after a short lag, the policy might be expected to raise interest rates. It would look like the Fed had switched from an easy to a tight money policy, but in fact we would simply be observing the delayed effect of the same easy money policy.

Furthermore, when considering even short-run changes in interest rates, it is important to distinguish between a reduction in interest rates caused by an increase in the monetary base, and a reduction in interest rates resulting from a decrease in money demand.

Consider again the period late 2007 to early 2008. During this nine-month stretch, the Fed aggressively cut its fed funds target from

5.25 percent to 2 percent. An economist explaining this policy to a class of economics students would naturally tend to treat these interest rate reductions as active Fed policy, increasing the money supply relative to a stable money demand. This is the traditional way of illustrating the liquidity effect. It just so happens, however, that the monetary base *did not* actually increase during this nine-month period. Instead, money demand decreased—and that is what reduced equilibrium short-term interest rates. The Fed adjusted its fed funds target just enough to keep the monetary base roughly constant. To put this somewhat differently, using the language of the equation of exchange, the Great Recession was not triggered by a fall in velocity; indeed, base velocity increased during the nine-month period in question. Instead, the recession was triggered by a sudden stop in the expansion of the monetary base.

The liquidity effect links short-term interest rates and the monetary base. Because the liquidity effect is often the most visible manifestation of monetary policy, it receives the lion's share of attention in any discussion of monetary policy, especially those focusing on current events. This leads to a sort of dual criteria for easy money: low interest rates *and* a rapidly expanding monetary base. At first glance, this dual criteria might seem to overcome the problem discussed above, in which rates fall not because of an increase in the monetary base, but rather because of a drop in money demand. Unfortunately, even this dual criteria is not reliable. To see why, let's consider the Great Depression.

During the 1930s, the demand for base money soared. This increased demand reflected two primary factors: ultra-low interest rates and financial market instability. When there is a near-zero opportunity cost of holding cash and bank reserves, and when alternative assets are viewed as increasingly risky and illiquid, the demand for base money tends to rise sharply. The Fed did increase the monetary base rapidly during the 1930s, but not fast enough to meet the rising demand for base money. Despite the Fed's efforts, monetary policy was tight and, as a result, prices and nominal GDP fell sharply. This episode suggests that the unreliability of low interest rates as an indicator of monetary policy tends to become entangled with the unreliability of the monetary base as an indicator of monetary policy precisely during those periods when interest rates are extremely low.

There is, however, one important difference between nominal interest rates and the monetary base: nominal interest rates tend to be an unreliable indicator of the stance of monetary policy during both deflation *and* hyperinflation. During deflation, nominal interest rates tend to fall close to zero, making monetary policy look expansionary at a time when it is actually far too contractionary to prevent deflation. During hyperinflation, meanwhile, nominal interest rates are also highly unreliable due to the Fisher effect.

In contrast, the monetary base offers a relatively reliable policy indicator during periods of hyperinflation, since a sustained period of hyperinflation is almost always accompanied by rapid growth in the monetary base. But the base is not a reliable indicator of the stance of monetary policy during periods of falling prices and/or output. When nominal GDP declines, interest rates fall close to zero. In that environment, the demand for base money increases very sharply, as a share of GDP. In most cases, central banks will at least partially accommodate this demand, carrying out aggressive quantitative easing (i.e., large-scale asset purchases) in an effort to increase the monetary base rapidly to prevent a more severe depression. We saw this in the United States during the 1930s, in Japan during the early 2000s, and in the United States after 2008. In each case, the monetary base rose rapidly after interest rates fell close to zero, but in none of these cases did that mean that money was easy.

To summarize, when inflation rates are extremely high, base money provides a more reliable indicator of the stance of monetary policy than nominal interest rates. In contrast, when there is a drop in nominal GDP, both nominal interest rates and the monetary base become highly unreliable indicators of the stance of monetary policy. Unfortunately, these currently fashionable indicators of monetary policy—nominal interest rates and quantitative easing—tend to become less and less reliable at the extremes, which is, of course, precisely when a reliable indicator is most desperately needed. This perverse state of affairs mirrors the well-known problem with interest-rate targeting: it becomes ineffective at the zero bound, which is exactly when monetary stimulus is most needed.

Economists Need a Better Indicator of the Stance of Monetary Policy

In this article, I have referred many times to events that took place during the Great Recession. One implication of my hypothesis is that monetary policy might have been too contractionary during this period. However, that is not my primary focus here. Instead, my focus is on the need for clearer thinking about the stance of monetary policy. It may or may not be the case that monetary policy was too contractionary during 2008. But, either way, the economics profession should not have summarily dismissed this possibility merely on the basis of the claim that monetary policy was "obviously" highly expansionary.

So how should economists think about the stance of monetary policy? In a sense, all judgments about easy and tight money are *relative*. Thus one appealing criterion would be to judge the stance of monetary policy relative to the policy goal, say inflation or nominal GDP growth—as Ben Bernanke has suggested. On the other hand, it would also be useful to be able to talk about the stance of monetary policy in real time. Unfortunately, inflation is measured with a long data lag, while the lag for nominal GDP growth is even longer. What's more, when we are thinking about the proper stance of monetary policy, what we really care about is inflation and nominal GDP growth going forward. All this suggests we might want to look at asset price indicators that are available in real time—as Frederic Mishkin has recommended.

I see merit in the proposals of both Mishkin and Bernanke. It is useful to think about the stance of policy relative to policy goals such as inflation and nominal GDP growth. It is also useful to have the sort of real-time policy indicators that the asset markets might be able to provide. But is there any way of bringing these two goals together?

One possibility is that the Federal Reserve could create, and subsidize trading in, a highly liquid nominal GDP futures market. Previous studies have shown that artificial prediction markets can be created at relatively low cost—say, less than one million dollars (see Hanson 2006; Hanson, Oprea, and Porter 2006). Given the huge costs associated with macroeconomic policy errors, it should not be difficult to justify the expense involved in creating a macroeconomic futures market.

Of course, if the Fed wanted to stick with an inflation target, or its dual mandate approach, it could create futures markets in inflation, real GDP, and unemployment. Yet there are powerful arguments in favor of using nominal GDP growth as an indicator of monetary policy. Recall that monetary policy directly affects aggregate demand, which then impacts prices and output. In contrast, changes in the price level can reflect monetary factors (aggregate demand), or nonmonetary factors (supply shocks). Moreover, inflation and nominal GDP growth are likely to give different readings during periods dominated by supply shocks. An adverse supply shock will tend to raise prices and reduce output—as a result, the impact on the price level is often much more pronounced than the impact on nominal GDP. In contrast, expansionary monetary policy raises both prices and output, with nominal GDP rising even faster than inflation. Here, nominal GDP growth gives a clearer reading of the sort of demand shocks that might be generated by changes in monetary policy.

Naturally, I don't expect all economists to agree with my claim that nominal GDP futures are the most useful indicator of the stance of monetary policy. But surely we can agree that there are serious problems with relying on nominal interest rates and/or the monetary base. Let's not forget that most economists would have been very dismissive of the idea that interest rates were a useful indicator during the German hyperinflation. And as recently as 2007, most economists would have rejected the notion that the monetary base was a useful indicator of the stance of monetary policy. So even if nominal GDP futures are not the optimal indicator, we can do much better than relying on interest rates and monetary base growth, which have dominated discussion of the stance of monetary policy over the past decade.

A recent study from the Federal Reserve Bank of San Francisco made me much more optimistic about the prospects for rethinking the stance of monetary policy. Its author, Vasco Curdia (2015) makes the following observation:

> This *Economic Letter* analyzes the recent behavior of the natural rate using an empirical macroeconomic model. The results suggest that the natural rate is currently very low by historical standards. Because of this, monetary conditions remain relatively tight despite the near-zero federal funds rate, which in turn is keeping economic activity below potential and inflation below target.

Curdia also shows that the natural rate of interest has been well below zero since 2008, suggesting that the fed funds target of 2 percent during April to October 2008 was actually an extremely contractionary monetary policy.

Of course, measuring the stance of monetary policy is not exactly the same as setting a policy target. But there may be an underlying linkage. Consider Bernanke's suggestion that nominal GDP growth or inflation were the best indicators of the stance of monetary policy. It seems plausible that this suggestion was at least partly motivated by the assumption that nominal GDP growth and inflation are plausible monetary policy targets, and that defining the stance this way would provide a metric for determining whether policy was too expansionary or too contractionary. If the Fed began defining "easy money" as expected nominal GDP growth exceeding 4 percent, and "tight money" as expected nominal GDP growth of less than 4 percent, then it's pretty clear that the public would begin to see 4 percent nominal GDP growth as a sort of benchmark for stable monetary policy.

In his recent memoir, Bernanke (2015) made a similar argument regarding inflation targeting. There was initial resistance within the Fed to an explicit inflation target. So instead, Bernanke set up a system where each Federal Open Market Committee (FOMC) member provided a long-range forecast of inflation (three years out) assuming "appropriate" monetary policy. Bernanke believed that markets would infer that those long-run forecasts represented each FOMC member's view as to the appropriate inflation rate. A few years later, Bernanke succeeded in getting the FOMC to agree on an explicit 2 percent inflation objective, which was roughly the average of those long-run forecasts.

Ultimately, the Fed might not choose nominal GDP growth as its criterion for the stance of monetary policy, but I don't see any obviously superior candidates. In any case, once they have told us their definition of the stance of monetary policy, the next step is to make the Fed more accountable.

How to Make the Fed More Accountable

As noted earlier, Fed officials don't like the idea of a rigid policy instrument rule, such as the Taylor rule. They don't even like simple policy targets, such as 2 percent inflation or 5 percent nominal GDP growth, to be achieved in any fashion the Fed chooses. Currently, the Fed operates under a dual mandate, which gives it a great deal of latitude.

For instance, the Fed recently reduced its estimate of the natural rate of unemployment. A few years ago, the estimate was 5.2 to 6.0 percent. Then it was reduced 5.2 to 5.5 percent. Now the estimate is

5.0 to 5.2 percent. These reductions point to the fact that there are other variables the Fed cares about, outside of inflation and unemployment. The Fed looked at variables such as part-time employment (now unusually high) and nominal wage growth (now unusually low) and determined that the labor market has more slack than the official (U-3) unemployment rate indicates. This led the Fed to continue holding interest rates below the levels consistent with the Taylor rule.

So the Fed doesn't seem to want to be told what to do. And it doesn't even seem to want to be told by Congress to come up with its own rigid policy rule. Yet it remains true that the Fed must in some sense want to do *something*. It must have some sort of policy objectives. And that means it ought to be possible, in principle, to ascertain how effectively the Fed has achieved those objectives, at least in a qualitative sense.

The Fed accepts the notion that it impacts inflation and unemployment by shifting the aggregate demand (AD) curve to the left and right. It does not control aggregate supply. In that case, once all the data comes in, it ought to be possible to ascertain whether the outcome has been too much spending—or too little spending—relative to the Fed's hard-to-define policy objectives. This is what I will call the *minimum level of accountability*.

Suppose that after each meeting, the Fed was instructed to provide a brief summary of the outcome of its previous monetary policy decisions, based on the latest available economic data. Again, recall that the Fed must be trying to achieve something, even if the objective is complex. Its only way of achieving these objectives is by shifting AD to the left and right. So after each meeting, the Fed ought to tell us whether, in retrospect, it would have been desirable for AD growth to have been higher or lower than what actually occurred.

This minimum level of accountability would not force the Fed to come up with any specific composite variable for its various inflation and employment goals. Rather, it would merely require the Fed to tell us whether, in retrospect, demand had been stronger or weaker than it would have liked, and, if so, by how much.

I see this as a first step toward accountability. It provides an absolute minimum level of accountability for a democratic society that delegates an important policymaking role to an unelected committee. But my hope is that this first step will also help the Fed to clarify its own thinking on monetary policy. Obviously, it would be awkward to undershoot your AD target for 30 or 35 consecutive meetings (as the Fed arguably did after the fall of 2008). It would also help to clarify decisions such as the ending of the QE1 and QE2 programs. My point is not that the Fed couldn't end these programs while AD was below its objective. In fact, it could have done so based on forecasts of the future direction of aggregate demand. But then the Fed would have to evaluate those forecasts at a later date. In retrospect, was it wise to end QE1? How about the decision to end QE2?

Fed accountability would also help Congress. If the Fed said, "On balance, AD is about where we'd like it," then Congress would know that it would be pointless to engage in fiscal stimulus. If the Fed said, "AD is lower than where we'd like it to be," then Congress could have a more intelligent conversation with the Fed. "Why is AD too low?" "Are you guys out of ammunition?" "Do you want us to do more fiscal stimulus?" "Do you need more tools?" "Are you afraid to do more QE because of possible future capital losses—and thus more concerned about the possible embarrassment of having to ask Congress for a bailout than about mass unemployment?" At present, Congress does not engage in these sorts of conversations, mostly because Congress doesn't understand what monetary policy targeting is all about. Accountability would help to educate Congress and thus make the policymaking process more rational.

The Fed does not currently evaluate whether its decisions from the recent past were wise, even in retrospect. However, individual members of the Fed do occasionally admit to the Fed's making mistakes in previous decisions. Bernanke has admitted that the Fed mistakes contributed to both the Great Depression and the Great Inflation of 1966–81. But those errors occurred decades ago. We need an official vote of the entire FOMC, preferably all 19 decision-makers, including nonvoting members: was AD stronger or weaker than desirable? Even more accountability would be desirable, but that minimum level of accountability is a good first step.

In my view, accountability would eventually lead the Fed to settle on a simple metric for whether AD grew too fast or too slow. Perhaps not surprisingly, I think nominal GDP is the ideal measure of AD. Again, this does not require strict NGDP targeting. The Fed might regard 4 percent nominal GDP growth as appropriate in one year, too high the next, and too low the year after that. But if the Fed did settle on NGDP growth as its way of providing accountability for previous policy decisions, then it's easy to imagine this variable gradually taking on the role of policy target. Later the Fed might start target-ing the forecast—that is, setting its policy instrument(s) in such a way that it expects its AD proxy to grow right on target.

Guardrails for Monetary Policy

Elsewhere, I've argued that the Fed should engage in "level tar-geting"that is, policymakers should promise to return to the previous trend line if they miss their target during a given year. Ben Bernanke once recommended a level targeting (of prices) approach to the Bank of Japan (Bernanke 1999). But when Bernanke joined the Fed's Board of Governors, he found an institution that was reluctant to commit to a specified trend line for prices.

Level targeting removes much of the discretion from monetary policy. Under growth-rate targeting, a central bank that misses its tar-get (perhaps due to unforeseen circumstances) has many options, including continuing along a new trend line with similar slope but higher or lower level. Under level targeting, the central bank has no such flexibility. If the economy is moving increasingly far away from the trend line, it clearly exposes a monetary policy failure. As an exam-ple, the GDP deflator in Japan has rarely moved by more than 1 per-cent during any recent year (mostly lower). But between 1993 and 2013, the GDP deflator fell by more than 15 percent in total. Under level targeting, the failure of the Bank of Japan to maintain price sta-bility is much more apparent than under growth-rate targeting.

Level targeting has many advantages. It gives business people and investors a much clearer idea of the future path of monetary policy. Even the Fed recognizes some advantages to level targeting. For instance, during the deflation of 2008–09, a price-level target path rising at 2 percent per year would have given Fed policy much more "traction" at zero interest rates. Markets would have viewed QE as being significantly more permanentthat is, more likely to lead to future inflation. This would have lowered real interest rates and sped up the economic recovery.

Here I'd like to suggest a compromise, a sort of "guardrails" approach to level targeting. Suppose we are back in 2007 and early 2008, when the Fed saw an unstable economy, but was equally wor-ried about recession and higher inflation. The Fed's central forecast is for continued 5 percent NGDP growth as far as the eye can see, but it wants the discretion to adjust to things like a change in trend real GDP growth (which seems to have slowed after 2007.) Locking into 5 percent trend nominal GDP growth is too risky in the Fed's view, as it could lead to above target inflation. On the other hand, the Fed would certainly like to prevent the sort of steep drop in nominal GDP, and high unemployment, that actually occurred in 2008–09.

My compromise would be for the Fed to set "guardrails" at a band around 5 percent—say between 4 and 6 percent, or 3 and 7 percent. These band lines might extend out three to five years, at which time the Fed would reevaluate the trend, based on new information about real GDP growth in the United States. The idea is that the lower bound (let's say 4 percent) would be a floor on nominal GDP growth, and the Fed would commit to, *at a minimum*, returning to that trend line if growth fell below 4 percent. Ditto for an overshoot of 6 percent. If the economy were still outside the band at the end of the specified target period, then the Fed would continue to push the economy back into the nominal GDP target range. That doesn't mean it commits to return exactly to the original 5 percent trend line, rather it would commit to do *at least* enough to get back within the 4 percent to 6 percent trend guardrails.

If the Fed had adopted a five-year, 4 to 6 percent nominal GDP target in late 2007, then the U.S. economy would likely have suffered from a period of stagflation—higher than 2 percent inflation and lower than normal real GDP growth. Unemployment would have risen, but nowhere near as high as the 10 percent rate reached in October 2009. By the end of 2012, the economy would probably have experienced something closer to 4 percent nominal GDP growth than 6 percent (which would still be considerably higher than what actually occurred). By this time, the Fed would have realized that real GDP growth had permanently shifted to a lower track and adopted a new 4 percent growth rate, with a 3 to 5 percent band. This would reflect its estimate that trend real GDP growth had fallen to 2 percent.

At one level, this compromise might seem pointless. If the Fed doesn't want to have its hands tied, why would the guardrails approach be any better than a single nominal GDP–level targeting trend line of 4 or 5 percent? The answer is that while the Fed doesn't want its hands tied, it also genuinely doesn't like wild swings in nominal GDP growth. Recall that these swings make its job much harder and put it in the spotlight as it adopts emergency policies like QE to deal with the severe undershoot in nominal GDP growth. Conversely, the Fed would need very high and unpopular interest rates to deal with an overshoot of 6 percent nominal GDP growth. It would prefer to avoid these extremes, and guardrails would help them to do so.

My claim is that the Fed itself sees, or should see, a tradeoff. Yes, it wants discretion, but it also wants success. There is some band so wide that the Fed would view movements outside that band as unacceptably large. I claim that 2008–09 was one of those periods of unacceptably large swings in nominal GDP. But because it didn't already have a guardrail regime in place, the Fed had trouble communicating a policy that could get us back into the acceptable range. That communication would have had to use the existing inflation targeting language (see Paul Krugman's [1998] recommendation for 4 percent inflation, for example), or perhaps would have required an amount of QE that was politically unacceptable. With 4 and 6 percent guardrails, the Fed could have promised to "do whatever it takes" without seeming to violate previous commitments.

Over time, the Fed would become more comfortable with this policy approach, and the guardrails would gradually narrow. And as nominal GDP growth, not inflation, became better understood as "the real thing," the Fed would become more and more comfortable with keeping its nominal GDP target stable, even as trend real GDP growth (and hence inflation) fluctuated. Or perhaps it would adjust the nominal GDP target only for labor force changes, which would move us closer to George Selgin's productivity norm—a policy approach that's probably superior to simple nominal GDP targeting.[4]

Clear Thinking Leads to Better Decisions

The economics profession lacks a clear indicator of the stance of monetary policy. And yet the concept of money being either "easy" or "tight" clearly plays an important role in the way we think about policy—and indeed the way we think about causation. Did tight money cause the Great Recession? And more importantly, why do so many economists view the question as being absurd?

---

[4]In my view, nominal GDP targets should be adjusted only for changes in labor force growth rates, not productivity growth rates. As George Selgin (1997) showed, some variation in inflation is appropriate when productivity growth fluctuates. See also Selgin (1995).

Paralleling the lack of clear thinking about monetary policy is the Fed's reluctance to embrace any clear metric for accountability. The Fed refuses to tell us which numbers would show that its policy decisions in 2008 and 2009 were too expansionary, too contractionary, or about right. The beauty of nominal GDP is that it can do both. It can provide us with a robust measure of the stance of monetary policy, and it can provide a way of making policy accountable, of determining whether the Fed was doing its job.

Once nominal GDP becomes the accepted way to think about whether monetary policy is appropriate, we need to gradually move toward an explicit nominal GDP target path. Putting guardrails on nominal GDP growth is a way of gradually phasing in nominal GDP level targeting, while still providing the Fed with some discretion to deal with cases where previously targeted nominal GDP growth may later seem inappropriate. For any new policy framework to be politically acceptable, it must first be acceptable to central bankers.

History shows that institutional reforms tend to occur incrementally, not all at once. In this article, I have tried to show how three modest reforms could nudge the Fed toward nominal GDP targeting. At least the first two reforms are, or should be, completely uncontroversial. Who can object to the Fed clearly explaining what it means by the language it uses? Economists frequently discuss the "stance" of policy, so why shouldn't we define this term? And who can object to a minimum level of accountability—the Fed evaluating the effectiveness of its past decisions by any metric it chooses? And yet I can't help thinking that these three seemingly innocuous reforms could go a long way toward setting the stage for full-blown nominal GDP level targeting.

References

Bernanke, B. S. (1999) "Japanese Monetary Policy: A Case of Self-Induced Paralysis?" Manuscript, Princeton University.

_____ (2003) Speech given at the Federal Reserve Bank of Dallas Conference on the Legacy of Milton and Rose Friedman's *Free to Choose* (October 24).

_____ (2015) *The Courage to Act: A Memoir of a Crisis and Its Aftermath*. New York: W. W. Norton.

Curdia, V. (2015) "Why So Slow? A Gradual Return for Interest Rates." Federal Reserve Bank of San Francisco *Economic Letter* (October 12).

Friedman, M. (1997) "Rx for Japan: Back to the Future." *Wall Street Journal* (December 17).

Friedman, M., and Schwartz, A. J. (1963) *A Monetary History of the United States, 1867–1960*. Princeton, N.J.: Princeton University Press.

Hanson, R. (2006) "Foul Play in Information Markets." In R. W. Hahn and P. C. Tetlock (eds.), *Information Markets: A New Way of Making Decisions*, 126–41. Washington: AEI–Brookings Press.

Hanson, R.; Oprea, R.; and Porter, D. (2006) "Information Aggregation and Manipulation in an Experimental Market." *Journal of Economic Behavior and Organization* 60: 449–59.

Hetzel, R. L. (2009) "Monetary Policy in the 2008–2009 Recession." Federal Reserve Bank of Richmond *Economic Quarterly* (Spring): 201–33.

_____ (2012) *The Great Recession: Market Failure or Policy Failure?* New York: Cambridge University Press.

Krugman, P. (1998) "It's Baaack! Japan's Slump and the Return of the Liquidity Trap." *Brookings Papers on Economic Activity* 2: 137–87.

Kydland, F. E., and Prescott, E. C. (1977) "Rules Rather than Discretion: The Inconsistency of Optimal Plans." *Journal of Political Economy* 85 (January): 473–91.

McCallum, B. T. (1985) "On Consequences and Criticisms of Monetary Targeting." *Journal of Money, Credit, and Banking* 17: 570–97.

Mishkin, F. (2007) *The Economics of Money, Banking and the Financial Markets*. 8th ed. Upper Saddle River, N.J.: Prentice Hall.

Plosser, C. I. (2014) "A Limited Central Bank." *Cato Journal* 34 (2): 201–11.

Robinson, J. (1938) "A Review of *The Economics of Inflation*." *Economic Journal* (September): 507–13.

Selgin, G. (1995) "The 'Productivity Norm' vs. Zero Inflation in the History of Economic Thought." *History of Political Economy* 27: 705–35.

_____ (1997) *Less Than Zero: The Case for a Falling Price Level in a Growing Economy*. London: Institute of Economic Affairs.

Sumner, S. (2012) "The Case for Nominal GDP Targeting." Arlington, Va.: Mercatus Center, George Mason University.

_____ (2015) "Nominal GDP Futures Targeting." *Journal of Financial Stability* 17 (April): 65–75.

Svensson, L.E.O. (2003) "What Is Wrong with Taylor Rules? Using Judgment in Monetary Policy through Targeting Rules." *Journal of Economic Literature* 41 (2): 426–77.

Taylor, J. B. (1993) "Discretion versus Policy Rules in Practice." *Carnegie-Rochester Conference Series on Public Policy* 39: 195–214.

PART 4

INTERNATIONAL MONETARY REFORM

16

TOWARD A RULES-BASED INTERNATIONAL MONETARY SYSTEM
John B. Taylor

Over the past few years I have been making the case for moving toward a more rules-based international monetary system (e.g., Taylor 2013, 2014, 2015, 2016a, 2016b, 2017). In fact, I made the case over 30 years ago in Taylor (1985), and the ideas go back over 30 years before that to Milton Friedman (1953). However, the case for such a system is now much stronger because the monetary system drifted away from a rules-based approach in the past dozen years and, as Paul Volcker (2014) reminds us, the absence of a rules-based monetary system "has not been a great success."

To bring recent experience to bear on the case, we must recognize that central banks have been using two separate monetary policy instruments in recent years: the policy interest rate and the size of the balance sheet, in which reserve balances play a key role. Any international monetary modeling framework used to assess or to make recommendations about international monetary policy must include both instruments in each country, the policy for changing the instruments, and the effect of these changes on exchange rates.

Using such a framework, I show that both policy instruments have deviated from rules-based policy in recent years. I then draw

John B. Taylor is the Mary and Robert Raymond Professor of Economics at Stanford University and the George P. Shultz Senior Fellow in Economics at the Hoover Institution. This article is reprinted from the *Cato Journal*, Vol. 38, No. 2 (Spring/Summer 2018).

the policy implications for the international monetary system and suggest a way forward to implement the policy.

Regarding policy interest rates, there has clearly been an international contagion of deviations from monetary policy rules that have worked well in the past, as I argued in Taylor (2009, 2013).[1] This international contagion is due in part to a concern about exchange rates. If a foreign central bank with global financial influence cuts its interest rate by a large amount, then the currencies of other countries will tend to appreciate unless the other central banks react and adjust their interest rates. Central bank reactions may also include exchange market interventions, capital flow restrictions, or some form of macroprudential actions aimed at international capital flows. These actions and reactions accentuate the deviation of monetary policy from traditional policy rules. To be sure, the international contagion of policy interest rates may be due to omitted factors that push interest rates around for many central banks. However, there is considerable econometric evidence that the deviations from policy rules are caused by unusual interest rate changes in other countries. There is also direct evidence from many central bankers who admit to these reactions. Norges Bank reports on monetary policy, for example, show that its policy interest rate is adjusted in relation to interest rate decisions at the European Central Bank (ECB), as described in Taylor (2013).

Regarding central bank balance sheet operations, there has also been international contagion, and this is also likely due to exchange rate concerns. Here an important distinction must be made between the central banks in large open economies and central banks in small open economies. In large open economies, the effects of balance sheet operations on exchange rates have been harder to detect than for central banks in small open economies. However, as I show in this article, there is now empirical evidence provided in Taylor (2017) of statistically significant impacts on exchange rates of the balance sheet operations by the Federal Reserve, the Bank of Japan (BOJ), and the ECB. There are also exchange rate effects in the small open economies where explicit foreign exchange purchases are often financed by an expansion of reserve balances.

---

[1] See also Carstens (2015), Gray (2013), Hofmann and Bogdanova (2012).

A Framework and an International Policy Matrix

To investigate the international aspects of central bank interest rate and balance sheet policies, it is necessary to introduce a simple framework that captures key features of the recent economic policy environment. In the framework I use here, central banks have two separate policy instruments: the short-term interest rate and reserve balances. By paying interest (either positive or negative) on reserve balances, central banks can separately set the interest rate and reserve balances. This enables the central bank to intervene in other markets for a variety of reasons. In fact, in recent years, central banks in large open economies have purchased domestic securities denominated in their own currency through their quantitative easing (QE) programs. The stated aim has often been to raise the price and reduce the yield of these domestic securities, though there are sometimes references to exchange rates. In contrast, the central banks in smaller countries have purchased foreign securities denominated in foreign currency. The explicit aim of these foreign exchange purchases is to affect the exchange rate.

To operationalize this framework in Taylor (2017), I examined the balance sheets of three central banks in large open economies—the Fed, ECB, and BOJ—and a central bank in a relatively small open economy—the Swiss National Bank (SNB). Most of the purchases of assets by these banks are financed by increases in reserve balances. For the Fed, purchases of dollar-denominated bonds are financed by dollar reserve balances. For the Bank of Japan, purchases of yen-denominated securities are financed by yen-denominated reserve balances. For the ECB, purchases of euro-denominated securities are financed by euro-denominated reserve balances. For the SNB, purchases of euro- and dollar-denominated securities are financed by Swiss franc–denominated reserve balances. In addition, each of these central banks sets its short-term policy interest rate, which in the case of the Fed is the federal funds rate. The private sector holds securities and deposits funds (reserve balances) at the central bank. Prices and yields are determined by market forces. The exchange rates between the dollar, the yen, the euro, and the Swiss franc are determined in the markets just as is the price of other securities.

The framework thus includes eight different policy instruments for the four central banks: the balance sheet items (R for reserve balances) R_U, R_J, R_E, and R_S, and the short-term policy rates (I for interest rate) I_U, I_J, I_E, and I_S, where the subscripts indicate the United States (U), Japan (J), Europe (E), and Switzerland (S). The actual data used in this article to compute international correlations and create time series charts were obtained directly from the central banks' databases.[2]

Table 1 is an international policy matrix that gives the cross correlations of the eight policy instruments in the four countries using monthly data for the dozen years from 2005 to 2017. Observe the strong positive correlation between the reserve balances in each country. This could indicate either a contagion of such policies or that they have been reacting to a common shock. Observe also the strong positive correlation between the interest rate instrument in each country, which is consistent with the recent literature on interest rate contagion. The most highly correlated of all the entries in the policy matrix in Table 1 is between the SNB policy rate and the ECB policy rate with a correlation coefficient of 0.93.

The international policy matrix also reveals a strong negative correlation between the two policy instruments *within* each central bank: when the interest rate is lower during this period, reserve balances are higher. This is likely due to the assumption at central banks that the impact of the two instruments is similar: a lower policy rate and an expanded balance sheet with higher reserve balances are assumed to increase aggregate demand, raise the inflation rate, and depreciate the currency.

Note also the negative correlation between reserve balances and the interest rates *across* countries. These are simple correlation coefficients, so the negative effect could be due to a negative correlation within each country coupled with a positive

[2]The specific data series are

R_U = total reserve balances maintained with Federal Reserve Banks (millions of dollars)

R_J = BOJ current account balances (100 millions of yen)

R_E = current accounts + deposit facility (millions of euros)

R_S = sight deposits of domestic banks + sight deposits of foreign banks and institutions + other sight liabilities (millions of Swiss francs)

I_U = effective federal funds rate

I_J = call rate, uncollateralized, overnight average

I_E = interest rate on deposit facility

I_S = Swiss Average Rate Overnight (SARON)

TABLE 1
INTERNATIONAL MONETARY POLICY MATRIX

	R_U	R_J	R_E	R_S	I_U	I_J	I_E	I_S
R_U	1.00							
R_J	0.72	1.00						
R_E	0.49	0.64	1.00					
R_S	0.89	0.85	0.69	1.00				
I_U	−0.77	−0.36	−0.44	−0.58	1.00			
I_J	−0.53	−0.45	−0.37	−0.48	0.49	1.00		
I_E	−0.81	−0.57	−0.51	−0.71	0.76	0.87	1.00	
I_S	−0.81	−0.62	−0.57	−0.72	0.83	0.81	0.93	1.00

NOTE: Each entry in the matrix is the correlation coefficient between the policy instrument on the vertical axis and the policy instrument on the horizontal axis over the months from January 2005 through May 2017. The policy instruments for the central banks—United States (U), Japan (J), Europe (E), Switzerland (S)—are reserve balances R_U, R_J, R_E, R_S, and the policy interest rates I_U, I_J, I_E, I_S.

contagion effect of either the interest rate or reserve balances in each country.

The underlying reasons for the numerical correlations between reserve balances in the different countries can be better understood by studying the actual paths of reserve balances for the Fed, the BOJ, the ECB, and the SNB. During this period, the Fed was out in front with large-scale asset purchases of U.S. Treasuries and mortgage-backed securities in 2009 following the short-lived liquidity operations during the panic in 2008. These large-scale purchases, commonly called QE I, II, and III, were financed with the large increases in reserve balances. For the past few years, reserve balances have started to decline in the United States as securities purchases were reduced in size and then were ended. Currency demand has grown, also reducing the need for financing the stock of securities with reserve balances.

This expansion of reserve balances in the United States was followed by a similar move by the BOJ at the start of 2013. Soon thereafter the ECB started increasing reserve balances. Throughout the period the SNB was expanding reserves as it purchased euros and dollars to counter the appreciation of the Swiss franc against these currencies. In other words, the positive correlations between reserve balances in the matrix are due to Japan's following the increase in reserve balances in the United States, the ECB's following Japan and the United States, and the SNB's responding to all three. In the end, the increase in global liquidity was much larger than if there had not been this contagion.[3]

The correlations between the interest rates in the matrix are similarly due to central banks' following each other as they make their policy decisions about their policy interest rate. This contagion has been documented with interest rate reaction functions in empirical work by Taylor (2009), Carstens (2015), and Gray (2013). With such functions, one can measure the reaction of central banks to other countries' interest rates by including the foreign central bank's interest rate in the reaction function. This is more difficult in the case where the balance sheet is the instrument.

Exchange Rate Effects

While the policy matrix shows a close association between the policies, there is a question about whether central banks were jointly trying to provide liquidity or whether the actions were part of a competitive devaluation process. As mentioned above and reported in Taylor (2017), I found statistically significant exchange rate effects in estimated regressions of exchange rates on reserve balances. To summarize, the regression equations showed that (1) an increase in reserve balances R_J by the Bank of Japan causes the yen to depreciate against the dollar and the euro, (2) an increase in reserve balances R_U by the Fed causes the dollar to depreciate against the yen and the euro, and (3) an increase in reserve balances R_E by the ECB causes the euro to depreciate against the yen and the dollar.

These results confirm the policy narrative presented in Taylor (2016b): Following the global financial crisis and the start of the U.S. recovery, the yen significantly appreciated against the dollar as the Fed extended its large-scale asset purchase program financed with increases in reserve balances. At first there was little or no response

---

[3]The paths of reserve balances described in this and the previous paragraph can be seen in the time series graphs in Figures 1, 2, and 3, where I examine the effects on the exchange rate.

from the BOJ, but the yen appreciation became a key issue in the 2012 Japanese election. When Shinzo Abe was elected, he appointed Haruhiko Kuroda under whom the BOJ implemented its own QE. A depreciation of the yen accompanied the change in monetary policy. The subsequent moves by the ECB toward QE were also due to concerns about an appreciating euro. At the Jackson Hole conference in August 2014, Mario Draghi spoke about these concerns and suggested QE, which soon followed. This shift in policy was followed by a weaker euro.

The timing of reserve balances and exchange rate movements is illustrated in Figures 1, 2, and 3. The top part of each figure shows the time series patterns of reserve balances for the three large central banks with scale on the right-hand vertical axis measured in units of the local currency—millions of dollars, hundreds of million yen, and millions of euros. The lowest line in the three figures shows the exchange rate between the dollar, the yen, and the euro using the scale on the left-hand vertical axis.

Figure 1 shows the dollar getting weaker against the yen following the increase in reserve balances in the United States, until the BOJ increased its own reserve balances and the dollar then strengthened against the yen. Figure 2 shows the yen getting weaker against the

FIGURE 1
YEN–DOLLAR EXCHANGE RATE AND RESERVE BALANCES
(R_U, R_J, R_E), 2005–17

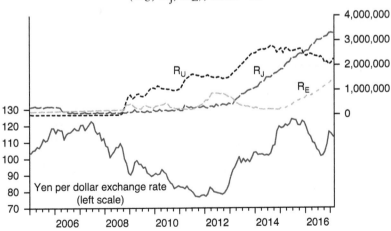

FIGURE 2
DOLLAR–EURO EXCHANGE RATE AND RESERVE BALANCES
(R_U, R_J, R_E), 2005–17

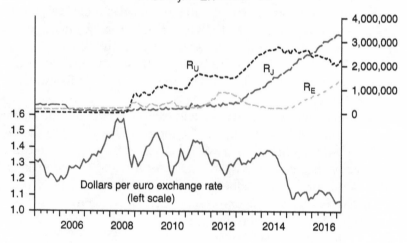

FIGURE 3
YEN–EURO EXCHANGE RATE AND RESERVE BALANCES
(R_U, R_J, R_E), 2005–17

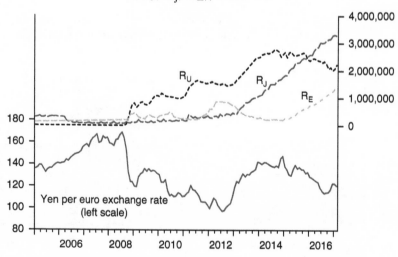

euro as reserve balances are increased in Japan and a reversal when reserve balances are increased by the ECB. Figure 3 shows the weakening of the euro against the dollar and the yen after the action by the ECB.

Note that the positive correlations between reserve balances over the whole period in the three central banks, which was reported in Table 1, is evident in these time series charts. The timing of reserve balance changes is also evident with the Fed going first, followed by the BOJ and the ECB.

Exchange rate effects of reserve balance changes can also occur for small open economies, but they are normally due to direct intervention on the currency markets. In the case of Switzerland, for example, reserve balances are used to finance direct interventions in foreign exchange markets. Vector autoregressions can then be used to examine the impacts. In fact, according to empirical results reported in Taylor (2017), there is significant two-way causality between the Swiss exchange rate and reserve balances. More specifically, the hypothesis that R_s does not Granger-cause the Swiss franc–euro exchange rate is rejected with an F-statistic of 4.74; the hypothesis that the Swiss franc–euro rate does not Granger-cause R_s is rejected with an F-statistic of 4.04. In other words, changes in the exchange rate Granger-cause an expansion of reserve balances, and the expansion of reserve balances Granger-causes a change in the exchange rate. In addition, I have found that a similar pattern of causality exists when the policy instrument is the interest rate rather than the balance sheet.

Policy Implications

For both policy instruments, the empirical results show that exchange rate considerations have helped cause deviations from rules-based policy in the international monetary system. To the extent that the deviations take policy away from the better performance observed in the 1980s and 1990s, they are a source of instability to the global economy. Moreover, there appears to be a "competitive devaluation" aspect to these actions as argued by Meltzer (2016). To the extent that the policies result in excess movements in exchange rates, they are another source of instability in the global economy as they affect the flow of goods and capital and interfere with their efficient allocation. They also are a source of political instability as they raise concerns about currency manipulation. Moreover, as countries have used balance sheet operations to affect currency values, actual balance sheets have grown throughout the world, and this has raised concerns about the global impact of unwinding them.

A counterfactual exercise using the estimated regressions mentioned above shows that exchange rates would have been significantly less volatile without the balance sheet operations. For the yen/dollar equation, the standard error of the regression is 7.27 and the standard deviation of the dependent variable is 14.11, indicating that the movements in reserve balances have nearly doubled the volatility of the exchange rate. Using the yen/euro equation and euro/dollar equations in the same way shows that movements in reserve balances have increased the volatility of the yen–dollar exchange rate by 60 percent and the euro–dollar exchange rate by 40 percent.

There is other evidence that exchange rate volatility and capital flow volatility have increased in recent years. According to Rey (2013), Carstens (2015), Coeuré (2017), Taylor (2016b), and Ghosh, Ostry, and Qureshi (2017), exchange rate volatility and capital flow volatility have increased recently. Rey (2013) found that a global financial cycle, which was driven in part by monetary policy, affected credit flows in the international financial system. Carstens (2015) documented a marked increase in the volatility of capital flows to emerging markets in recent years. To be sure, there are other explanations for this increased volatility. Ghosh, Ostry, and Qureshi (2017) argue that the volatility has increased because of international externalities and market imperfections. Nevertheless, the evidence provided here and in other recent studies suggests that a deviation from rules-based monetary policy has been part of the problem.

The main policy implication is that the international economy would be more stable if policymakers could create a more rules-based international monetary system. The approach that I favor would be for each central bank to describe and commit to a monetary policy rule or strategy for setting the policy instruments. These rules-based commitments would reduce exchange rate volatility and uncertainty, and remove some of the reasons why central banks have followed each other in recent years. The strategy could include a specific inflation target, an estimate of the equilibrium interest rate, and a list of key variables to react to in certain specified ways. The process would not impinge on other countries' monetary strategies. It would be a flexible exchange rate system between countries and between currency zones.

Each central bank would formulate and describe its strategy, so there would be no reduction in either national or international independence of central banks. The strategies could be changed or deviated from if the world changed or if there was an emergency, so a commonly understood procedure for describing the change and the reasons for it would be useful. It is possible that some central banks will include foreign interest rates in the list of variables they react to so long as it is transparently described. But when they see other central banks not doing so, they will likely do less of it, recognizing the amplification effects.

The process would be global, rather than for a small group of countries, though, as with the process that led to the Bretton Woods system in the 1940s, it could begin informally with a small group and then spread out. The international rules-based approach I suggest here is supported by research over many years, for example, in Taylor (1985). It is attractive because each country can choose its own independent strategy and simultaneously contribute to global stability.

The major central banks now have explicit inflation goals, and many use policy rules that can describe strategies for the policy instruments. Explicit statements about policy goals and strategies to achieve these goals are thus feasible. There is wide agreement that some form of international reform is needed. In any case, a clear commitment by the Federal Reserve to move in this rules-based direction would help. A prerequisite would be for the international monetary system to normalize. Getting back to balance sheets with reserve levels such that policy interest rates are determined by the supply and demand for reserves—rather than by paying interest on excess reserves—will facilitate a rules-based international system because the balance sheet decisions and interest rate decisions would be linked.

The biggest hurdle to achieving such a rules-based system is a disparity of views about the problem and the solution. Some are not convinced of the importance of rules-based monetary policy. Others may doubt that it would deal with the problems of volatile exchange rates and capital flows. Still others believe that the competitive depreciations of recent years are simply part of a necessary process of world monetary policy easing.

Such a disparity of views has existed for generations of economists and central bankers. Indeed, the current discussion of reforms in the international monetary system reminds one of the debate about exchange rates and capital flows that occurred in the 1940s and 1950s, which Eichengreen (2004) has written about. Nurkse (1944) argued that destabilizing speculation inherent in the market system was the cause of exchange rate and capital flow volatility; his solution was government controls on capital flows and fixed exchange rates. Friedman (1953) argued that monetary policy actions were the cause of the volatility; his solution was an open international monetary system with transparent monetary policy rules and flexible exchange rates. The experience over the years since that time—the improvements in economic models, the enormous volume of research on policy rules, and, especially, the poorer performance in the past dozen years as policy has deviated from a rules-based system—suggests that the answer is a more open, transparent, and rules-based international monetary system in the future.

References

Carstens, A. (2015) "Challenges for Emerging Economies in the Face of Unconventional Monetary Policies in Advanced Economies." Stavros Niarchos Foundation Lecture, Peterson Institute for International Economics, Washington (April 20).

Coeuré, B. (2017) "Monetary Policy, Exchange Rates, and Capital Flows." Speech given at the 18th Jacques Polak Annual Research Conference hosted by the IMF, Washington, D.C. (November 3). Available at ecb.europa.eu.

Eichengreen, B. (2004) *Capital Flows and Crises.* Cambridge, Mass.: MIT Press.

Friedman, M. (1953) "The Case for Flexible Exchange Rates." In *Essays in Positive Economics*, 157–203. Chicago: University of Chicago Press.

Ghosh, A.; Ostry, J.; and Qureshi, M. (2017) *Taming the Tide of Capital Flows: A Policy Guide.* Cambridge, Mass.: MIT Press.

Gray, C. (2013) "Responding to a Monetary Superpower: Investigating the Behavioral Spillovers of U.S. Monetary Policy." *Atlantic Economic Journal* 21 (2): 173–84.

Hofmann, B., and Bogdanova, B. (2012) "Taylor Rules and Monetary Policy: A Global 'Great Deviation'?" *BIS Quarterly Review* (September): 37–49.

Meltzer, A. H. (2016) "Remarks" in "General Discussion: Funding Quantitative Easing to Target Inflation." In *Designing Resilient Monetary Policy Frameworks for the Future*, 493. Kansas City, Mo.: Federal Reserve Bank of Kansas City.

Nurkse, R. (1944) *International Currency Experience: Lessons of the Inter-war Period.* Geneva: Economic, Financial, and Transit Department, League of Nations.

Rey, H. (2013) "Dilemma Not Trilemma: The Global Financial Cycle and Monetary Policy Independence." In *Global Dimensions of Unconventional Monetary Policy.* Jackson Hole Conference, Federal Reserve Bank of Kansas City.

Taylor, J. B. (1985) "International Coordination in the Design of Macroeconomic Policy Rules." *European Economic Review* 28: 53–81.

_____ (2009) "Globalization and Monetary Policy: Missions Impossible." Originally presented at an NBER conference in Gerona, Spain. In M. Gertler and J. Gali (eds.) *The International Dimensions of Monetary Policy*, 609–24. Chicago: University of Chicago Press.

_____ (2013) "International Monetary Coordination and the Great Deviation." *Journal of Policy Modeling* 35 (3): 463–72.

_____ (2014) "Nice-Squared." Presentation at "Bretton Woods: The Founders and the Future," conference sponsored by the Center for Financial Stability. Available at www.youtube.com/watch?v=XGMmJ2IAHJs.

_____ (2015) "Recreating the 1940s–Founded Institutions for Today's Global Economy." Remarks upon receiving the Truman Medal for Economic Policy, Kansas City (October 14).

_____ (2016a) "Rethinking the International Monetary System." *Cato Journal* 36 (2): 239–50.

_____ (2016b) "A Rules-Based Cooperatively Managed International Monetary System for the Future." In C. F. Bergsten and R. Green (eds.) *International Monetary Cooperation: Lessons from the Plaza Accord after Thirty Years*, 217–36. Washington: Peterson Institute.

_____ (2017) "Ideas and Institutions in Monetary Policy Making: The Karl Brunner Lecture." Swiss National Bank, Zurich (September 21).

Volcker, P. A. (2014) "Remarks." Bretton Woods Committee Annual Meeting (June 17).

17

SOME THOUGHTS ON INTERNATIONAL MONETARY POLICY COORDINATION

Charles I. Plosser

It is a pleasure to be back here at Cato and to be invited to speak once again at this annual conference. This is one of the premier ongoing monetary policy conferences, and the participants, both at the podium and in the audience, attest to its prominence.

This is a session on international monetary arrangements, and there has already been an interesting discussion. I find myself in substantial agreement with the comments of John Taylor, so I do not wish to repeat his points. What I will try to do is put the rules-based approach to international monetary policy coordination in a context that I hope will help us understand some of the past failures so we might avoid them in the future. In many ways, I will simply be reminding us of some principles we all have known for some time, yet which we seem to forget all too frequently.

A Little History of Efforts at International Central Bank Coordination

The dream of international coordination or cooperation among central banks is not new. Through much of the late 19th and early 20th centuries, we witnessed an international rules-based effort grounded in the classical gold standard. The idea was that each

---

Charles I. Plosser is a Visiting Fellow at the Hoover Institution at Stanford University and former President and CEO of the Federal Reserve Bank of Philadelphia. This article is reprinted from the *Cato Journal*, Vol. 38, No. 2 (Spring/Summer 2018).

country was expected to maintain convertibility of its paper currency into gold at an agreed-upon nominal rate. The foundation of the system was grounded in the parities agreed upon by the countries involved. These parities amounted to the specification of a fixed exchange rate regime among the participating countries. Of course, like any fixed exchange rate regime, it meant that pressures arising from the external balance could put limits on domestic monetary policy and fiscal policy options. This reality ultimately proved to be the regime's undoing.

The arrangement mostly worked during the early 20th century. The outbreak of World War I, however, placed enormous strains on the finances of the warring countries. The European nations had to finance large deficits through a combination of external borrowing and inflation. In most cases, the countries suspended convertibility to prevent large gold outflows. Following the war there was a strong interest in Europe to restore the prewar parities. Unfortunately, external debt and high inflation made this virtually impossible. Despite years of effort, including meetings (public and private), and conferences among central bankers attempting to coordinate actions, misalignments persisted, requiring massive gold flows, particularly from Great Britain to France and the United States. This undermined the credibility of the regime, and it never fully regained the success or stability it once enjoyed. By 1933, the entire system had collapsed. The United States abandoned its peg to gold in April 1933 because of the constraints it placed on domestic monetary and fiscal policies seeking to address the Great Depression.

Later, following World War II, world leaders again sought to create a new framework for international financial coordination. The Bretton Woods system laid out rules to bring stability to exchange rates and international capital flows. The new system once again attempted to establish an essentially fixed exchange rate regime by requiring that each country commit to maintaining a targeted exchange rate within a narrow band. It also created the International Monetary Fund to help nations borrow to ease balance of payment problems in the short run. It took a long time, but the Bretton Woods system was finally fully implemented in 1958.

Despite the apparent different words and institutional arrangements, the Bretton Woods regime sought to control exchange rates in order to manage international capital flows and current account fluctuations much like the old gold standard era. Gold convertibility continued to play a role but only internationally, not domestically. The flaw was that the new arrangements still demanded that domestic monetary and fiscal policies take a back seat to the exchange rate regime. One might have guessed that, like the international gold standard regime, Bretton Woods would fail for the same reason, that being that the fixed regime was incompatible with the incentives of sovereign nations to have their own independent monetary and fiscal policies—and, of course, it did. The pegged exchange rate regime faced pressures that resulted in large but infrequent adjustments in the rates. These adjustments encouraged speculative attacks on some currencies as the credibility and the commitment of participants to follow through with the necessary policy actions was undermined. As a result, credibility of the entire regime came into question. The system was abandoned after about 15 years, shortly after the United States abandoned convertibility.

The Importance of Credibility and Commitment

A major challenge for any rules-based regime is attaining and preserving the credibility and commitment of all parties to follow the rules. In establishing a rule, it is desirable to ensure that it is one that is incentive compatible. The international arrangements discussed above were not well designed in the sense that targeting a fixed exchange rate is fundamentally inconsistent with a nation's retaining full sovereignty with respect to domestic monetary and fiscal policy. It was this inconsistency that undermined credibility and doomed both the gold standard and the Bretton Woods system's attempts to coordinate international monetary policy. Put slightly differently, a challenge for rules-based systems is how to enforce a commitment to the rule. In these previous efforts there was no mechanism to enforce the rules, particularly when they ran strongly counter to the self-interest of an individual country. This suggests that we must think carefully about the scope of what we can expect to achieve from such coordination efforts. To be effective, the institutional arrangements and the incentives they create must be understood when considering any rule or set of agreements among central bankers.

At Cato's 31st Annual Monetary Conference, in November 2013, I spoke to some related issues in a paper entitled "A Limited Central Bank" (Plosser 2014). I stressed that there were ways to increase the chances of achieving commitment with the right institutional design, and to some degree we see such efforts in practice. For example, many central banks around the world face constraints on what types of assets they can buy and hold. The Fed is generally limited to holding only assets that are guaranteed by the federal government, although there are many loopholes. For example, during the financial crisis the Fed exploited Section 13(3) of the Federal Reserve Act to purchase private sector securities (e.g., enabling the rescue of Bear Stearns and AIG). Such purchases constitute a form of off-budget fiscal policy and proved highly controversial. The consequence was that the Dodd-Frank legislation imposed additional limits on what the Fed could do under Section 13(3). I have argued that the Fed should be limited to an all-Treasuries portfolio to restrain its discretion to conduct credit policy through asset purchases.

Another way of constraining options is to provide more narrow and clear objectives that are achievable and clearly measurable. Discretion and multiple objectives permit central banks to pursue varying goals at different times. Broad objectives often allow for great discretion to address one goal or another depending on economic conditions or political pressures. This can undermine the credibility and commitment to achieve specific tasks, such as employment, price stability, or exchange rate targets. By narrowing an institution's objective function, it is easier to demonstrate and maintain commitment and achieve credibility. It also improves the accountability of the institution. In the case of the Fed, I argued that a narrow mandate focused on price stability was desirable. It is a narrow and achievable objective that is directly observable making accountability more effective.

A Brief Refresher on Fixed vs. Flexible Exchange Rates

As I have noted, the historical efforts at international coordination have generally focused on achieving exchange rate "stability," often a code word for fixed exchange rates. The argument for fixed rates usually follows from the advantages of a common currency. A common currency promotes trade across regions of a nation as well as efficient competition and integration of markets, both product markets and the markets for factors of production such as labor and capital. The case for fixed exchange rates, by analogy, is that they promote the integration of markets internationally with similar benefits. Such arguments were made repeatedly in support of the creation of the euro.

Yet the analogy has serious limitations. A major defect is the analogy fails to consider the important role played by the mobility of both products and factors of production. In order to achieve the market efficiencies of a common currency, goods, services, labor, and capital must be free to move throughout the market area. In the international context such free movement is rarely the case. On the product side, tariffs and other constraints are often present. In the case of labor, barriers are even more serious, including immigration policies, language, culture, and other domestic laws and practices. National policies also inhibit capital movements much like labor. So one of the prerequisites for gaining the benefits of a common currency is often absent in the international setting.

The benefits of a common currency domestically are also made possible by the existence of a common fiscal framework. This means that there is a fiscal means of addressing regional imbalances through transfers (for better or worse). A currency union of sovereign countries rarely has such mechanisms. In an international context, the failure of the gold standard and Bretton Woods highlighted all these weaknesses. In each case, the arrangements failed to adequately address the issue of mobility of either products or factors of production. Moreover, these systems did not address the fundamental challenge that each nation continued to want to conduct independent monetary and fiscal policy.

Economists have been aware of these points for a long time. Many economists voiced skepticism regarding the prospects for the euro for many of these reasons. While the euro did create a common central bank, it failed to adequately address the free movement of labor and capital. It also failed to develop an adequate fiscal mechanism to address national shocks and imbalances. The current troubles in the eurozone were largely predictable and mirrored many of the failures of previous attempts to fix exchange rates.

Recent Efforts to Coordinate International Central Banks

The recent calls for international coordination among central banks are somewhat different from the past, yet somewhat the same. On the one hand, the calls from some sectors in the global economy are not, on their face, calls for fixed exchange rates. It seems likely that the weight of experience and empirical evidence is beginning to have an impact on international policymakers. The attention is mostly focused on the volatility of capital flows that may be a consequence of surprise or unusual changes in monetary policy. The source of the frustration stems from two factors. The first is that the Fed is arguably the most important central bank in the world and its decisions can have important effects, "spillovers" they are often called, on the exchange rate and trade balances with other countries. The second factor is that the severity of these "spillovers" for individual countries is often a consequence of the country's own choice of policies and institutional arrangements.

Countries with large fiscal deficits, heavy external debt, and high inflation likely will have more trouble contending with spillovers and thus complain about a U.S. policy decision. They then press for greater consideration of their circumstances in U.S. monetary policy decisions. Countries maintaining sound fiscal policies, low inflation, and a commitment to flexible exchange rates are less affected.

While calls for coordination on interest rate decisions from some countries do not explicitly argue for fixed exchange rates, that seems mostly what they long for—they just don't say it. On the other hand, the major central banks were playing a somewhat different tune. The sequential adoption of quantitative easing (QE) by one major country after another was mostly cited as a domestic policy action, yet the undercurrent was about exchange rate effects. They didn't call it a currency war, or even competitive devaluations, because everyone understood such strategies are ineffective and undesirable. Nonetheless, it seems to have been the unspoken strategy that no one wanted to admit.

These different strategies highlight the underappreciated challenge to the case for international coordination among central banks. Our models usually don't deal with a world in which there are many different exchange rate regimes or many different fiscal regimes. How should the United States coordinate monetary policy in a world in which different countries experience differential impacts from a given monetary policy decision by the Fed? Which countries' outcomes matter, and which do not? For example, the Fed's response to an inflation shock in the United States can have different impacts on a country that ties its currency to the dollar and has a balanced current account than on a country that operates a floating exchange to a broad basket of foreign currencies but runs a persistent current account deficit and imposes capital controls. Which countries should be taken into account in the Fed's decision, and which should not?

Should U.S. monetary policy play favorites? How should it decide which countries' consequences demand consideration and which do not?

So, from my perspective, the concept of coordinated monetary policy is deeply problematic. Moreover, as I argued at the outset, any regime that attempts to target exchange rates among sovereign countries is most likely to fail if those countries desire an independent monetary policy.

Conclusion

I agree with John Taylor that the best results are likely to arise in more rule-like regimes with flexible exchange rates and capital mobility (Taylor 2018). With regard to monetary policy, the rule matters. Rules that require multiparty coordination to "stabilize" exchange rates are likely to fail and cause more problems than they solve. Rules that are incentive compatible with independent monetary and fiscal policy are more likely to be followed, and further reducing the discretionary options permitted monetary policymakers would enhance the commitment and credibility of the rule-like behavior.

References

Plosser, C. I. (2014) "A Limited Central Bank." *Cato Journal* 34 (2): 201–11.

Taylor, J. B. (2018) "Toward a Rules-Based International Monetary System." *Cato Journal* 38 (2): 347–59.

18

THE CASE FOR A NEW INTERNATIONAL MONETARY SYSTEM
Judy Shelton

How often do we hear references to the notion that we live in a rules-based global trading system? Addressing the World Economic Forum at Davos in January 2017, British Prime Minister Theresa May praised liberalism, free trade, and globalization as "the forces that underpin the rules-based international system that is key to our global prosperity and security" (Martin 2017). Chinese President Xi Jinping likewise extolled the virtues of a rules-based economic order at Davos, winning widespread praise for defending free trade and globalization (Fidler, Chen, and Wei 2017).

But could someone please explain: What exactly are those rules? Because if we are going to invoke the sentimentality of Bretton Woods by suggesting that the world has remained true to its precepts, we are ignoring geopolitical reality. Moreover, we are denying the warped economic consequences of global trade conducted in the absence of orderly currency arrangements. We have not had a rules-based international monetary system since President Nixon ended the Bretton Woods agreement in August 1971. Today there are compelling reasons—political, economic, and strategic—for President Trump to initiate the establishment of a new international monetary system.

Judy Shelton is a Senior Fellow at the Atlas Network and author of *Money Meltdown: Restoring Order to the Global Currency System*. This article is reprinted from the *Cato Journal*, Vol. 38, No. 2 (Spring/Summer 2018).

An Inspiring Vision of Future Prosperity

To fully appreciate how far we have strayed from the high-minded objectives that motivated the 1944 multilateral currency accord forged at Bretton Woods, New Hampshire, it's useful to reflect on the fundamental principles that defined its purpose and to consider the historical context for its acceptance.

The United States had been attacked at Pearl Harbor scarcely a week before Treasury Secretary Henry Morgenthau asked his deputy, Harry Dexter White, to prepare a paper outlining the possibilities for coordinated monetary arrangements among the United States and its allies. The primary goal was to provide the means, the instrument, and the procedure to stabilize foreign exchange rates and strengthen the internal monetary systems of the Allied countries (Horsefield 1969a: 12).

Why was it deemed so important to ensure stable exchange rates at a time of war when the very survival of Allied nations was at stake? The answer: struggling nations required assurances that a more prosperous economic future was in store if they could summon the will to prevail over Axis powers. During the 1930s, countries had engaged in competitive devaluations to gain an export advantage over their trade partners. As the gold standard was serially abandoned, international trade succumbed to the vicissitudes of unpredictable changes in exchange rates and retaliatory tariffs. Global depression had followed.

But now the United States was suggesting that something new would be done in the sphere of international economic relations—something "powerful enough and comprehensive enough to give expectation of successfully filling a world need" (White 1942, in Horsefield 1969b: 46). By establishing new rules to ensure a level monetary playing field as the logical foundation for expanded free trade and the optimal use of financial capital, America would be providing those needed assurances that would "unify and encourage the anti-Axis forces, to greatly strengthen their will and effort to win" (ibid., pp. 38–39).

Did it work? Less than four weeks after Allied forces landed at Normandy on June 6, 1944, the Bretton Woods conference was convened. Representatives from 44 Allied nations hammered out rules for participating in an international monetary system based on fixed exchange rates anchored by a U.S. dollar convertible into gold. The Axis powers surrendered the following year.

Did adoption of a stable monetary platform deliver as promised? The Bretton Woods era would be characterized by remarkable economic growth rates, extraordinary productivity gains, and decreased inequality of wealth.

Losing the Dream

The period of exceptional world economic performance was ended in 1971. Some blame the closing of the gold window on American domestic budget exigencies. Others attribute the collapse of Bretton Woods to the "Triffin dilemma"—a failing inherent in its dependence on a single reserve currency country. In any case, the vision of providing a solid monetary foundation for global free trade was shattered by Nixon's decision to suspend gold convertibility of the dollar.

Paul Volcker, serving as undersecretary for monetary affairs at the Treasury department, felt anguished at the time. He was concerned that the initiative would be seen as a humiliating change in U.S. domestic policy and a derogation of duty in the international monetary arena (Volcker and Gyohten 1992: 78–79). Volcker had advised Nixon to make the move as a temporary decision to redress the flaws of Bretton Woods. Nixon himself had told the American people in his televised speech on August 15: "We will press for the necessary reforms to set up an urgently needed new international monetary system" (Nixon 1971).

But a novel theory was being promoted by members of the emerging group of monetarist economists associated with the Chicago School—led by Milton Friedman—arguing that floating exchange rates were preferable to the fixed-rate Bretton Woods system. Keynesians quickly seized the opportunity to pursue fiscal activism without the constraints imposed by balanced budgets and the discipline of gold convertibility.

The new approach that emerged in the vacuum left by the dissolution of Bretton Woods was to have *no* international monetary system—that is, no rules or coherent mechanism for maintaining exchange-rate stability among national currencies.

The free-for-all approach to determining exchange rates is sometimes promoted as a "free market" solution. However, if exchange rates are truly determined by market forces alone—not subject to government intervention or manipulation—why are governments allowed to build up massive foreign currency reserves? Theoretically, the exchange rate between a nation's currency and other currencies should be determined at any given moment by the forces of demand and supply. Instead, governments not only accumulate reserves as a bulwark for thwarting market forces, but also use monetary policy to deliberately manipulate their currencies to gain an advantage over trade partners.

The currency disorder that reigns today is anathema to any notion of free and fair trade. Nations can blatantly target the exchange rate they desire—in pursuit of strategic objectives. Deliberate depreciation is used to boost exports; it's the customary definition of currency manipulation. However, financial capital flows may figure more importantly for some nations, in which case they may instead choose to manipulate their currencies upward to attract foreign investment. Deliberate appreciation also enables a nation to maximize the purchasing power of its currency for purposes of obtaining strategically important assets abroad.

Central banks play a major role in either case. They are the main players when it comes to currency manipulation, even when monetary officials claim that the exchange rate consequences of their policies are merely incidental to achieving domestic economic objectives.

The lack of any kind of rules-based monetary system to uphold the legitimacy of global free trade is provoking economic tensions among powerful nations. It is fueling the fundamental dissonance between monetary policy and the credit demands of the real economy.

In short, we have the worst of all worlds in the currency arena. It should not require the threat of war this time to spur an American initiative for international monetary reform.

The Imperative of U.S. Leadership

Just as the United States rose to the challenge of providing inspiration to desperate nations with a promise to establish stable and trustworthy monetary rules to undergird international commerce in compliance with free trade principles, the needed initiative falls once again to America. And just as then, the advantages of a sound money approach to ensure a level playing field that maximizes the rewards from true competition—by preventing currency manipulation through government intervention—will serve our own best interests.

It's a pivotal moment. The challenge these days is to inspire strug-gling nations to continue to believe in the advantages of democratic capitalism, to embrace free market ideas and support entrepreneur-ial endeavor. The United States is the only country that can mean-ingfully address the status quo disarray in monetary arrangements. According to Jacques de Larosiere (2014), former managing director of the International Monetary Fund, what we have today amounts to an "anti-system."

The current monetary regime permits governments to knowingly distort exchange rates under the guise of national monetary auton-omy while paying lip service to avoiding trade protectionism. It empowers central banks to channel the benefits of monetary policy decisions to some people at the expense of others, pitting wealthy investors against average savers. It facilitates cheap government borrowing. The shift toward increasing government influence over economic outcomes is anathema to the free market doctrines pro-pounded by Friedman.

If the United States does nothing to restore a rules-based approach to international monetary relations, our values come into question. We lose credibility by failing to challenge an international monetary anti-system that condones cheating by governments and central banks. We acquiesce to the fiction that enforceable rules exist to ensure against currency manipulation—even as we complain about trade imbalances contrived through exchange-rate targeting.

Dangerously, we pretend that today's speculative gaming in for-eign exchange markets by the world's largest banks somehow vali-dates the casino of floating rates—as if the $5.1 trillion daily turnover does not vastly exceed the amounts necessary to finance international trade and finance. The U.S. dollar is involved in 88 percent of the trades (BIS 2016: 3) in a currency market exhibiting "rising instances of volatility outbursts and flash events" (Murphy 2016).

Preemptive International Monetary Reform

America has long had the luxury of issuing the world's most dom-inant currency without having to guarantee its integrity. But with the dollar's popularity come financial risks: Widespread use of our nation's money for structuring complex derivatives, or for denomi-nating debt to foreign borrowers, sets up America's economy for unanticipated repercussions. Financial fallout from regional defaults triggered by a surge in the value of the dollar against other currencies would impact bank and nonbank institutions, and in turn constrain the availability of credit to domestic borrowers.

More concerning is the exposure to a broader global financial crisis brought on by liquidity pressures in the foreign exchange market due to the sheer volume of dollar-denominated currency swaps and related contracts. Staggering levels of such instruments—some $58 trillion, according to the Bank for International Settlements—are not recorded on balance sheets even though they function as debt-like obligations (Borio, McCauley, and McGuire 2017).

President Trump has demonstrated his resolve to meaningfully address the problems caused by currency disorder. Early in his campaign he called attention to the unfairness of currency manipulation by governments. He defined himself as a "free trader" while nevertheless insisting that trade had to be conducted on a level playing field. He denounced currency depreciation as cheating and vowed to punish offenders for "stealing" American manufacturing jobs (Holland and Lawder 2017).

Now he has an opportunity to restructure existing international monetary arrangements—to implement a rules-based approach—through decisive action.

The political imperative for President Trump derives from both his criticism of domestic monetary policy and his identification of currency manipulation as a violation of free trade principles. As a candidate, he acknowledged that the extraordinarily low interest rates of accommodative monetary policy were punitive for ordinary savers—they were "getting creamed"—even as developers such as himself had access to extremely low-cost funding from banks (Davidson and Taylor 2016). As an experienced businessman, Trump also expressed disapproval of the Federal Reserve for fueling "a big fat ugly bubble" in financial markets through low interest rates (Crutsinger 2017).

On the international front, besides identifying the distorting impact on trade and economic performance caused by currency manipulation, Trump has publicly expressed concern over whether government policies were supportive of the dollar as a trustworthy currency and reliable measure of value. In September 2011 he accepted gold bars in lieu of payment in dollars as a security deposit on commercial space in one of his properties, publicly stating: "Obama's not protecting the dollar at all." Trump has expressed positive views on the gold standard, noting during a 2015 televised town hall that there was something "solid" about the United States when its currency was linked to gold—though he conceded that restoring it would be difficult (McElveen 2015).

Still, when asked by *GQ* magazine to give his spontaneous reaction to the notion of a gold standard, Trump responded: "Bringing back the gold standard would be very hard to do, but boy, would it be wonderful. We'd have a standard on which to base our money."[1]

Trump's views on monetary policy and his concern for the integrity of the dollar clearly resonated with American voters; accusations that he was "politicizing" the Fed by criticizing the negative aspects of low rates did not seem to hurt his political popularity, nor did the usual "goldbug" epithets. Economic forces had combined with social tensions in the aftermath of the 2008 financial crisis to incite people on both the right and the left over the perception that a "rigged" system had bailed out the perpetrators at their expense. From the Tea Party movement to Occupy Wall Street, long-simmering grievances over economic inequities came to a head in the 2016 election.

President Trump's economic imperative now is to initiate reform both at the Federal Reserve and in conjunction with the international community to redefine monetary relations. The extraordinary measures of accommodative interest rate policy enacted by the Fed over an extended period have exacerbated income inequality, an issue to which Federal Reserve Governor Lael Brainard recently alluded (Torry 2017). The task for the next Fed chairman to be nominated by Trump is to craft an interest rate glide path that will soothe markets while supporting a pro-growth economic agenda. At the same time, given that economic and financial outcomes are highly vulnerable to currency shifts, such finesse in formulating monetary policy must include direct consideration of the dollar's value relative to other currencies.

What's needed is a comprehensive approach for linking the money supply to increases in productive output—the restoration of sound money principles for economic growth. It's time to reassert the primary functions of money as (1) a medium of exchange, (2) a unit of account, and (3) a store of value. Workers hurt by the consequences

---

[1] See the GQ website at https://thescene.com/watch/gq/donald-trump-weighs-in-on-marijuana-hillary-clinton-and-man-buns?mbid=marketing_paid_cne_social_facebook_scene_gq_dp_28.

of the 2008 financial market meltdown need to be assured that they will not be punished by a future bubble; no more monetary favoritism. It is also imperative that global monetary turmoil not undermine what currently passes for economic recovery.

Ultimately, the compelling reason for the Trump administration to undertake the challenge of structuring a new international monetary system is that democratic capitalism is unlikely to survive another blow on the scale of what has been endured this past decade. And having been so critical of currency manipulation and its deleterious impact on trade flows, it is incumbent on President Trump to propose what would constitute a better approach to exchange rate relations. The United States cannot point an accusing finger without defining the ameliorating change in behavior—or better yet, the set of new rules—it would require trade partners to accept.

The role of the dollar as the world's dominant reserve currency is a matter of national strategic importance: it is the strongest tool in our soft power arsenal. Yet the dollar's vulnerability to uncontrollable developments in foreign exchange markets is a potential weakness; it could perversely become a deterrent to effective domestic monetary policy. It would be negligent to permit currency shifts to undermine the hard-sought growth benefits of tax and trade reform.

Thus it falls to the United States under President Trump to champion the noble cause of restoring order to international monetary relations—so that free trade does not fall victim to the demoralizing effects of having economic and financial outcomes altered through exchange rate machinations.

Playing to Our Strengths

Proposing a new approach in keeping with the Trump administration's emerging national security strategy doctrine, which emphasizes the primacy of national sovereignty, engages our strong suit of financial supremacy to good purpose in the international economic arena.

Timing is important to ensure that a future monetary system is not governed by a global body; such a development would be distinctly at odds with Trump administration objectives. The International Monetary Fund long ago abandoned its responsibility for maintaining a stable international exchange rate system anchored by a gold-convertible dollar. Yet today it flirts with the notion of serving as the main platform for regulating cryptocurrencies. Citing the organization's "mandate for economic and financial stability" as rationale, IMF Managing Director Christine Lagarde (2017) proposed recently that the IMF take a strong role in overseeing the advent of virtual currencies and also move forward toward creating a digital version of the SDR.

Such a bold move to assert control over monetary policy at the global level would constitute a challenge to the continued reign of the U.S. dollar and undermine our own nation's sovereign power and influence in global financial markets. America needs to have a better idea—one that readily accommodates and creatively uses evolving advances in fintech capabilities.

If the appeal of cryptocurrencies is their capacity to provide a common currency, and to maintain a uniform value for every issued unit, we need only consult historical experience to ascertain that these same qualities were achieved through the classical international gold standard without sacrificing the sovereignty of individual nations. To the contrary: gold standard rules permit nations to participate voluntarily by operating in accordance with the discipline of gold convertibility of their own currencies.

A modern version of this approach—one that permits the issuance of virtual currencies in tandem with government-issued currencies, adapting legal tender laws to permit healthy currency competition—should be put forward.

Golden Opportunity

The United States is the world's largest holder of official gold reserves. Comprising 8,311.5 tonnes or 261 million troy ounces, those reserves are carried at a book value of roughly $11 billion. Notably, the market value is significantly higher at $345 billion (based on the London Gold Fixing for September 30, 2016) as cited in the Treasury's report filed June 30, 2017 (U.S. Department of the Treasury 2017).

In proposing a new international monetary system linked in some way to gold, America has an opportunity to secure continued prominence in global monetary affairs while also promoting genuine free trade based on a solid monetary foundation. Gold has historically provided a common denominator for measuring value; widely accepted at all income levels of society, it is universally acknowledged as a monetary surrogate with intrinsic value.

Speaking in February 2017, former Federal Reserve Chairman Alan Greenspan defined gold as the "primary global currency" and further added, "We would never have reached this position of extreme indebtedness were we on the gold standard, because the gold standard is a way of ensuring that fiscal policy never gets out of line" (Oyedele 2017). To confront U.S. indebtedness, we need to restore fiscal discipline and sound money through gold convertibility.

We make America great again by making America's money great again.

References

BIS (Bank for International Settlements) (2016) "BIS Triennial Central Bank Survey: Foreign Exchange Turnover in April 2016." Monetary and Economic Department, Bank for International Settlement (September). Annex tables revised on December 11, 2016. Available at www.bis.org/publ/rpfx16fx.pdf.

Borio, C.; McCauley, R. N.; and McGuire, P. (2017) "FX Swaps and Forwards: Missing Global Debt?" *BIS Quarterly Review* (September).

Crutsinger, M. (2017) "Will Trump Drop His Grumbling about Fed and Favor Low Rates?" *AP News* (January 30).

Davidson, K., and Taylor, M. (2016) "Trump Claims Yellen Is Holding Rates Low to Aid Obama." *Wall Street Journal* (September 12).

de Larosiere, J. (2014) "Bretton Woods and the IMS in a Multipolar World?" Keynote Speech at Conference on "Bretton Woods at 70: Regaining Control of the International Monetary System," Workshop No. 18 (February 28). In *Workshops: Proceedings of OeNB Workshops,* 180–85. Vienna: Oesterreichische Nationalbank.

Fidler, S.; Chen, T. P.; and Wei, L. L. (2017) "China's Xi Jinping Seizes Role as Leader on Globalization." *Wall Street Journal* (January 17).

FOXBusiness (2011) "Trump Accepts Gold Instead of Dollars from Tenant." *FOXBusiness* (September 15).

Holland, S., and Lawder, D. (2017) "Exclusive: Trump Calls Chinese 'Grand Champions' of Currency Manipulation." *Reuters* (February 24).

Horsefield, J. K. (1969a) *The International Monetary Fund, 1945–1965: Twenty Years of International Cooperation*. Vol. 1: *Chronicle*. Washington: International Monetary Fund.

_____, ed. (1969b) *The International Monetary Fund, 1945–1965*. Vol. 3: *Documents*. Washington: International Monetary Fund.

Lagarde, C. (2017) "Central Banking and Fintech: A Brave New World." Speech presented at Bank of England conference, London, September 29.

Martin, W. (2017) "Theresa May Davos Speech: Full Text." *Business Insider*. Available at www.businessinsider.fr/uk/theresa-may-davos-speech-full-text-2017-1.

McElveen, J. (2015) "Conversation with the Candidate: Donald Trump (Web Extra)," hosted by Josh McElveen, WMUR television, New Hampshire (March 27).

Murphy, H. (2016) "Dealmaking Surge Dominates the Year in Market Structures." *Financial Times* (December 29).

Nixon, R. (1971) "Address to the Nation Outlining a New Economic Policy: The Challenge of Peace" (August 15). Available at www.presidency.ucsb.edu/ws/?pid=3115.

Oyedele, A. (2017) "Greenspan: The U.S. Cannot Afford to Spend on Infrastructure Like It Wants to Because It's Not on the Gold Standard." *Markets Insider* (February 16).

Torry, H. (2017) "Torry's Take: Mind the Wealth Gap." *Wall Street Journal/Pro: Central Banking* (September 29).

U.S. Department of the Treasury (2017) "Status Report of U.S. Government Gold Reserve," Current Report (June 30). Washington: Bureau of the Fiscal Service, Department of the Treasury.

Volcker, P., and Gyohten, T. (1992) *Changing Fortunes: The World's Money and the Threat to American Leadership*. New York: Times Books.

White, H. D. (1942) "Preliminary Draft Proposal for a United Nations Stabilization Fund and a Bank for Reconstruction and Development of the United and Associated Nations" (April). In J.K. Horsefield (ed.) *The International Monetary Fund, 1945–1965*. Vol. 3: *Documents*. Washington, International Monetary Fund.

INDEX

Note: Information in figures and tables is indicated by f and t; n designates a numbered note.

About the Editor

James A. Dorn is Vice President for Monetary Studies, Editor of the *Cato Journal*, Senior Fellow, and Director of Cato's annual monetary conference. He has written widely on Federal Reserve policy and monetary reform, and is an expert on China's economic liberalization. He has edited more than ten books, including *Monetary Alternatives: Rethinking Government Fiat Money*, *The Search for Stable Money* (with Anna J. Schwartz), *The Future of Money in the Information Age*, and *China in the New Millennium*. His articles have appeared in the *Wall Street Journal*, *Financial Times*, *South China Morning Post*, and scholarly journals. He has been a columnist for *Caixin* and writes for *Forbes.com*. From 1984 to 1990, he served on the White House Commission on Presidential Scholars. Dorn has been a visiting scholar at the Central European University and Fudan University in Shanghai. He holds a PhD in economics from the University of Virginia.

About the Cato Institute and Its Center for Monetary and Financial Alternatives

Founded in 1977, the Cato Institute is a public policy research foundation dedicated to broadening the parameters of policy debate to allow consideration of more options that are consistent with the principles of limited government, individual liberty, and peace.

The Institute is named for *Cato's Letters*, libertarian pamphlets that were widely read in the American colonies in the early 18th century and played a major role in laying the philosophical foundation for the American Revolution.

The Cato Institute undertakes an extensive publications program on the complete spectrum of policy issues. Books, monographs, and shorter studies are commissioned to examine the federal budget, Social Security, regulation, military spending, international trade, and myriad other issues. Major policy conferences are held throughout the year.

The Cato Institute's Center for Monetary and Financial Alternatives was founded in 2014 to assess the shortcomings of existing monetary and financial regulatory arrangements, and to discover and promote more stable and efficient alternatives.

In order to maintain its independence, the Cato Institute accepts no government funding. Contributions are received from foundations, corporations, and individuals, and other revenue is generated from the sale of publications. The Institute is a nonprofit, tax-exempt, educational foundation under Section 501(c)3 of the Internal Revenue Code.

Cato Institute
1000 Massachusetts Avenue, N.W.
Washington, D.C. 20001
www.cato.org

CPSIA information can be obtained
at www.ICGtesting.com
Printed in the USA
FFHW020251051218
49767702-54242FF